The Eighties have b
money era, the faste
 aring   ties.

(Continued from front flap)

collapse. For survivors of the coming bust will be the next boom's winners. Read *Boom and Bust* and make sure you are one of them.

© Adolfo Doring

CHRISTOPHER WOOD is *The Economist's* New York–based financial correspondent. Formerly with the *Far Eastern Economic Review* of Hong Kong, Christopher Wood has worked as a financial writer in New York, London, Hong Kong, and Tokyo. He was educated at Eton College and Bristol University in England.

BOOM AND BUST

BOOM AND BUST

Christopher Wood

Atheneum   New York
1989

Atheneum
Macmillan Publishing Company
866 Third Avenue, New York, NY 10022

Library of Congress Cataloguing-in-Publication Data
Wood, Christopher, 1957–
    Boom and bust/Christopher Wood. — 1 American ed.
       p.   cm.
    Bibliography: p.
    Includes index.
    ISBN 0-689-12070-2
    1. Business cycles – History – 20th century. 2. Economic history – 1971– 3. Finance – 20th century. 4. Stock Market Crash, 1987.   I. Title.
HB3716.W73   1989
338.5′42′0904 – dc19   89-30773
                                   CIP

Macmillan books are available at special discounts for bulk purchases for sales promotions, premiums, fund-raising, or educational use. For details contact:

Special Sales Director
Macmillan Publishing Company
866 Third Avenue
New York, NY 10022

First American Edition 1989

10 9 8 7 6 5 4 3 2 1

Printed in the United States of America

To Kathleen and Justine

CONTENTS

Contents

ACKNOWLEDGMENTS

Boom and Bust is the result of countless interviews conducted all over the globe in the course of six years of weekly financial journalism. Clearly it is impossible to name all the people who have given me ideas and inspiration. However, thanks are due in particular to my present employer, *The Economist*, for providing me with the opportunity to meet so many interesting people. Naturally, all views expressed here are my own.

Much of this book was written before the worldwide stock market crash of October 1987. Thanks are due to Gill Paul and Robert Smith at Sidgwick & Jackson for encouraging me to press on to conclusion. I soon realised the wisdom of this advice when it became clear that despite that historic event most people remain extraordinarily complacent.

Finally, thanks to Stephen Brown, Philip Manduca and Hugh Sloane for swopping ideas over the years and for reading the raw manuscript.

All exchange rate conversions are as at 31 December 1987.

STILL STORMY
An Introduction and Update

Financial mania was not dealt a killer blow by the October 1987 worldwide stock market crash. In pockets of the money world the fever has continued.

This may not be obvious to the armies of disillusioned brokers, traders and analysts toiling on Wall Street and in most of the world's other financial centres. The decline in trading volume and commission revenue was constant until the end of 1988, more than a year after the crash. Indeed business was so lacklustre that many sensed the carnage in the securities business had only just begun. They knew the reduced volume of business could not possibly support the staggering overhead costs built up during the 1980s' global bull market. Still the composition of the American securities industry has not been substantially altered. The 15,000 jobs which have so far been lost on Wall Street represent only 5 per cent of the national head count of 300,000. Cutting the first 5 per cent in any organization is always the easiest part. It then becomes progressively tougher. If trading volumes do not recover soon Wall Street and other financial centres will be forced to cut much deeper.

The investment banks have been able to hang on and avoid further retrenchment thanks to continuing deal mania. If markets have been generally boring, Wall Street has been able to reap huge fees in 1988 advising on, investing in and lending to leveraged buy-outs (L.B.O.s). This climaxed in December when Kohlberg, Kravis & Roberts won an auction to L.B.O. food-tobacco giant R.J.R. Nabisco. The $25bn. price tag was an incredible $12bn. more than the company was worth in the stock market before the

L.B.O. merchants set to work on it. It was by a huge margin the largest takeover ever, and it would involve saddling R.J.R. Nabisco with more than $20bn. of debt, including $5bn. worth of junk bonds. These were staggering sums even for macho Wall Street. They also involved heroic assumptions on the part of the protagonists for the deal.

America's stock market remained bogged down at the end of 1988 in a trading range 25 per cent below its high of August 1987; yet eager L.B.O. punters, investment banks, commercial banks and insurance companies were conspiring to put a value on selected companies nearly 100 per cent higher than the shares original trading price.

The question to ask (and few do) in a case such as this is which valuation is likely to be proved wrong? The answer is rarely known to those conspirators eager for any deal, including the investment bankers who were competing for some $500m. in fees in the R.J.R. mega-deal. Those most in the know are the mass of investors, sobered by the recent crash, by an indebted economy and by America's inability to get a grip on its own housekeeping.

In their eagerness to do L.B.O.s at such huge premiums to the stock market's valuation, L.B.O. merchants, and the banks and insurance companies that lent to them, were displaying incredible arrogance. In effect, they were saying they knew a company's valuation better than the stock market did. And the optimistic assumptions behind their deals meant they were betting that the economy would continue to grow, though by the end of 1988 America had already enjoyed six years of continuous economic growth.

The sheer size of the R.J.R. Nabisco deal may have made even cynical Wall Street gasp. At the same time, it made the rest of America angry. The company's chairman, Mr Ross Johnson, became a national symbol of greed: he was featured unflatteringly on the cover of *Time* magazine as the man who had hoped to put his company deep in hoc and make $100m. for himself in the process. The deal marked the watershed when L.B.O.s went from the business section to the front page.

When Wall Street captures such publicity a political reaction is seldom far behind. Washington could put an end to the excesses of L.B.O. fever in an instant by changing the tax laws, as Federal Reserve chairman Alan Greenspan suggested in October 1988. As it stands L.B.O.'d companies can deduct interest payments on their mountain of debt, whereas companies with little debt pay dividends to shareholders out of after-tax earnings. America's tax system therefore has the perverse effect of encouraging debt over equity.

The R.J.R. Nabisco deal involved some ultra-aggressive investment banking. Drexel Burnham, for example, agreed to lend $3.5bn. of its own capital in a bridge loan to help finance the K.K.R. bid; though, at the same time, the investment firm was locked in a life-and-death legal battle with federal prosecutors.

The Securities and Exchange Commission declared war in September 1988 in the form of a 182-page civil complaint which listed a litany of securities offenses against Drexel. Criminal indictments are now expected to follow. Most ominously for Drexel, the government was threatening racketeering charges against junk-bond supremo Michael Milken and others, and perhaps even against Drexel itself under the 1970 Racketeer Influenced and Corrupt Organisation (R.I.C.O.) act. A law originally designed to counter organized crime, R.I.C.O. gives government prosecutors huge discretion and huge leverage. The government could, for example, seize a large portion of Drexel's assets under this statute.

Many lawyers are of the opinion that no investment bank could survive the stigma of a R.I.C.O. charge, which is why Drexel decided to settle in December 1988. This decision was not without cost: first, it meant abandoning Michael Milken, who made most of the firm's money, and second, it meant admitting a felony and so paving the way for a wave of multi-billion-dollar civil lawsuits from the sixteen companies whose shares Drexel manipulated according to the S.E.C. complaint. Either way, Drexel will emerge a much diminished force.

The endurance of L.B.O. fever, however, was in a sense only appropriate. For Wall Street in the 1980s has succeeded in casting much of the world around it in its own image.

In a sense the financial condition of America at the end of 1988 mirrors the status of its largest companies: the country is one vast L.B.O. In the first quarter of 1988 America's domestic nonfinancial debt to its nominal gross national product (G.N.P.) reached 181.4 per cent. After hovering at around the 140 per cent level from 1940 to 1983, the debt load is again at levels not seen since the early 1930s when the G.N.P. collapsed.

This dangerous position of indebtedness makes it increasingly tough to earn a dollar of cash flow to pay a dollar of debt service, especially as the United States (unlike most L.B.O.s) has continued to borrow as if there were no tomorrow. Hypothetically, if America's domestic nonfinancial debt and nominal G.N.P. were to continue to grow at the average rate that they grew between 1984 and 1987 – namely, an 11.8 per cent increase in debt (assuming an average interest cost of 8 per cent) and a 5.9 per cent increase in G.N.P., then it would take thirty-six years before 100 per cent of America's G.N.P. would be used up paying interest on debt. Such is the impeccable logic of compound interest. Clearly this will not happen. The simple point is that the current trend is unsustainable.

The sad news for Americans is that more and more this debt is owed to foreigners and not just to fellow Americans. Increasingly these creditors are not private foreign investors, who in 1987 virtually stopped buying foreign dollar securities, but foreign central banks. As of 20 April 1988 foreign central banks owned $229bn. worth of American treasury securities, which was more than the Federal Reserve itself owned. How long will these foreign central banks be prepared to go on printing money to finance America's deficits? And, with that slice of America's debt, how long will they retain faith in the dollar as the world's reserve currency?

These risks continued to hang stubbornly and ominously over the financial markets at the end of 1988 despite deal mania. They explain why most world stock markets did not bounce back strongly after the crash and why many investors remain cautious waiting for that other 'shoe' to drop.

The economy may have continued to roll along in 1988 but that happy fact failed to please many investors. Perversely, they do not want to see a strong economy. Rather they want signs of an orderly economic slowdown which will reduce the rate at which Americans consume and borrow.

The trick is to produce a soft landing that manages to avoid the shock of recession. The outstanding problem plaguing the monetary authorities is that such a slowdown risks triggering debt defaults and so turning on a destructive deflation.

More than one year after the crash, the deflationary argument remains valid. Indeed it has become more valid as the debt load has continued to grow and, in fact, has continued to outpace economic growth in 1988, albeit at a slower pace.

The problems warned of in this book have, if anything, worsened since the crash. The long-ignored financial catastrophe in America's savings and loans is only now meriting the crisis treatment it deserves.

Toward the end of 1988 it became blatantly obvious that no one, least of all the responsible regulators, knew the extent of the financial black hole in America's thrift industry. This ignorance spreads from two points. First, the regulators are reluctant to sell the assets of dud thrifts onto a weak market and so realize huge losses on them. Second, they are still far too keen on tolerating smoke-and-mirrors accounting to obfuscate the problem.

There is, however, a sore rule of thumb that can be applied in the savings and loan – or thrift, as it is otherwise ironically known – industry. The gloomiest of private analysts have in recent years consistently been too low in their guesstimates of how much money the thrifts have been losing. By the end of 1988 these same private analysts were saying that some $100bn. of taxpayers' money would be required to liquidate and pay back depositors in all the insolvent thrifts, the financial world's equivalent of the living dead. This is not a puny sum. If such spending had been voted by Congress in 1988, it would have meant adding about two thirds to that year's expected federal budget deficit. The industry managed astoundingly to lose this sum of money after six years of economic growth and falling interest rates. What, it may be asked, will happen in the event of a national recession and/or falling house prices?

The thrift problem has been deteriorating for obvious reasons. The insolvent F.S.L.I.C. (Federal Savings and Loan Corporation), the industry's deposit insurance fund, is reluctant to put the basket cases out of business by closing down savings and loan institutions because it does not have the funds to pay back depositors. Yet because it has continued to try to hide from Congress the inevitable need for huge dollops of taxpayers' money to keep its commitment to depositors, F.S.L.I.C. has only ensured that the ultimate bill facing the taxpayer will be even greater.

The lengths to which the regulators will go to avoid facing the harsh facts of the thrift crisis became dramatically clear in the autumn of 1988 with the infamous Southwest Plan. This was the grandiose name given to the crackpot scheme thought up by the Federal Home Loan Bank Board, F.S.L.I.C.'s overseer and regulator. The idea was to merge lots of little-bust thrifts into big-bust thrifts (many of them in depressed Texas) in hopes of finding buyers willing to put in some new money. This marked yet another attempt to buy time with federal free lunches entailing massive costs for F.S.L.I.C. – costs that will end up with the taxpayer. That is, unless Congress ever balks at voting the necessary funds, an event which would risk precipitating depositor panic.

xiii

The details of these deals bear spelling out since they highlight the costs tomorrow of suppressing today's problem. First, F.S.L.I.C. guarantees to pay back to the buyer after ten years the principal on all the sick thrift's dud assests, and in some cases on any more assets, loans, which may turn bad during the first two years of ownership. Second, the new owner is guaranteed also an income for ten years on these dud assets. This so called 'yield maintenance agreement' starts at 260 basis points, or more than 2.5 per cent over Texas cost of funds, which has been as high as 4 per cent over the national cost of funds. (Dodgy Texan thrifts have to pay a premium to attract hot-money deposits.) That premium scales down over ten years to a still exorbitant 160 basis points.

In return for these incentives, the regulators demand only that the buyer invests the equivalent of 1.5 per cent of the thrift's total assets in new cash. Take the example of one deal which was on the table in September 1988 – a $1bn. thrift in which the buyer proposed to invest $15m. of new money. He would get that money and more back at the end of the first year. Based on an agreed yield of 260 basis points over Texas cost of funds, the buyer would be paid some $26m. in the first year of ownership, or $11m. more than he had paid for the whole thrift. Not a bad return!

The buyers of these too-good-to-be-true sickly thrift deals are really only taking two risks. First, that the already insolvent F.S.L.I.C. runs out of credit and Congress refuses to honour its commitments. Second, that opportunistic buyers become the target of congressional wrath when knowledge of the true cost of these deals to the taxpayer becomes widespread. Then from being hailed as 'rescuers' of the Texas thrift industry they risk suddenly being viewed as pariahs ripping off the taxpayer.

Another fundamental problem with these deals is that they create no incentive for the thrift to try renting out space in buildings gained from defaulting borrowers. These spaces remain empty because the thrift owner's guaranteed yield is paid after the subtraction of any rental income earned by these dud assets. So the more space rented, the less received in guaranteed yield from F.S.L.I.C. Why go to the trouble of renting out space when you can receive the income direct from the government?

This flawed arrangement undermines the comfortable bureaucratic argument that the Southwest Plan is buying time to work the problem out. Its only practical effect is to ensure that the Texas property market remains in a condition of suspended animation.

Huge amounts of property will be kept off the market preventing prices from bottoming out naturally. For the harsh truth is that no market can bottom until the weakest holders dump at fire-sale prices. To postpone this liquidation simply delays the recovery making everyone worse off. That is why the final bottom in Texas property will not be reached until a national recession hits across America. At that point it will soon be beyond F.S.L.I.C.'s meager capacity to defer the liquidation of the sickest thrifts. There will by then be far too many fires to put out.

The hope is that Washington will have devised a national strategy for managing the thrift crisis *before* the losses become even more astronomical. This is not impossible though it requires considerable political will as well as taxpayer funds. By the end of 1988 there were encouraging signs that the incoming administration of George Bush was preparing to give the thrift issue top priority. It clearly deserves it.

The thrift problem is a dramatic illustration of how deposit insurance has bred a dangerous illusion of stability in America's financial system, just as portfolio insurance created an illusion of liquidity in its stock market prior to 19 October 1987. Deposit insurance is a time bomb waiting to explode.

The institution of deposit insurance was controversial even at the time of its origin. It became law in 1933 in the midst of the Great Depression, a period when many unfortunate people lost their life savings in banks through no fault of their own. Despite that trauma an unlikely alliance of Democrat Franklin Roosevelt and the predominantly Republican American Bankers Association opposed the reform. They argued that deposit insurance was dangerous because it would take the discipline out of banking. By removing the penalty of not being able to pay back depositors, deposit insurance would tempt bankers to bet their depositors' money in speculative lending and gambling in the financial markets. This is just what has happened.

The result is a peculiar situation where the financial markets no longer worry when American banks fail. (And by the end of 1988 there had been a wholesale failure of banking as an industry in Texas). The markets are so sanguine because they assume (so far correctly) that the government will bail out all depositors. Pain will be suspended and panic prevented.

The only logical conclusion to draw from this is that the federal government in effect has nationalized all the liabilities (that is what banks call their deposits) on the balance sheet of America's nearly

15,000 banks and 4,000 thrifts. Perhaps this item should be added to the list of the federal government's contingent liabilities.

The problems facing America's credit system reveal that financial mania and financial excesses have not just been confined to the securities industry. America's economy may have remained much stronger throughout 1988 than it was in 1930. But its financial structure looks a whole lot weaker. It is not reassuring when markets do not worry when banks fail. In fact it is scary. Pain suspended usually means more pain tomorrow. Just as many investors have now lost faith in the stock market as a home for their savings, so America's depositors could lose faith in their much-abused banking system.

So far depositors have proved extraordinarily willing to keep their money in institutions that are known to be bust. They have continued faith that the federal government will honour its obligations. It is equally true, though, that this faith should neither be taken for granted nor abused. For if and when confidence is ever lost, it would be awfully hard to convince people to put their money back into banks.

The one area of the money world where the global stock market crash has barely dented financial fever is Tokyo. There the crash only caused a 'healthy' 20 per cent correction in the Japanese stock market. The Nikkei Index has since gone on to make new highs, nearly hitting the 30,000 level in early December.

This spectacular performance not surprisingly has led the Japanese to keep more of their investment funds at home. Foreigners are also investing more there simply because it is the only major stock market that continues to perform. The Japanese economy has been booming as domestic growth has, largely, taken over from export-led growth. March through September 1988 compared to the same period the previous year shows that Japanese companies' operating profits have risen 58 per cent. In this sense the huge valuations in the Tokyo market have been justified by phenomenal earnings increases. There also remains a huge pool of liquidity in Japan to fuel speculation, a prerequisite of any sustained bull market. Nomura, Japan's largest securities firm, now has 48 trillion yen in its clients' accounts, corporate and personal. That is the equivalent of $400bn. or 8 per cent of American G.N.P. Daiwa, Japan's second largest broker, has just under 40 trillion yen, or over $300bn. or 6 per cent of the G.N.P. These clearly are awesomely large numbers.

There remain many troubling signs of excess in Tokyo. In

October 1988 Japan suffered its third-largest postwar bankruptcy when an Osaka-based stock market and property firm named Nihon Tochi went bust to the tune of $1.2bn. Simultaneously, the company's president was charged with possession of firearms and swords. The same month a former head of research at one of Japan's top stockbroking firms, Cosmo Securities, was found dead in a cement mixer. The unfortunate man had disappeared along with a colleague in February. His mistake was to have agreed to manage money for Yamaguchi Gumi, a gang in the Japanese underworld of organized crime. Clearly his investment performance during the crash did not please his clients. Yet these were isolated incidents within the context of a continuing boom, much like the Ivan Boesky scandal that broke a year before the crash.

Tokyo's importance is hard to exaggerate since this is the centre of world liquidity. Turn the hose off and the impact will be felt everywhere capitalists gather. The best guess is that the bubble – and it surely is a bubble – will only burst when Japan faces a real inflation scare and an upward spike in interest rates.

For the main reason the Japanese stockmarket commands such high valuations is because Japanese inflation and interest rates are so low. If inflation in Japan rose to 4 per cent from its present level of 1 per cent, and long-term government bond yields from the 4 per cent level to over 7 per cent, that alone would be sufficient to cause a 30–40 per cent downward rating in the Tokyo stock market.

Given that the Japanese economy is growing flat out and the very low Japanese interest rates, that drop is unlikely to occur until well into 1989. By then their current monetary policy expansion will have translated into price increases. The inflation threat could be accelerated by a rising dollar. The big surprise of 1989 might be such a rally in the dollar as the American economy slows and the trade deficit consequently contracts. It would be deflationary for America and inflationary for Japan, forcing higher interest rates.

If the Western economies do slow in 1989 while Japan continues to record stronger growth, as may well happen, that could conceivably lead to one large upward move in the Tokyo stock market as its performance looks better and better vis-à-vis other lacklustre markets. The more out of line Tokyo valuations become, the greater the danger subsequently of a powerful deflationary crash, an event that would precipitate a credit contraction worldwide since it is Japanese purchasing power that is behind so much buying at the margin, be it Picasso paintings, Waikiki condominiums or American Treasury bonds.

The Japanese, who long ago became smug if not downright arrogant about their economic success and soaring stock market, should not be expected to react well in such circumstances. Japan is not a culture suited to managing failure. The consensus society risks degenerating into a Gadarene swine–like panic.

Back in the West the October 1987 crash seemed a distant if not irrelevant memory to many on the occasion of its first anniversary (save for those employed in the securities industry who were still suffering from the hangover). By then there were already clear signs that deflation was beginning to pick up momentum. These signs could not, however, be found in the newspaper headlines. Instead weak gold and oil prices – the money world's two most sensitive commodities – have hinted at the oncoming deflation. Gold closed on 30 September at $394 an ounce. This was well below the $500 level it had begun 1988 at. That performance hardly suggested rising inflation fears. The same applied to oil which in September hit $12 a barrel, compared with $18 at the start of 1988.

Despite this evidence in the financial markets most economists continued to fight yesterday's war and talk about the threat of higher inflation, not looming deflation. Even though the Federal Reserve's and/or the credit markets' move to increase short-term interest rates during the summer of 1988 had clearly added to deflationary pressure. Despite these higher short-term rates – which by then were higher than they were prior to the October 1987 crash – the Treasury thirty-year bond market behaved in a manner that suggested that bond investors were much less concerned about inflation than either the Fed or most economists appeared to be. For thirty-year Treasury bonds continued to yield nearly 1.5 percentage points less than they did prior to the crash. So investors were demanding less of a premium to invest in long-term debt. Their decreased expectation pointed to an economic slowdown ahead, not a boom and higher inflation.

True, monetary growth picked up in the first half of 1988, reflecting the Fed's dramatic easing at the time of the crash. But by July 1988 it had turned flat again. By the end of 1982 America's money supply was growing at its slowest rate in twenty years. Whether the Fed was being deliberately tight or whether the system was deflating of its own accord, no one could tell. One point was sure: monetary conditions looked the opposite of inflationary.

Meanwhile, the Fed has continued to perform its unenviable

balancing act. Because of America's dependence on foreign credit, Greenspan has had to keep one eye on the value of the dollar and the bond market, the other on the condition of the economy. Indeed the Fed has increasingly found itself obliged to follow the whims and neuroses of the markets, not the other way round. This is not so surprising. Capital must be placated. Such is the priority of a debtor nation.

A further sign of deflation was a weakening property market throughout nearly all of America, except in still-booming California. In 80 per cent of the metropolitan areas surveyed by America's National Association of Realtors at the end of June 1988, the increase in house prices year after year had already fallen behind the rate of inflation. In a third of those areas surveyed they were actually falling.

The historical evidence of what a deflation can do to property values is not reassuring to a generation used to rising house prices. In 1933 America's Department of Commerce price index for private homes fell below the level it had stood at nineteen years earlier in 1914. So the 1930s' depression wiped out all the gains in property prices during the preceeding inflationary boom after the end of the First World War. A repeat performance would cause property prices to fall back to levels prevailing in 1969, which is a scary thought for the 55 per cent of American households whose equity in their homes represents more than 50 per cent of their private wealth.

There is also the huge rise in mortgage debt to worry about. Total mortgage debt in America is now around $3 trillion. It has been growing too fast, soaring by $1.3 trillion since 1982. Home equity loans are another crazy scheme denuding people of the remaining equity in their homes so that banks can sustain their book profits. Between May and December 1988 home equity loans grew at more than a 30 per cent annual rate at a time of a softening property market. The madness continues.

This book has at its core a deflationary premise: that inflation breeds deflation; that prices rise and also fall. This argument is viewed as doomsday nonsense by the majority of contemporary economists, who consider that deflation in the sense of falling prices is impossible in an age when government spending forms such a large part of the modern economy and central banks are willing and able to print money at the first sign of any financial panic.

The economists' assumption that prices have only to rise is

based on a too-rosy view of the power of government. Its debunking will have shattering consequences for the self-confidence of economists everywhere and for the prestigiousness of this very modern profession. During the second half of the twentieth century economists have become the equivalent of the high priests of previous centuries. They indulge in the same internecine theological disputes over dogma, and they are the natural advisors of the governing classes. But the lessons they preach and their mumbo-jumbo jargon may turn out hardly more relevant than the religious schisms of an earlier age. Economics was a healthier pursuit when it was considered an art and not a 'science'. Modern man has asked too much of the modern technocratic economics. He is likely to be disappointed.

Such reservations were worrying few in December 1988. Fashionable contrarians argued that there could not possibly be a depression because there were too many doomster books predicting it, just as they had agreed in the summer of 1987 that there could not be a crash because there were too many people talking about similarities with 1929.

It is true that there are many Cassandras, just as there are many Pollyannas, like the so-called 'New Wave' economists, who argue that there will never be another recession. Many of today's doomsters colour their dire forecasts with politically loaded socialistic messages that depression is caused by too much wealth in too few hands.

I have no such political manifesto and would dearly love to be more optimistic. Capitalism is the most efficient and most moral economic system known to man, and the one most suited to get the best out of human nature. Financial markets reflect the ebb and flow of capitalism and its natural tendency to advance in cycles, to undershoot and overshoot.

This is where modern economics goes terribly wrong. It assumes economic equilibrium, whereas the real forces are cyclical, a truth accepted by modern physics which increasingly rejects the notion of equilibrium and continuous relationships in complex systems. Modern economists are as straightjacketed by their mind-sets as were those scientists of an earlier age who swore the world was flat.

The harsh truth is that throughout economic history inflation has bred deflation. The cause of deflation has always been too heavy a burden of debt. But the Central banks' and governments' prevention of a potential credit crunch six years ago in August 1982 when Mexico came to the brink of default, haulted the natural flow of the credit cycle from playing out. So this period of credit has been artificially extended by central bank bail-outs and blanket deposit insurance. In the meantime the debts have been allowed to mount inexorably as if the prosperity was genuine rather than bought on borrower time.

It is not necessary to be a Calvinist to know that pain suspended today usually means more pain tomorrow. Still modern 'democratic' society has no tolerance for pain. The problem is that capitalism always entails failure as well as success. By pretending that it can give free lunches to all, governments have stimulated expectations and encouraged financial irresponsibility. Clearly not all debt is bad. Indeed debt is a tremendous generator of economic growth. However, since all debt must be paid back there comes a point when debt ceases to be a stimulating force and turns into a negative drag. We reached that point long ago.

The worry now is that because governments have not allowed the credit cycle to play out, the deflation will be that much more severe when the natural course of the credit cycle finally overwhelms the forces governments are throwing at it. When that occurs the capitalist system – and not just particular governments – risks being terminally discredited. That would be a terrible price to pay for a few years of lingering on borrowed time.

FINANCIAL FEVER

'The markets are driven by liquidity and silly young men. I am not sure which is more dangerous or which is more fickle.'
Richard Thornton, money manager, 1986

The game is up. We were living in a time of fast money. The press had already coined their epitaphs. A cover story in America's *Fortune Magazine* called it 'The Money Society'. A *New York Times* article on young Wall Street investment bankers ran the headline 'Feeling Poor on $600,000 a Year'. It was often true. As the 1980s drew to a close, so the financial fever intensified in which the only score card that counted was the number in your bank account.

Nowhere was this mentality more prevalent than in the money business itself, the world of high, or perhaps low, finance. In Wall Street, the City of London, Tokyo's Marunouchi district or any of the world's lesser financial centres, the different national cultures had been increasingly submerged in a uniform lusting for material prosperity. The spiritual was out. Toys were in. The baubles may have differed – a house in Chelsea and a manor house in Gloucestershire for the upwardly mobile City slicker; a Park Avenue coop and a Long Island mansion for the striving Wall Street yuppie; a golf club membership at $2m. a time for the obedient Tokyo eager-beaver. But the goal was the same.

This turbocharged atmosphere developed for two reasons: first, the amazing worldwide bull (rising) market in financial assets in the 1980s, the biggest since the 1920s; second, the deregulation and globalization of the world's financial markets. This meant a once in a lifetime boom for those working in the money business. Bumper salaries and jumbo bonuses were paid as the various securities firms geared up for the impending global battle from which only a few of the players would emerge as survivors, let alone winners.

1

This book is about that financial jungle; about the players in it and the markets they dealt in. It is also about how they functioned in a climate of false prosperity. The 1980s boom in trading pieces of paper, optimistically known as securities, could not last. But because it is in the nature of free-wheeling markets to test extremes, it was only to be expected that financial mania would lead to greedy excesses. Only then could there occur the inevitable sobering hangover. This boom-bust cycle is as old as man himself.

Until October 1987 the prophets of doom had been discredited. Their warnings of an impending débâcle had gone unfulfilled and everyone had continued to make merry and make money. That came as no surprise to savvier investors who understood that it takes years, not months, for cycles to turn. The bull market, which only really began in the summer of 1982, continued more than five years later. However, the party was drawing to a close. The debate among more sophisticated investors was more concerned with when rather than whether the revellings would end. The proper analogue was a good party where all the guests were enjoying themselves, but all knew they had to be at work the next morning. The question was whether it was 2 a.m., 4 a.m., or still only midnight.

The Collapse of 1987

Dawn broke on 19 October 1987 when the Dow Jones Industrial Average collapsed 508 points to 1,738.74, a 22.6 per cent decline in a single day on the then record trading volume of 604m. shares. This was truly the stuff of history. It dwarfed the 12.8 per cent fall on the fabled Black Tuesday of October 1929. It also came after days of falling share prices. From its peak of 2,722.42, reached on 25 August, the Dow had collapsed a breathtaking 36 per cent. The sheer scale and speed of the crash made a nonsense of the conventional wisdom that a 1929 could never happen again. Even so, that did not stop nearly all the pundits and top Wall Streeters from at once proclaiming that this time round a stock market crash would not lead to a depression because of 'safeguards' in the system. Do not believe them. They will be as wrong about that as they were about the impossibility of a repeat of the 1929 stock market crash. Rather, the reverse is true. The stock market crash in late 1987 was twice as bad in percentage terms as 1929 and the subsequent depression or slump, call it what you will, promises to be twice as bad too.

A few more historically minded commentators had for some time been pointing out the extraordinary similarity of current events with those of the 1920s, especially in the behaviour of the financial markets. History never repeats itself that neatly, of course. Even though details may differ, however, the trend remains the same and the trend is what matters, especially to the investor.

The pessimists who predict that the 1990s will be at least as unpleasant as the 1930s neither expect nor want to be believed. Indeed the disbelief has to be there for the cycle to happen. For if the majority of market participants felt that another depression was at hand, then the price of bonds, shares and property would already have collapsed and the prophecy would be self-fulfilling. It would already be too late to sell.

Fortunately for the sceptical few, the main concern until the October stock market crash and even after was that 1970s-style inflation would return. People have short memories. They have continued to worry about last decade's problems – double-figure inflation – when the world has been sliding in the opposite direction of deflation during the 1980s. Deflation means a contraction of the money supply and credit, falling prices and a general economic slump. Because it last occurred two generations ago, most people have difficulty in grasping what a deflation would mean.

A useful definition was provided by John Rothchild in the glossary of investment terms found in his satirical 1987 book *A Fool and his Money*. He contrasted an inflationary period, which he defined as a period 'when things are worth more than money, and you have more of the latter', with a deflationary period, 'when things are worth less than money and you have more of the former'. In a deflation the best asset is cash since it is about the only thing which increases in value.

Yet investors have continued to fight yesterday's war. Their main concern right until the October crash was a return to higher inflation. Indeed these worries – and not, as the press reported, the budget or trade deficit – were the catalyst that sparked the world-wide stock market rout. Exaggerated inflationary concerns bid up long-term interest rates in the bond market until American treasury bonds were yielding nearly 10.5 per cent. It was this rise in interest rates which broke the back of the bull market in shares. As soon as shares crashed, government bonds soared and interest rates plunged as the markets anticipated a weakening economy ahead and investors fled to quality.

At the time of writing most investors still believed in the ability of governments to head off depression when all the signs point to disintegrating economic cooperation between the major economic powers of America, West Germany, and Japan and the looming outbreak of dog-eats-dog protectionist economic warfare. In trying to put pressure on the West Germans by talking down the dollar the weekend before the 19 October crash, American Treasury Secretary James Baker made this only too clear to foreigners. The name of his game was competitive devaluation. It was simply another version of Smoot-Hawley, the 1930 protectionist legislation that historians have blamed for sending the world into the Great Depression. Baker's policy doubtless has short-term benefits for America's exporters, but in the long run it is a dangerous gamble. It is betting the integrity of the dollar, which is still the world's reserve currency as witnessed by the willingness of foreigners to hold it. For how long?

The extent of most investors' current faith in the ability of governments to alter destiny is touching, if misguided. They cannot. It also suggests that the politicians and central bankers were somehow solely to blame last time round. They were not. For when a deflation sets in, the central bank can print all the money it likes but will increasingly find itself 'pushing on a string' since the money supply can only expand when borrowers want to borrow and lenders want to lend. In a deflation this does not happen because both are too scared. That is why the money supply will contract as debts are liquidated, just as it did during the 1930s, despite the best efforts of the central bankers and their printing presses.

In fact it is just the sort of financial excesses in evidence today which have historically been a prelude to deflation, above all the accumulation of debt and its subsequent liquidation when borrowers default and capital is written off, just as $1 trillion was wiped off American share values in October's Wall Street crash.

In 1936 near the trough of the Great Depression, Freeman Tilden, an obscure American novelist, wrote a remarkable book called *A World in Debt*. Today it makes more compelling reading than a pile of commentaries from professional economists. Indeed, Tilden write his book because he could find nothing in the writings of contemporary economists about debt. The same is true today. Keynsians are obsessed with creating demand, monetarists with the money supply and supply-siders with cutting taxes. Where are the economists writing about the economic consequences of debt? Tilden was less reticent. He wrote: 'There is one cause, and only one cause, of all panics and depressions in the economic world. That cause is debt. Credit is debt.'

Many modern economists would like to dismiss this idea that debt has to be repaid as old fashioned. As one of them put it to me in July 1987, 'Rolling debt gathers no loss.' There is danger in such an attitude, however. Economics is no science; it is a best-guess art of studying how human beings squabble over the resources available. Debt, as any housewife knows, is debt. When people finally lose faith in the banking system and the debt pyramid, as they lost faith in the stock market in October 1987, there will be a worldwide scramble for cash. Debts will be called in, borrowers will default, and liquidity will contract.

That said, the accumulation of debt has meant prosperity for most of this decade for the stockbrokers, investment bankers, and others who inhabit the financial jungle. To see why, we need to set the context in which the world's financial markets boomed.

The Speculative Bubble

If Vietnam and hippy flower power are dominant folk memories of the 1960s, and inflation and the Organization of Petroleum Exporting Countries (OPEC) of the 1970s, the 1980s will be remembered for yuppies and the cult of the financial asset. In virtually every capitalist country the price of these financial assets (shares of companies and bonds issued by governments and companies) soared in value. As prices rose, more people felt comfortable about investing and still more became interested in it. Just what was this suddenly glamorous, if mysterious world of finance? Who were these men in the pinstripe suits, these shufflers of pieces of paper? How did they make so much money, making money out of money?

These were the questions which spawned a whole new industry. From America and Britain to Japan, Australia and Italy, books and magazines specializing in personal finance mushroomed. Business news suddenly became sexy and financial news even more so.

This kind of literature is traditionally associated with America with its greater financial sophistication and strong investment sub-culture arising from the greater amount of private wealth there. The interest in the markets and investing now became a global phenomenon helped, as in Britain, by privatization, the politically and financially profitable business of selling state-owned companies on the stock market. Until the October 1987 crash, which unhappily coincided in London with preparations for the sale of £7.2bn.-worth of shares in the partly government-owned BP (British Petroleum), everyone had benefited from privatization. The government received windfall revenue and the investor (unless the financial advisers really messed it up) a guaranteed quick profit.

Nor could the fashionable interest in all things financial be ignored, even by those who professed no interest in it. Indeed, only the very poor, the unemployed and the 'seriously rich' (to use money industry parlance) can afford to indulge in such disdain. For money men are not like oil men, motor-car men or computer men. They trade not in just another commodity or product but in what glues capitalist civilization together. Money serves both as society's standard of value, its store of value, and as its medium of exchange. Its integrity is all important, as is the integrity of those who deal in it. Like it or not, anyone enrolled in a private pension scheme or a life insurance policy has a stake in this financial game. His pension rises if the stock market does. His future security is threatened, right down to the value of his home, if the money industry crashes as will now happen, bringing the markets down with it.

The world has seen speculative excesses before. Markets are, in essence, nothing more than day-to-day measures of crowd psychology, which swing between alternating bouts of greed, fear, and sheer boredom. In the 1980s we have been operating at the greedy end of the scale. Financial history is littered with speculative bubbles that burst. Back in 1841 the poet and journalist Charles Mackay penned a classic with the memorable title *Some Extraordinary Popular Delusions and the Madness of Crowds*. His purpose was to chronicle some of history's more insane manias, such as England's South-Sea Bubble, France's Mississippi Scheme, and Holland's Tulipomania.

The question now is how great the 1980s' excesses have been. Have we been living in a bubble? Certainly it has been a period increasingly mesmerized by all forms of speculation. The world's stockbrokers and money managers, (known as fund managers in England, portfolio managers in America, and henceforth described as money managers) were the central protagonists. The brokers sold the paper. The money managers bought it. These two groups, known in the securities business as the sell side and the buy side respectively, were at the epicentre of this speculative whirl and the much talked about 'new era' of global financial markets and twenty-four-hour trading from Tokyo to London to New York and back to Tokyo again.

Indeed by 1987 'global' had become the clichéd buzz word of the financial markets, and with good reason. Electronic communications and the information revolution (the world of the Reuters screen) had made the global market a reality. Like most innovation, that had a good and a bad side. Good because investors could move their money quickly from market to market. Bad because, just like an electricity grid, shocks are felt virtually simultaneously everywhere money flows freely and dealers watch Reuters screens. So this was also a bubble which could burst on a global scale with all the frightening chain-feeding reactions.

This became only too clear in October 1987 when, following the Wall Street crash, shock waves were immediately felt everywhere shares were traded. Fear was back and global greed had turned overnight into global panic. Tokyo fell 15 per cent in a day, London 22 per cent in two days, while casino Hong Kong resorted to closing its market altogether. When it reopened a week later, the result was a one-day 35 per cent plunge. So as far as the financial markets were concerned, technology had bred a monster.

The Flood of Liquidity

The gathering hordes employed in the money industry should have been aware of these dangers. The wiser (and usually older) ones were. The problem was that more and more get-rich-quick Charlies were gatecrashing the party and quantity did not breed quality. The money business had continued to grow, fuelled by the flood of liquidity (cash or borrowed cash) which was being spent on financial assets. This had pushed stock markets ever higher, sometimes, as in Japan, seemingly regardless of underlying economic activity. The result was a perverse deviant of the 1970s phenomenon, financial asset inflation, the speculative bubble which disguised the underlying deflationary forces ravaging the world economy.

Money always needs to find a home. In the 1980s it went increasingly into financial instruments, as much for a lack of other suitable investment choices as for the attractions of stocks and bonds. During the 1970s it paid off to invest in real assets. For both individuals and companies it made sense to borrow money, be it to buy a home or build a factory, because the cost of borrowing (interest rates) was well below the rising rate of inflation. It paid to be in debt. The more conservative, who frowned on the seductive lure of the overdraft or the mortgage, lost out badly, seeing their capital wiped out by the erosion in the value of money. That is why inflation, which penalizes the prudent, saving classes, is so politically and morally damaging.

The watershed for inflation came with the advent of a restrictive monetary policy in America in 1979. That began with the decision by Paul Volker, the then chairman of the Federal Reserve (America's central bank, also known as the Fed), to impose a severe monetary squeeze. American interest rates soared to the 20 per cent level as inflation was squeezed out of the system.

This amounted to a change in the game's ground rules, the results of which are still unfolding. It affected marginal producers everywhere. In the 1970s booming commodity prices had encouraged a tremendous flurry of production. In the 1980s much of this relatively new production capacity became uneconomic and there were supply gluts everywhere. The world had too much of everything. Oil was perhaps the most dramatic example of supply and demand at work, of shortage turning into excess. A whole host of commodities and industries were similarly affected; from sugar to tin, steel to ships, semiconductors to motor-cars, from farmland to labour (and consequently unemployment) everywhere. Compounding the pain for producers, new technology made the use of raw materials many times more efficient which meant fewer of them were needed. It even threatened to make some industrial commodities redundant.

This outcome vindicated those believers in the free market who, in the depth of the 1970s oil crises, amid mass hysteria about energy shortages, argued that supply and demand would work much more efficiently than production controls. Their simple message was to sit back and watch the OPEC cartel price itself out of the market. That is just what happened. Even in early 1988 oil only hovered around $17 a barrel because of the willingness of Saudi Arabia to curb its own production drastically. It is a form of masochism that cannot last. That country has 110 years of proven oil reserves which can be pumped at a cost of only 50 US cents a barrel.

To the would-be investor this world of glut has one key message: that there are few attractive areas in which to invest spare cash in new productive capacity. As a result, liquidity piled up on the sidelines. Indeed, money was encouraged to stay idle because of the high real interest rates ('real' in the sense of being above the level of inflation) which were available to depositors as a consequence of Volker's tight money policy. Whereas in the 1970s savers who deposited money in the bank saw the value of their capital eroded by inflation, in the 1980s they have earned a return comfortably above the falling inflation rate. If they invested in bonds, they have also made spectacular capital gains. The price of a bond appreciates in value when interest rates fall. When American long-term treasury bond yields plunged from around 14 per cent in the early 1980s to nearly as low as 7 per cent in April 1986, the biggest bull market in bonds for fifty years resulted.

Industrialists drew the same conclusions as investors. With their industries suffering from excess manufacturing capacity, company executives increasingly realized that it made more sense to invest their spare cash buying financial assets. In America numerous companies have bought back large quantities of their own shares or bought the shares of other companies. Hence the huge profits earned on Wall Street from the takeover boom. In Japan when the soaring yen in 1985–7 made many exports uncompetitive, traditional exporting companies had to look for a new way to make money. Many found it by using their spare cash to speculate in the local stock market. Even riskier, some borrowed money to speculate as a way of propping up earnings. The rationale was the same in all cases. Financial assets promised a superior rate of return to the business of producing goods and selling them.

This swamp of liquidity led to today's financial scourge and nowhere more so than in America. That is the explosion of debt. With gluts everywhere, monetary authorities have had to keep printing money to keep the economy growing. Contrary to the conventional monetarist theories espoused by Professor Milton Friedman of the University of Chicago and others, that has not been inflationary because of the prevailing overcapacity.

The problem with debt is that it puts an economy on a treadmill. Once on, it is hard to step off. The bigger the debt overhang, the more money that must be earned to pay back the interest on that debt and the less left over for profit. Today there is a debt culture. There is debt at the individual level: the credit card, the instalment loan, the home mortgage, the purchase of shares on a 50 per cent margin account or, more scary, the buying of futures contracts where, before the stock market crash, speculators needed only to put down 5 per cent or so of the sum risked. There is debt at the corporate level and debt at the governmental level.

At the end of 1987 America's federal government alone had a total debt of $2.35 trillion, and state and local governments another $550bn.-worth. In 1987 America's federal government spent around $165bn. servicing its debt and state and local governments another $55bn. Conservative estimates put America's national debt at $4 trillion by the year 2000, which would mean interest payments running at $1bn. a day. These figures do not even include private-sector debt. Government and private-sector, non-financial debt in America, a definition which excludes the banks, is now reckoned to total around $8 trillion.

The Debt Bomb

The growth in outstanding obligations has been called the debt bomb and with good reason. Debt is growing much faster in the American economy than money is being made. In the past three years debt increased more than three times as fast as profits. This trend is unsustainable. Either debt slows through the liquidation of existing debts because borrowers cannot pay the interest or profits must increase enormously to service the debt. Unfortunately, the odds favour default and liquidation which is, of course, highly deflationary. Moreover, the longer the debt is allowed to accumulate through political fixing, the worse the eventual liquidation and the longer the subsequent depression.

The figures for the American government's debt do not, of course, include that great debt hangover from the 1970s, sovereign debt. Brazil, Mexico, and Argentina, to name only the worst cases, and other Third World countries still face an outstanding debt burden of some $700bn. which they are never going to repay in full, a fact which the biggest American bank creditors at last began to recognize in 1987, five years after the crisis first made headlines. These banks will have to pay for this loss by writing off their loans. No one yet knows by how much though it seems bound to be more than the 25–30 per cent the big New York banks have so far reserved for. Because the American government has insured depositors in these banks up to $100,000 per head through federal deposit insurance, the cost of bailing out the banks concerned will eventually fall on the government, which means the taxpayer. Just as it was the taxpayer who paid for the multi-billion-dollar bail-out of Chicago's Continental Illinois in 1984. The Federal Reserve not only bailed out depositors up to $100,000 on that occasion, as deposit insurance requires, but all depositors, even if they lived in Switzerland, in what amounted to effective nationalization. With 50 per cent of the deposits in the American banking system held by foreigners, the Federal Reserve presumably feels it has little choice in such emergencies.

Nor can we blandly assume that the debtor nations will go on paying interest. Since the sovereign debt crisis erupted in August 1982 with Mexico's declaration of insolvency and threatened default, an event which coincided with the start of Wall Street's bull market, the debtor countries have for most of the period gone on paying interest. Since bankers have been unwilling to lend new money after bad unless it was coming straight back to them in interest payments, there has been a one-way flow of money from the poor debtor countries to the rich creditor countries. From 1983 to 1987 there was a cumulative net drain of $140bn. out of the most heavily indebted countries. No wonder the stock markets of London, New York, Tokyo and elsewhere were booming. The money has had nowhere else to go. Stockbrokers have been profiting at the expense of undernourished peasants in the Third World.

Since 1982 the accumulation of debt in other areas of the economy has been such that sovereign debt has become just one aspect of the overall debt problem. That does not make it any less serious. New debt problems have simply been piled on top of old ones. But when Brazil in February 1987 stopped paying interest on $68bn. it owed to foreign bankers at the time out of its then total $113bn. of foreign debt, it pushed sovereign debt back into the headlines.

The pertinent question is how long the debtor countries will continue to tolerate the political dynamite of a one-way flow of capital out of their country without declaring outright default. History – most of these countries defaulted in the 1920/30s period – suggests that practical default, if not outright repudiation, is inevitable. The point at issue then becomes one of timing. The final straw for these countries will probably be when they find their export markets closed to them either through protectionism and the erection of trade barriers or because of a recession in America. Take away the ability to trade and you remove the incentive not to default.

As always, there is a broader political context to America's debt burden. That is the change in the political power equation.

America might still have the guns but it no longer has the money. And, save in the most desperate circumstances such as a threat to default, a country deeply in debt does not enjoy great political bargaining power.

In 1985 America became the world's biggest debtor nation, overtaking Brazil. Much of this borrowing was financed by the new wealth of Japan which finds itself, to its increasing embarrassment, with a vast cash surplus. Then in April 1986 Japan's admittedly wildly inflated stock market overtook America's as the world's largest.

These events passed almost unnoticed by an American public happy (at least until the disclosure in late 1986 of arms' sales to Iran) with the patriotic rhetoric of President Ronald Reagan. Yet what could be at stake is nothing less than an end to Pax Americana, to the supremacy of the English-speaking world.

In June 1987 David Hale, an economist with the Chicago-based Kemper Financial Services, published an interesting paper called 'The Twilight of Anglo-American Power'. In it he argued that the Reagan period would go down in history as 'an Indian summer reprieve from America's imperial retreat'. Hale calculated that at its current rate of borrowing America was likely to have an external debt of $1 trillion by the early 1990s as compared with an external investment surplus of $200bn. in 1982. That swift turnround in circumstances becomes increasingly analogous to the rise of America as the world's dominant economic power and the eclipse of Britain, a development which was complete by 1945 and the end of the Second World War. The only difference is that this transition has occurred much faster, and Britain's wealth was dissipated in fighting Hitler, not in consuming.

The worry is that when the American people wake up to the consequences of what has actually been happening during the Reagan years, their reaction will not be positive. Hale wrote:

Once the full consequences of this adjustment becomes apparent to the public, there is a danger that the resurgent American confidence of the Reagan era could degenerate into a frustrated nationalism, spawning a new political mood conducive to isolationism, protectionism, and withdrawal of American military forces from Europe and Asia.

This danger is less a possibility than a probability.

So far these developments have been confined mostly to the business pages. But to anyone who believes that economics determines politics, they mark a watershed. Could American government treasury bonds become at the end of the twentieth century the equivalent of Russia's Tsarist loans at the start of it; pieces of paper to adorn the mantelpiece? The question is not as absurd as it would have seemed five years ago; even if the losses are not through outright default but rather through a wholesale depreciation in the value of the dollar or, say, a unilateral reduction in interest rates paid to foreign bond holders.

However, it would be unfair to single out America's problem. The debt culture is not confined to Uncle Sam. Figures prepared by Ed Hyman, an economist at C. J. Lawrence, a New York stock-broking firm, show the affliction is global. Total domestic non-financial debt at the end of 1987 in Japan was 239 per cent of that country's gross national product, compared with 205 per cent of GNP in Britain and a comparatively modest 178 per cent in America. There is another comfort for the United States. America should be spared the worst of any depression since as a large continental economy (especially if Canada and Mexico are included in a trade zone) it would weather a protectionist climate far better than the Asian and western Europeans who have become so dependent on exporting to America. In short, America has the market.

Such matters are the largest of issues but they connect directly with our theme. Wall Street and the City of London were direct beneficiaries of this explosion in debt because they dealt in the multiplicity of debt instruments. Indeed, the very prosperity through debt trading was a function of the underlying false prosperity.

Wall Street's top investment banks such as First Boston, Goldman Sachs, Merrill Lynch, Morgan Stanley, Salomon Brothers, and Shearson Lehman offered, in the context of the money business, state-of-the-art technology. Employing the best brains from the business schools, they led the way in devising ever more complex debt securities to satisfy investors' every whim. The result was a seemingly constant generation of new product. The investment bankers expanded these services as trading in the debt markets exploded. In 1987 the daily average volume in America's long-term government bond market was $17bn. according to Salomon Brothers figures. The daily average trading in treasury bond futures was an even bigger $22bn. The same pattern was evident in London. After Big Bang deregulated the markets in October 1986 the daily trading average in long-dated gilts (British government bonds) was up threefold on the 1986 figure to around

£3bn. In Tokyo daily average spot trading in yen government bonds reached $20bn. in 1987, and in the Tokyo bond futures market $46bn.

Securitization

A by-product of this frenzied trading was securitization, an ugly term used to describe the process by which traditional bank loans were replaced by tradeable securities. Investors could now buy all manner of securitized debt, from companies' commercial paper to securitized mortgages, car loans, credit card loans, even securitized federal government loans.

Here again the going was made by Wall Street's investment bankers who had a natural incentive to securitize because of the 1933 Glass-Steagall Act. Conceived in the Great Depression, this separated commercial banking (making loans) from investment banking (underwriting and trading securities). The politicians passed the legislation because they blamed the banks for selling bonds to the general investing public. There was particular outrage that National City Bank of New York (now called Citibank) securitized its Peruvian loans and sold them to retail investors shortly before Peru defaulted. Many other such bonds defaulted during the 1930s. The effect of Glass-Steagall was to split financial institutions into two. Thus Wall Street's most famous private bank at the time, J. P. Morgan, divided into Morgan Guaranty, the commercial bank, and Morgan Stanley, the investment bank.

Despite continuing piecemeal erosion, the substance of this legislation remains intact today, though a bill to repeal Glass-Steagall was before Congress during 1988. It means that the most aggressive commercial banks, such as Citibank or Morgan Guaranty, still cannot underwrite or trade in corporate securities at home, an activity they have long practised in London's free-for-all Euromarkets. This offshore market began in 1963 as a means of bringing together European investors who owned dollars with European borrowers who wanted to borrow dollars. It has since mushroomed, being used by governments, companies, and banks to raise long-term debt in all the world's leading currencies. Because companies have found it cheaper to raise money by selling bonds rather than by borrowing from the bank, America's commercial banks have lost their clients and, increasingly their very franchise, to the investment banks.

Legal protection has then allowed Wall Street firms to enjoy windfall profits. Commercial bankers might have enjoyed the boom business of the 1970s, namely the recycling of OPEC petro-dollars via sovereign lending, but for most of the 1980s it has been investment bankers trading debt securities who have prospered.

That bonanza has not gone unchallenged. Since there is no good reason why an investment banker can underwrite or sell corporate securities and a commercial banker cannot, Glass-Steagall will surely fall by the wayside. In their arguments for abolition, America's commercial bankers like to claim that securitization is a new technology which has replaced traditional bank lending. It is nothing of the sort. Although this generation's crop of clever young Wall Streeters might have devised some fancy new gim-micks, there is nothing fundamentally new, let alone technologic-al, about securitization. Financing by selling bond issues was common in the nineteenth century.

Nor is securitization quite the panacea its advocates claim. They argue that because securities are more liquid (i.e. they can be easily sold in the marketplace) they are safer than loans. Yet here again history teaches a different lesson. Listen to George Moore, the down-to-earth former chairman of New York's National City Bank (the forerunner of Citibank), America's biggest com-mercial bank. In his memoirs, published in 1987, the then eight-two-year-old Moore described how banks in the 1920s were not only big issuers of corporate bonds but also big investors in them, as were their clients. He observed that the arguments in favour of securitization today reminded him of the arguments used then. 'The fact is, of course, that when your bank needs the cash all the other bondholders need cash, too, and the market price of the bonds goes down – if you can sell them at all.' The last point is not academic. For the record, 50 per cent of the foreign government bonds issued between 1925 and 1929 defaulted, as did 28 per cent of the domestic corporate bond issues and 21 per cent of the urban home mortgage loans. Unlike bank loans, bonds cannot easily be rescheduled.

So today's buyers of debt paper, which include insurance companies and pension funds, would do well to pause and ask themselves a few basic questions. Tilden's account of an earlier débâcle again merits repetition.

Bolivian promises, stocks of gigantic but creaking financial institu-tions, real-estate bonds based upon mad valuations or dishonest ones, notes of foreign corporations whose very names were strange to the purchasers – all were swept into the bank vaults by the same broom and on the same 'guaranty' – a warrant which proved to be originated either in ignorance or guile, with a touch of arrogance for seasoning.

The following chapters will describe that blend of ignorance, guile, and arrogance which remains an eloquent description of many of those who have been inhabiting the financial markets. They will also show that, just as the stock market has crashed, so will the debt markets. Indeed, the damage will be worse. Many bonds issued in the 1980s will never be repaid. The debt is global, oppressive, and unpayable, which is why we face the gloomy prospect of a deep and long-drawn-out depression.

WALL STREET

'Wall Street is always the same: only the pockets change.'
Jesse Livermore, speculator, 1877–1940

The Insider-Trading Scandal

For humbug it was hard to beat. In a signed statement released in November 1986 to coincide with the announcement that he had confessed to insider trading following a Securities and Exchange Commission (S.E.C.) investigation, Ivan Boesky, a celebrated speculator in shares of companies involved in takeovers, declared: 'I know that in the wake of today's events, many will call for reform. If my mistakes launch a process of re-examination of the rules and practices of our marketplace, then perhaps some good will result.'

To the many cynical observers on Wall Street, who did not believe in divine conversions on the road to Grand Central Station, this indicated rather that Boesky, who had been fined $100m., ordered to pay back another $100m. in ill-gotten gains and banned for life from dealing in American securities, would make damn sure others did not have any fun either. Hence the widespread fears about where his revelations to the S.E.C. would lead. The American judicial process known as 'plea bargaining' gave Boesky every incentive to sneak on as many big fish as he could in order to reduce his own sentence, which is just what he proceeded to do.

The Boesky scandal, and its resulting fall-out in terms of more insider-trading cases, unleashed a torrent of press comment and industry posturing on the need to improve ethics on Wall Street. Only more detached observers grasped the true significance of the headline coverage, namely that such scandals always occur near

17

the end of all great periods of speculation. For during a time of fast money, money goes into the hands of those who play fastest and closest to the edge.

Insider trading is part and parcel of markets because information, plus emotion, is what they trade on. Note the witty if cynical aphorism coined by Daniel Drew, the nineteenth-century speculator in railroad shares: 'Anybody who plays the stock market not as an insider is like a man buying cows in the moonlight.' That sentiment may have been expressed over a century ago but it remains pertinent today. To pretend that everyone participating in the financial markets is doing so with the same amount of information is to deceive the general investing public. Better they be warned of the risks as well as lured by the rewards of investing.

Boesky fell, not because he was doing something no one else was doing but because he was doing it on a gargantuan scale which made it inevitable he would get caught. Greed begets hubris and Boesky and his friends were merely a symptom of that greed which knows no limits, and hence of a market which was nearing its peak. Had Boesky still been active almost a year later, he would doubtless have been wiped out in the stock market crash of October 1987. The takeover stocks which he speculated in were probably the biggest losers in that débâcle. In such a rout prior knowledge of a thousand impending takeover deals is of no help whatsoever. Indeed, the greater the knowledge of inside information, the bigger the subsequent loss because the arbitrageur will be invested in more deals which are subsequently called off.

The Role of the Investment Banks

Wall Street lived increasingly off both fear and greed during the 1980s bull market. Investment bankers may have pulled in million-dollar-plus salaries and business-school graduates may have rushed, lemming-like, to join the fashionable industry of the day, but the wiser members of America's financial community had long ago begun to worry about the consequences of this remorseless growth.

The securities industry anywhere is not, in essence, complex. It deals in one commodity – money. Just as it prospers when there is plenty of it around, so it hurts when the supply contracts. The ebb and flow of credit, which is just another word for debt, is as cyclical as ever, and by 1987 Wall Street, as the world's leading financial centre and a leading manufacturer of debt, was approaching the high point of the cycle. None of this was new to hard-headed Wall Streeters. Their problem was that being deal-driven, they found it hard if not impossible to turn business down just because a hunch told them a bear market (a period when the prices of shares fall) was just round the corner. That mentality bred a competitive frenzy to hire more and more staff and to chase deals at ever lower profit margins.

To complicate matters, there was a new twist to this cycle, the biggest bull market the world had seen since the 1920s. That was the perception and increasing practice of a global financial market. After decades of myopia, virtually all Wall Street's top managers were suddenly prepared to acknowledge they were operating within a global marketplace and that New York was but one prong of a three-dimensional time zone that also included London and Tokyo.

In order to turn this strategic vision into commercial reality, New York's top investment banks used some of their recent years' profits to build an international business at a frantic pace. Big operations in London and Tokyo were built up in just two or three years. The result was huge increases in operating costs and numbers of people employed. A major investment bank, Salomon Brothers, the New York bond-trading house, grew in 1986 by an astonishing 40 per cent. Some 36 per cent of the trainees it recruited were non-Americans, mainly Europeans or Japanese. Less than a year later and a mere week before the October 1987 stock market crash Salomon announced it was dismissing 800 people (or 12 per cent of its workforce of 6,500) in an attempt to bring under control seemingly runaway costs. The execution of that decision could be brutal. One Salomon municipal bond trader was called up at 4 a.m. in Honolulu on the first night of his honeymoon to be told that he would no longer be in a job which the year before had paid him some $300,000. Fortunately, his wife worked for Salomon as well and kept her job.

Much worse was to come. By March 1988 some 15,000 people had been fired on Wall Street. Most dramatic was the 6,000 or so jobs lost at stockbroker E. F. Hutton when it was bought by Shearson Lehman in January 1988. However virtually no firm was immune. Indeed business was so bad, as measured by declining securities trading volumes, that many Wall Streeters sensed that the carnage had only just begin. For when revenues fall in the money business, management's immediate response has always been to cut costs. The past five years' glamour profession was fast degenerating into the next five years' sob story.

Wall Street's commitment to being global may have been laudable but it has meant a change in the rules of the game for the top Wall Street investment banks, a move into uncharted waters. That presented a commercial as well as a management challenge. For despite their undoubted aggression and comfort in managing risk, *the* business of the investment banker, the big Wall Street houses have continued to prosper at home in a protected environment because of the Glass-Steagall Act.

Glass-Steagall, combined with securitization, has caused the commercial banks to lose their clients in droves to the investment banks. In the deregulated global market this is an anomaly which cannot last, a point that was highlighted by London's Big Bang in October 1986. For, while Tokyo's financial system remains regulated in both pricing and structure, with interest-rate ceilings on bank deposits and fixed stockbroking commissions intact, London has become the financial industry's laboratory with commercial and investment bankers free to compete.

That has left Wall Street as the half-way house. Fixed stockbroking commissions disappeared as long ago as 1 May 1975. This resulted in much greater industry concentration, a dramatic fall in commissions for big institutional investors and, to cater for retail investors, the rise of the discount broker who charged investors bargain-basement commissions but provided no investment advice. However, thanks to Glass-Steagall, the structural aspect of regulation remained intact. So for the moment America's top investment banks still preside over what has amounted to a lucrative oligopoly. Wall Street's select group of investment banks, the so-called 'bulge-bracket' firms, namely First Boston, Goldman Sachs, Merrill Lynch, Morgan Stanley, Salomon Brothers, and Shearson Lehman, continued in 1987 to enjoy a dominant 80 per cent or so share of the business.

Since they now realize deregulation at home is coming, whether piecemeal fashion or by wholesale legislative reform in Congress, these Wall Street firms spent some of this cycle's profits building their global muscle in both the trading and selling ('distribution') of securities. It is a game where not everyone can emerge the winner. Senior financiers give differing estimates as to how many full-service global financial middle men the world has room for. The optimists say twenty-five; the pessimists fifteen at best.

Even that higher number would mean many of today's players either dropping out, being taken over or declining, voluntarily or involuntarily, into niche operators. For, if deregulation means anything, it means everyone competing on everyone else's patch where banks (commercial banks) can own brokers (investment banks) and vice versa. At some stage, insurance companies may even be allowed in too.

For now, the challenge for the Wall Street investment banks is that they increasingly find themselves competing against the world's commercial-banking giants, as well as foreign securities companies. Most of the banks long ago set up global operations and are already experienced in running large, diffuse organizations. That does not only mean a Citicorp or Chase Manhattan. It also means the likes of Dai-Ichi Kangyo (Japan's and the world's largest bank), Zurich-based Union Bank of Switzerland (Switzerland's largest), and Frankfurt-based Deutsche Bank (West Germany's largest). That is not to mention Japan's 'Big Four' securities houses: Nomura, Daiwa, Nikko, and Yamaichi, all of whom in terms of their 1988 stock market capitalizations, dwarf the biggest Wall Street firms.

The bulge-bracket firms also face pressure from below their ranks. Drexel Burnham Lambert is a good example. By refusing to play the bulge-bracket game, it muscled its way to prominence by pioneering and becoming leading player in the 'junk-bond' market. Junk bonds are high-yield bonds (i.e. bonds paying above average interest rates) issued by companies which are below investment grade as measured by the credit-rating agencies, Moody's and Standard & Poors. The word junk, however, is a misnomer. Drexel reckons that more than 95 per cent of the more than 22,000 American companies with over $35m. in annual sales would be rated investment grade.

By 1988 junk had grown up into a $160bn. market. Drexel, by providing access to finance through bond issues, had therefore helped a lot of companies and managers grow, stay afloat or even get rich when other investment banks were not interested in helping, which is surely what capitalism and Wall Street should be about. This is why so many Drexel clients have, so far, remained conspicuously loyal, despite highly publicized government insider-trading investigations into the firm which continued throughout 1987 and 1988. These have centred on the firm's Beverly Hills office and in particular junk-bond chief Mike Milken, the man credited with creating the 1980s junk-bond phenomenon.

Drexel's refusal to play by Wall Street's established rules, in particular not sharing business with other firms, did not make it many friends within its own industry. Members of the Wall Street establishment always complained they could not relax on a deal because Drexel was always so aggressive, constantly looking to score points. That explains why when, post-Boesky, it became known that Drexel was being investigated, the rest of Wall Street positively gloated, competing to spread rumours about how Drexel would be laid low by the scandal. 'They're just a bunch of schmucks. There won't be a lot of guys at their wake,' was the not untypical comment of a president of one top firm, quoted anonymously in a trade weekly. None the less, such sentiments have not stopped most top firms from building their own junk-bond efforts. Still Drexel remains the leader in junk.

If Drexel has been the star newcomer in this cycle, there are other aspiring competitors too. Prudential Bache (owned by America's biggest insurance company), Dean Witter (owned by the huge retailer Sears Roebuck), and Kidder Peabody (owned and, following the firm's embroilment in insider-trading scandals, managed by industrial giant, General Electric) are examples of middle-ranking broking firms which have been bought by deep-pocketed parents. In a risk-taking business whose need for capital had become increasingly rapacious, these all presented competitive threats. They also put further downward pressure on profit margins.

So by the time of the stock market crash investment banking on Wall Street had already all the attributes of a vogue industry which everyone was stampeding into at the top of the cycle. It was ripe for a fall. Even if the momentum now somehow continues, which it will not since that would depend on an unsustainable explosion in the issue and trading of debt, the increased competition would still translate into lower returns on capital. That is one reason why the publicly traded Wall Street firms were selling even before the stock market's historic plunge for as much as a 50 per cent discount to the industrial companies that make up the widely followed Dow Jones Industrial Average. Investment bankers may have enjoyed 'revved-up' earning power in a fashionable industry but their companies' share prices during 1987 told a different story. Familiarity appears to have bred self-contempt as it was these same investment banks which analyse and trade in other companies' shares. The stock market's message was that the industry's headlong expansion and explosive rise in costs was destined to end in tears.

As the 1980s' securities boom unravels, it is possible that it will be the investment bankers, rather than the commercial bankers, who will suffer the worst shocks because they are more exposed to the violent swings of deregulated financial markets. That could leave the commercial banks free to buy up the pieces, assuming not only that they survive the looming default on their foreign debt exposures, which is a big if, but also that Congress repeals Glass-Steagall. That would be an ironic outcome given the current spectacle of commercial banks desperately trying to break down Glass-Steagall and Wall Street's lucrative cartel against the opposition of populists in Congress who, remembering the 1930s, do not like 'banks' dealing in securities. That traditional way of thinking has been exploited for years by artful Wall Street firms. They have proved much more adept at lobbying Congressmen (and contributing to their political campaigns) than their commercial-banking rivals. These skills have proved important since there is no practical difference in terms of potential damage done to the investor between a commercial bank and an investment bank selling dud securities to the public, which is why London's Big Bang abandoned the distinction. That will also soon happen in America. A bill to repeal Glass-Steagall was before Congress in 1988. It was co-sponsored by veteran Senate banking committee chairman William Proxmire, a long-term opponent of banking reform who only changed his mind on Glass-Steagall in 1987. Although this bill failed (and Proxmire, who retired at the end of 1988, is naturally pushing hard to have his name on historic banking legislation) the bear market will probably precipitate the end of Glass Steagall, particularly if big securities firms get into financial difficulties and need rescuing. For obvious American candidates to rescue them are the commercial banks. In fact Congress may end up begging the commercial banks to buy up ailing securities companies.

The investment banks are more vulnerable in the event of a financial crash for several reasons. First, America's commercial banks are protected by federal government deposit insurance. This effective blanket government subsidy may have caused many banks to be run carelessly. But it does provide an underlying comfort, at least for as long as depositors have faith in the federal government's credit and the dollar, two seeming constants which should not be taken for granted. There is, by contrast, no official lender of last resort to a Salomon Brothers.

Second, there is the growing risk of the firms' own principal capital in the business of investment banking. The Wall Street firms were competing with each other right up until October 1987 by betting larger and larger amounts of their own money. This is precisely what the stock market did not like. It saw these firms earning an ever increasing share of their profits from risking their own capital in securities' trading or by lending their own money to finance takeover deals, and ever less from old-fashioned advisory fee income.

As such America's investment banks have become the best example of the virtues and vices of modern finance. Their very energy and mental agility in stretching logic and financial leverage to their limits made it more than likely that the next big shock to the world's financial system would come from the international capital (stock and bond) markets. And since these markets were now global, the after shock would be felt everywhere money flows freely, as it was when Wall Street crashed.

Trading

Trading is at the heart of the dealings of the modern investment bank. It is an inherently risky business as every day the traders bet huge sums. The idea is to lock in a small spread between the buyer and a seller on every transaction and keep the flow of product moving. Imagine a double-ended funnel. Inventory in the form of bond and stock issues is taken in at one end when an investment bank underwrites an issue, and distributed at the other, hopefully after the trader has earned a profitable spread in the middle between the offer to buy and the offer to sell.

The salesman's job is to keep filling up both ends of the cone, so keeping the supply of paper moving. The risk is that some of the paper will get stuck on the neck of the cone, which means the firm's capital is at risk, because the market falls and traders hang on in the hope of a bounce in prices.

The all-important trading discipline is, therefore, to know when to take a loss. Since it goes against human nature to take a loss on any investment, because it means admitting one is wrong and losing money, this is a discipline which needs constant enforcing. It is also a business which needs managers who understand it (which usually means they must be ex-traders). That is why, in the best-run firms, the managers usually sit among the traders, constantly monitoring positions. Communication is vital. Hence the need for open-plan trading floors where everyone can be seen and no one can hide. Herbert Freiman, head of sales and trading at Shearson Lehman Hutton, is a comparative veteran by Wall Street standards. He has a rule of thumb he lives by. 'You can tell a worried trader when you look him in the eye,' he says.

But not all managers are so observant. In recent history Wall Street has suffered a number of lessons in just how painful trading can be. In May 1986 Wall Street firms lost an estimated $300m. when they calculated incorrectly that the Japanese would sell to them a new issue that they had bought at a treasury bond auction. The Japanese, however, delayed selling, catching the Wall Street houses short of the new issue. That precipitated a rush by the Wall Street firms to buy back the bonds and, therefore, a sharp rally in their price. In effect the Wall Street firms suffered a 'short squeeze' at the hands of the Japanese. Whether this was a deliberate strategy on the part of the Japanese, as some conspiracy theorists alleged, or just bad luck was not the point. Rather the episode underlined how exposed these firms had become to unexpected moves in interest rates. It also taught the American firms not to take on the Japanese.

The drama was repeated a year later, most spectacularly at Merrill Lynch. It managed to lose, before tax write-offs, $377m. or the equivalent of 12.5 per cent of its then $3bn. of equity on a single trading position. Merrill came unstuck dealing in one of the new-fangled securities dreamt up by the academics (known as 'quants' or 'rocket scientists') who have been employed in droves in recent years to pursue Wall Street's equivalent of product research. The problem is that these securities – Francis Jenkins, former head of sales and trading at First Boston, calls them 'green-eyed monsters' since they only really exist in quants' minds and on traders' electronic screens – can be so complex that they cannot be easily hedged in the futures markets to protect against a loss in value. Nor is there any guarantee that they can be easily sold. By contrast, it is always possible to find a buyer, at a price, for a run-of-the-mill treasury bond or I.B.M. shares.

In Merrill's case it was stuck with the principal-only portion of what is known as a 'stripped' mortgage-backed security during April–May 1986 when nearly all of Wall Street was caught off-guard by an unexpected sharp upward spike in interest rates. In these securities the seller auctions the interest and principal portions of the bond separately. The débâcle served to underline several points which were already becoming obvious to any sober observer. First, the sheer amounts of money that can be lost given the size of the positions. Second, the daunting task facing senior management in the sense of keeping an eye on what is going on. Third, the risks of dealing in complex securities.

Initially, Merrill sought to blame the loss on one dismissed trader exceeding his limit and concealing the position in what proved to be the vain hope that the market would bail him out. (This is known in the business as 'hiding the ticket in the drawer'. Every time a trader buys or sells he has to 'write a ticket'.) Even if the whole of the loss could have been blamed on this, which it could not, the responsibility lies with superiors which is why Merrill subsequently announced further resignations. Stopping such trading abuses is precisely what the managers are there to do.

That the Merrill trading position was open and bleeding for three weeks before the firm finally owned up to it in a public announcement also indicates that others inside Merrill aside from the individual trader knew about the deteriorating position but held off in the hope that the market would turn round. Such conspiracies of silence are fatal in the securities business. Investment bankers like to think of themselves as tough professionals. Real toughness is being able to cut a losing position. Any old fool can run a winning one. The lesson is clear. Given the mega bets these firms make every day in the markets, egos and emotions must always be kept firmly in line. The Merrill disaster may have been the biggest trading loss owned up to so far but it will not be the last. In October 1987 virtually every securities company lost money trading, often tens of millions of dollars worth, but there was no repeat of the scale of the Merrill débâcle despite the collapse in share prices.

Some firms are more natural trading houses than others. Until recently Salomon enjoyed the reputation of the best bond trader in the business and, not surprisingly, it prospered with the 1980s debt explosion. In fact when debt finally goes out of fashion so will Salomon, and the rest of Wall Street with it. In its trading strategy Salomon has traditionally had the confidence not to impose strict limits on traders. This did not mean it encouraged gambling but rather that it wanted to remain flexible. Salomon made a virtue of its minute-by-minute management of positions in fast-moving markets. The trick was to take a small spread on every deal and not to run losses. However, it has increasingly suffered a fundamental deterioration in its key businesses. Increasing competition has narrowed the trading and underwriting margins. Investment bankers used to enjoy far wider spreads between the issuer of a security and the buyer. These smaller margins tempted them to bet more money to compensate for lower spreads, a recipe for disaster during the fall in the bond market which occurred between April

1986 and October 1987. The result was that earnings suffered, Salomon's particularly.

Some firms remain uncomfortable with this most short-term of businesses. Take Goldman Sachs, which remains a private partnership. This means unlimited liability in the sense that each partner's capital is at risk. In April 1986 the firm lost a good deal in the bond market – market guesses ranged up to $200m. – though being privately owned, it was under no obligation to disclose the size of the loss. For some partners this apparently proved a rude awakening to the realities and risks of investment banking in the 1980s. They sensibly opted for early retirement, taking their depleted capital with them. Soon after Goldman decided to give itself some extra financial muscle, raising $500m. of capital by selling to Japan's Sumitomo Bank a right to 12.5 per cent of Goldman's profits.

That move once again underlined the importance of capital, which along with good people and state-of-the-art technology, are perceived as the three key ingredients of modern investment banking. Another one used to be volatility. Investment bankers grew fond of telling anyone with an ear to listen that they loved volatile markets because it gave them lots of opportunity to make money. By contrast, boring markets meant fewer chances for the traders to move in and out. The problem with this analysis is that big trading losses have since been sustained in just such volatile markets.

The truth is that volatility was fine so long as it was in the right upward direction. Until April 1986 volatility in the bond markets was predominantly in that one-way direction as investment banks made money out of falling interest rates and rising bond prices. The 'inventory' on their books, be it treasury bonds, mortgage-backed securities, municipal bonds or junk bonds, kept rising in value. An investment bank always tends to be a net owner of these paper debt securities. In such circumstances it is not difficult to make money.

From April 1986 bond prices started falling again. That tested the real skill of traders as well as their ability to hedge. For, if investment bankers tend to be net owners of securities, it is equally hard for them to be net sellers when prices fall.

If trading is intrinsically a risky business, it becomes all the riskier the greater the sums wagered. They grew ever larger up until the sobering experience of 19 October, as was clear from measuring the growth in the bulge-bracket firms' balance sheets.

In investment banking, a firm's 'assets' means the cash and securities it has bought with borrowed money (plus a few long-term investments); not, as in the case of an industrial company, bricks and mortar. Salomon, the biggest trading firm, regularly had assets on its books at the end of a trading day of some $80bn. That was money borrowed against its equity base at the end of 1987 of $3.4bn., or an assets-to-equity ratio of 22.5:1. That, if anything, is on the low side. America's Securities Industry Association calculated that in 1986 the assets-to-equity ratio for wholesale investment banks averaged 38:1. In the four years from 1983 to 1986 the assets of the big investment banks grew 240 per cent against a 47 per cent rise in the assets of all commercial banks. James Grant, a Wall Street Jeremiah, noted in his newsletter *Grant's Interest Rate Observer* that if Salomon was a commercial bank it would have replaced Morgan Guaranty as America's fourth largest bank in assets in 1986.

There are, however, some key differences. The only reason investment banks can be so highly borrowed – 'leveraged' or 'geared' to use Wall Street's or the City of London's respective jargon – is because their balance sheets are so liquid in the sense that they can be easily converted into cash by selling securities on the market. This reduces the risk of borrowing many times the firms' capital base. There is also another safety valve. An investment bank's assets are marked to market every night after the New York markets close. Commercial banks do not mark their assets (loans) to market every day, save for the securities they trade, which means that no one knows what they are really worth.

'Merchant Banking'

However, even that commendable daily discipline has become less of a source of comfort as the investment banks have increasingly committed substantial chunks of their own capital not in easily saleable securities but in altogether more illiquid investments. These can be equity investments in leveraged buy-outs (L.B.O.s), (a highly aggressive way of buying a company by using large amounts of borrowed money – five to twenty times the equity component – as the main source of financing), and/or bridge financing (short-term loans) lent to companies either to mount takeover bids or to buy back their own shares in a bid to fight off a hostile takeover bid.

This activity was the logical outcome of Wall Street's obsession with commitment of capital. it has been labelled 'merchant banking'. The phrase has stuck but most City of London merchant bankers would not recognize the label, nor be comfortable with the activity it describes.

They would be right to be both worried and sceptical. 'Merchant banking' Wall-Street style involves a quantum leap in risk taking for the investment banks. It has also been an extremely lucrative business where $100m. plus fees have been earned on a single deal. With industry cost exploding because of all those expensive M.B.A.s (Masters of Business Administration) crammed into costly office space, trading profits under pressure, and given the deal-chasing penchant of investment bankers, it has proved irresistible business. Perhaps more amazing, it has continued to prove irresistible business even after the crash. The reason for this is not hard to find. A couple of big 'merchant banking' deals can pay everyone's bonus in an otherwise lacklustre year.

Proof that 'merchant banking' was fashionable came in May 1987 when it merited a case study in the final exam at Harvard Business School. The subject was a counter offer by the aggressive British conglomerate, Hanson Trust, for America's S.C.M. Corporation, America's leading maker of typewriters, in response to an L.B.O. bid led by Merrill Lynch in which Merrill would end up as the biggest equity investor in S.C.M. How should the Wall Street firm respond? Most students answered that Merrill should counter with a better offer because the firm had to demonstrate its commitment to 'merchant banking' to remain at the forefront of the business. A minority argued that this move to acting as principal investor in takeovers put at risk the firm's traditional role as an independent advisor to companies in mergers and acquisitions (M. & A.).

Such, in a nutshell, is the debate over 'merchant banking'. Merrill, along with First Boston, led the way in this field. Of the two, First Boston was an already established leader in conventional M. & A. otherwise known as corporate finance. For Merrill 'merchant banking' was a way of aggressively using its capital to buy its way into the business.

More thoughtful advocates of 'merchant banking' like to argue that it is a natural evolution of traditional M. & A. They draw an analogue with stockbroking. It has evolved from a fixed-commission agency business (as pre-Mayday in America and pre-Big Bang in London) to a trading market-making business where capital is risked. Now they say the M. & A. business is following the same route from a fee-advisory business to a capital-commitment one.

There are two basic problems, however, with this kind of analysis. The first is the conflict of interest. In traditional corporate finance the main concern of the investment banker is his client company's balance sheet. In merchant banking it becomes his own firm's balance sheet. As Robert Pirie, president of Rothschild Inc., London's N.M. Rothschild's New York subsidiary, puts it: 'If my capital is at risk, I don't see how I can advise my clients about it. It is a conflict of interest and sooner or later the clients will wake up to it.'

The second point is that money is invested or lent in ways where it cannot easily be converted back into cash, unlike traditional securities' trading. Consider the two main forms of merchant banking.

First L.B.O.s where investment banks take equity stakes. Merrill Lynch, the most aggressive in this area, had by the middle of 1987 shareholdings in some forty companies bought as a result of L.B.O. deals. Effectively Merrill had become an industrial holding company. It is a moot point whether it understands quite what it has invested in but clearly this is a radical departure from its traditional business of stockbroking. The attraction of course for Merrill is that, not only does it earn good fees arranging the financing for these deals, but also that L.B.O.s are so highly leveraged that the return on equity invested can be correspondingly enormous. In the same way an investor makes a lot more money if he buys a share or futures contract with lots of borrowed money and the price goes up, so L.B.O.s are simply a device of buying a whole company on credit. The bigger the margin (the more money borrowed) the more that can be made. And, conversely, the more that can be lost if the company's prospects fade and the equity value falls. That is partly what happened in October 1987. The consequences to Merrill and others are still not clear though the risks are clearly great should the economy go into a severe downturn.

In bridge financing both the risk and the rewards can be even more spectacular. An example best illustrates the point. At the end of 1986 First Boston had more than its total capital of $1.4bn. committed to two deals: $865m. lent to a Canadian property company Campeau Corporation in its successful bid to take over the much bigger American company, Allied Stores, and $925m. lent to Union Carbide which needed the money to buy back its own shares.

First Boston successfully completed both deals though not without some awkward moments. It took four and a half months before it paid itself back the Campeau bridge loan by selling a Campeau junk-bond issue. Investment bankers argue that they would not take on such loans unless they were comfortable they could hold the loan until maturity. That is what they would have to do assuming they could not find buyers for the junk bonds. Still it is a prospect no one relishes. First Boston's former co-head of mergers and acquisitions, Jo Perella, who abruptly left the firm in February 1988 along with his colleague Bruce Wassertein following a highly publicized management dispute, recalls that when they put the Campeau deal before First Boston's four-man executive committee they were asked whether they would bet their careers on it. He and Bruce Wassertein, Wall Street's most famous corporate-finance duo, replied in the affirmative. Their reasoning was that Campeau was a safe bet because the collateral was secured on income from Campeau-owned buildings rented out to Canadian government tenants.

So even investment bankers need some persuading to lend nearly $1bn. or well over half their firm's capital to one company, even if it is only on a short-term basis. Still the fees that can be earned have made it that much harder to say no. First Boston made some $94m. on the Campeau Allied Stores deal alone, which compares with a paltry few million on an ordinary M. & A. advisory deal. Like any good professional advisor it made so much by billing for several different services. There was a traditional advisory fee (a mere $7m. in the Campeau deal), a commitment fee, a financing fee and a 'divestiture' fee for selling the junk bonds. In addition First Boston made money lending from the interest-rate spread between its cost of funds and the interest rate it charged Campeau. By such deals do investment bankers get rich.

Aside from the risks and the rewards, there is another aspect of 'merchant banking' worth mentioning. It is a further blurring of the divide between investment banking and commercial banking and so between lending and underwriting. It means investment banks moving into the business of lending money and making judgements on credit risks, the traditional preserves of commercial bankers. It also means the commercial banks moving into investment banking. For the banks are the senior lenders to L.B.O.s, usually accounting for at least half of the total financing. This means that in the event of a default the banks rank above the junior or subordinate debt of junk bonds and bridge finance. Sometimes the banks will also invest equity in a L.B.O., compounding both the potential risks as well as the rewards.

Peter Cohen, chairman of Shearson Lehman, has a neat definition of 'merchant banking'. He calls it 'commercial banking with securitization behind it', the difference being that investment bankers have the supposed expertise to arrange a way out by converting the loan into a piece of paper and selling it. But there is one key difference about 'merchant banking'. Usually an investment banker can relax when his deal closes. In bridge financing the risk begins at the close of the deal. Between taking on the bridge and selling the junk bonds the tension mounts inexorably. As one Wall Streeter put it: 'Everyone knows the clock is ticking against you.'

The risks of bridge loans were spelled out clearly by the credit-rating agency, Standard and Poors, in an early 1987 study. First, such deals represent huge concentrations of credit risk. Second, the takeover financing depends not only on the borrower's creditworthiness but also on conditions in the junk-bond market. Third, and most important, bridge loans are illiquid. They cannot quickly be converted into cash. To date the only reason investment bankers have been able to get away with leveraging up their balance sheets is precisely because their assets were so easily converted into cash and could be liquidated in a single day.

As with trading, the only real curb to excesses in 'merchant banking' is fear of loss. Market discipline will be imposed when somebody loses a sum of money that will dwarf Merrill's $377m. trading loss, or as Lou Perlmutter, a partner in the small, elite, and very profitable Lazard Frères, a firm which scorns this latest fad, puts its, 'when somebody gets caught with their hand in the cookie jar'. For now most firms would agree this is only a matter of time. But they all affect equal confidence that the casualty will not be their own firm.

The real catalyst to 'merchant banking' Wall-Street style was the phenomenal success of Drexel Burnham in the junk-bond market. That firm has been so successful in raising financing for takeovers through issuing so-called 'letters of comfort' (effectively a pledge to raise the required sum by selling junk bonds to its tight circle of investor clients) that more established rivals could no longer afford to ignore the growing loss of business. Their response was to come up with the money themselves.

In retrospect 'merchant banking' will probably be seen as Wall Street's final fling to extract every last dollar in this cycle's round of corporate restructuring, during which America's corporate landscape has been transformed by the 1980s takeover boom. By the autumn of 1987, even before the stock market's dive, there were signs that leveraged takeover activity was peaking. However, the crash has not yet caused a halt to 'merchant banking'. Rather, with trading revenues slumping as investors fled the markets and the investment banks themselves became less willing to bet as much of their capital trading securities, by early 1988 'merchant banking' had become the favourite hope of many on Wall Street of making big money that year. The arguments in favour of this activity were first, that post-crash share prices made L.B.O.s cheaper and second, the deals were less risky because lower share prices would mean that less debt would be needed to finance any deal. That may be. The real risk in L.B.O.s, however, is not the condition of the stock market but that of the real economy and how it affects the prospects of the companies which have taken on so much debt as a result of one of these deals. If the stock market has flashed the warning of an impending general economic downturn, then both investment and commercial banks should be pulling back rather than expanding into this inherently risky business which always involves the substitution of debt for equity.

L.B.O.s

Indeed the whole field of M. & A. had increasingly become the tail that wags the investment-banking dog, even before world stock markets crashed. That is yet another reason why the party on Wall Street is over. The revellers, however, will take some stopping. L.B.O. deals continued throughout 1987 right up until the stock market rout, even though high prices made them ever riskier. The Dow Jones Industrial Average had risen threefold since the bull market began in August 1982, making companies more expensive to buy, while the economic recovery was already five years old. Buying a cyclical company with lots of borrowed money after its share price has risen three times, and five years into an economic upswing, had to be riskier than doing the same deal back in 1982.

There was another pressure chasing deals and so pushing up prices. As is often the case when a business turns into a fad, the amount of money chasing L.B.O. deals had increased exponentially. Kohlberg, Kravis & Roberts (K.K.R.), the biggest L.B.O. partnership, was formed in 1976 when its founders left the medium-sized investment bank, Bear Stearns, to go it alone. K.K.R. started the first L.B.O. fund of $10m. the same year. In 1987 it found enough greedy institutional backers to put together a fund of some $6bn., money that would be leveraged ten and more times to do deals. It could do so because of its superb track record. Investors in K.K.R.'s 1986 $6.2bn. L.B.O. of food company, Beatrice, were estimated, just prior to the crash, to have earned a pre-tax paper profit of $3.8bn. or more than five times their total investment of some $700m.

K.K.R.'s fund was not the only pool of capital assembled. Morgan Stanley, for example, closed a $1.15bn. L.B.O. fund just six days after the crash. The money took six months to assemble from nearly fifty investors all over the world, including fifteen leading Japanese financial institutions. Despite the unfortunate timing, only one investor pulled out. In another example of business as usual Merrill Lynch approved a $500m. bridge loan only two days after 19 October. Although the deal never went through because the company subsequently changed its mind on the financing, Merrill's decision shows it still had the stomach for risk. More proof, if it were needed, came in February 1988 when First Boston said it would provide $1.1bn. in bridge financing to finance a second Campeau bid for another retailer, Federated Stores. The investment bank's move was seen as an attempt to demonstrate it was still in the 'merchant banking' business despite the abrupt departure of Wassertein and Perella. More cautious souls could only wonder that First Boston would contemplate such a risky deal only four months after the crash. Clearly it did not seem to believe in the stock market as a lead indicator of the future condition of the economy, a perhaps curious position for a securities firm.

Yet there were many others still keen to chase these deals. By mid 1988 some $25bn. had been raised in L.B.O. funds. Given that leveraged deals are usually geared with at least ten times as much debt as equity, that meant another $250bn. of fire power still on the hunt for L.B.O.s. A 28 January memo to clients from Wachtell, Lipton, Rosen & Katz, the top New York law firm which specializes in takeovers, observed: 'Bridge loans are still available and bank financing is more available than ever before.'

The point is clear. This area of the money business will only follow securities' trading into limbo when the real economy turns down and it will no longer be profitable for Wall Street to dismember and rearrange the various bits and pieces of corporate America. Nor will it be possible to find the insurance companies to buy the junk bonds. By then they will be worrying about the credit risks of those bonds they already hold. Nor will it be possible to find the commercial banks to lend. By then they will be concerned about the health of their existing L.B.O. loan portfolio. In short, L.B.O.s are just another financial fad which are sure to reap their own excesses. The amazing fact is that the game is still continuing. That again shows the deal-making mentality of most investment bankers. The potential rewards are so great that act first, think later is the only formula that counts.

This does not mean that a cyclical slump will mark the end of all L.B.O.s for ever, even if many of the latest deals do come unstuck. For, if the form has bred excesses, the mechanism itself is here to stay. The reason is that the L.B.O. is virtuously capitalistic because it gives managers a chance to be entrepreneurs and own a chunk of their own company at the cost of going heavily into debt. However, as experienced L.B.O. specialists always argue, quality of management is the vital ingredient determining whether most L.B.O.s turn out a success, not the details of the financing nor even the product. Deal-chasing investment bankers should have kept reminding themselves of that as they piled deeper into this very different kind of business. There is more to running a company than crunching a few numbers and manipulating a balance sheet.

Risk Arbitrage

If L.B.O.s are an example of one fad, risk arbitrage, the peculiar Wall Street business of speculating in takeover shares which Boesky made infamous, was another. Thanks to the killer blows of Boesky and then, eleven months later, the stock market crash, it went right out of favour. That shows, like Hollywood, how fickle Wall Street is. A hot area one minute becomes a pariah the next as the money merchants get cold feet. Thus the clumsy giant Merrill Lynch withdrew completely from the business after losing tens of millions in the sell-off following the Boesky announcement. It is just such changes in sentiment which the best investment bankers exploit. Bear Stearns, which has a deserved reputation for eschewing fashion, correctly saw the exit of Boesky and others as a money-making opportunity. The firm raised the amount of capital it commits to risk arbitrage by a hefty 50 per cent. Said its street-wise trader chairman Alan 'Ace' Greenberg: 'We were making a living when we were playing with cheats. We should do even better now.' Unfortunately Bear Stearns also dropped many millions in the October 1987 crash in this area, though by March

1988 risk arbitrage had recovered strongly again with the renewed takeover activity.

That sort of opportunistic, seat-of-the-pants response is the traditional genius of investment banking. But as the top Wall Street firms grew bigger and as the erosion of barriers between different forms of financial institutions gathered pace, these firms were, however reluctantly, being compelled to build bureaucracies and management controls. As Salomon has found out, creative anarchy was no longer an option.

The Response to the Challenge

How have the different Wall Street firms responded to the challenge? And how will they cope with the growing threat to their very survival? Brief sketches of five firms follow: one upstart with huge ambitions; one giant in trading that has plateaued; one blue chip that was forced to change itself to stay in the big league; one still-private entity fighting a rearguard battle to preserve its club-like culture; and one colossus, too big and diffuse to manage but also probably too strong to fail.

PRUDENTIAL-BACHE

Prudential-Bache's immodest goal is to be one of the world's top three investment banks. Its plan, pompously titled 'Project 89', has, not surprisingly, attracted much scepticism, if not plain ridicule, on Wall Street. That only increased as the firm, backed by a $1.2bn. investment from its wealthy parent, ventured forth, cheque book in hand, to lure away talent from rival firms.

Wall Street's doubts were understandable. Pru-Bache has not made money since the American Prudential, the country's largest insurance company, bought the ailing but venerable Bache (established in 1879) for $385m. in 1981. Bache was then in poor shape having nearly come unstuck as one of the unfortunate brokers in the Texan Hunt brothers' failed attempt to corner the silver market in early 1980.

Since then the firm has been slowly grappling its way back to profitability. But more interesting are its grandiose ambitions, which are backed by the wealthiest of parents. 'We're Bigger Than Life', the Prudential adverts declare. By its own reckoning, the Pru is the biggest farmer in America, the biggest investor in oil and gas, the biggest money manager with assets of $177bn. at the end of 1986, and the country's biggest owner of property after the federal government and the Catholic church.

As significant as its sheer financial clout, the Prudential is an investing institution sufficiently established to be able to take a long view and ride out the cycle. It has had to do just that with its oil and gas portfolio, much of which was bought in 1979–80 at the top of that market. It has probably made the same mistake in investment banking, though in the long term that will not matter, providing it has the stamina to stick to its investment and its goal of being one of the surviving global financial-service firms. Certainly, short-term profit considerations are not paramount. The Prudential is not a publicly quoted company which in America must report to shareholders every three months.

Why does the American Pru want to own an investment bank? Ted Fowler, Pru-Bache's co-head of investment banking and recruited to the firm from First Boston, tells an interesting story. When he was first approached by the firm, his instinctive reaction was that of most hardened Wall Streeters; namely that there was no way he was joining a second-rater like Pru-Bache. He changed his mind after visiting the Prudential's chiefs in Newark, New Jersey. They told him that one reason they were interested in investment banking was because the Prudential was no longer getting the service it wanted from Wall Street. As a big institutional investor it relies on Wall Street to bring it deals and investment ideas. Increasingly, however, Wall Street firms are taking the best deals for their own account. Fowler says: 'They realized they no longer had a competitive edge. Their money had become a commodity.' The Prudential concluded that it needed to start originating the deals itself.

Pru-Bache's strategy has been to build one strong product area and expand the rest of the business on the back of it. The chosen product is interest-rate 'swaps', a fancy financial gimmick where two parties, usually companies or banks, agree to exchange interest payments on each other's debt. The firm has enjoyed a competitive edge in the swaps business because it successfully persuaded its wealthy owner to back each swap with its own triple-A credit rating. This allows the swap team the considerable luxury of not having to find swap counterparties before committing to deals. The Pru simply takes swaps on to its own books, only later looking for a counterparty. This has given Pru-Bache the base on which to build the team required for a 'full service' global investment bank. Hence the frantic recruiting in all product areas both in America and overseas, all financed by the Prudential's cash. No one can say that Messrs Fowler and his fellow co-head of investment banking, Jim Crowley, have not been having fun.

They contend that Wall Street has a history of fallen angels. Firms rise to prominence and then fall precipitously from grace. The largest retail broker in the 1920s was Dillon Reid. Now it is in the second division. Pru-Bache hopes that the leading players in the 1990s will be radically different from today's bulge-bracket names, and it is probably right. Its guess is that the key change in the business will be the decline in profitability of the core trading business. The conventional trading orientation of a Salomon Brothers will no longer be enough. Disinflation and booming financial markets have disguised the dismal prosects of the sales and trading business and covered up a multitude of sins. Crowley says: 'Everybody in a bull market makes money in trading. Why do you make money? Because your inventories go up.'

If investment banks will have to go on trading as a basic function of their business, it is not an area where they will add value and make money. That will come from 'merchant banking'. The firm's strategy document claims: 'The winners of the 1990s will be more than underwriters, agents and advisors – they will control business as a principal.' And if this means capital tied up in illiquid positions that, according to Fowler, is just where tomorrow's investment bankers will add value. They will purchase an illiquid asset cheaply and use their 'financial technology' to make it saleable and so worth more. That, he rightly argues, is a very different kind of business from trading one hundredth of a percentage point spreads all day every day.

So uppity, gung-ho Pru-Bache reckons it is prepared for the upcoming concentration in the money industry as Glass-Steagall disintegrates and the commercial banking juggernauts and foreign competitors enter the fray. Nor, with its rich parent, does it fear a blow-out. Fowler argues: 'The best thing that can happen to our strategy is a dramatic depression. There is more opportunity for people like us to make money in a depression who have the capital and culture to build through the cycle. We are not a public company.'

Whether the Pru's senior officers sitting in suburban Newark, New Jersey, would quite put it like that is another matter. But there is no doubt that the deep-pocket strengths Fowler refers to could prove an advantage, so long as the Prudential has the stomach for the long haul. It will need it. In 1987 Pru-Bache lost $164m.

SALOMON INC.

Salomon Inc. is America's largest investment bank with some $3.4bn. of equity at the end of 1987. The firm's growth exploded in the 1980s thanks to its acknowledged prowess in trading in America's debt securities markets.

The more debt around, the more pieces of paper for Salomon to underwrite, trade, and distribute. This is ironic because the firm's former chief economist, Dr Henry Kaufman, who resigned in early 1988, long ago acquired the nickname Dr Doom because of his continued warnings about the dangers of America's addiction to debt. However correct he may have been to warn of the consequences, the fact remains that his own firm has been one of the biggest pushers, if not supplier, of this particular drug.

Salomon has also been creative in devising new paper debt products. Its biggest success has been mortgage-backed securities which, together with junk bonds, were the two big product bonanzas developed by Wall Street in this cycle. These are pools of mortgages bundled together into pieces of paper and sold as securities. Their big selling point for investors is that they are often guaranteed by the federal government but offer a higher interest-rate yield than treasury bonds. The yield is higher because the risk is greater. For mortgage-backed securities are not, like treasury bonds, just a play on interest rates. Their value also varies with the rate of mortgage pre-payments. An investor in a pool of mortgages which are suddenly paid off will suffer from a loss in income stream (because the monthly mortgage payments have stopped) and so a drop in the value of his principal.

Salomon was the pioneer in this market which exploded from nothing in the late 1970s to $600 bn. in 1987. It remains the market leader followed by First Boston. For years the two firms virtually shared the market between them. Indeed mortgage securities have in recent years been Salomon's most profitable product accounting for up to 30 per cent of profits.

But despite its success during the 1980s in the debt markets, Salomon is now fighting for its survival as an independent firm. Significantly, Salomon's share price peaked with the treasury bond market in April 1986 and has fallen ever since, even when the Dow was soaring. Investment banks may have been out of investment fashion during this period, but Salomon has suffered more than most. The first reason was the familiar one of rising interest rates. The second was that the market was, in hindsight, correctly worried that the firm did not possess the management structure in place to control its headlong international growth; that it simply did not know where it was going.

Since its founding as a money broker in 1910, Salomon has traditionally been content to ignore the views of outside pundits and get on with what it likes doing best, trading. However, with the poor performance of its share price and a bad run of earnings, it finally realized the need to start talking. In April 1986 the firm held a briefing for stock market analysts and the financial press. The event coincided with the day Merrill announced its record trading loss. Salomon's almost legendary chairman, John Gutfreund, was called out of the room and returned cigar in hand to read out the relevant Dow Jones press report to the assembled reporters adding gleefully that, as of that day, Salomon had not lost any money that month in mortgage-backed securities. (He did not know then that the trader blamed by Merrill was a former star at Salomon who had been lured away by Merrill for a reported three times increase in salary.)

Gutfreund's message at the briefing was simple. Salomon's goal was to be the premier investment bank globally. The official line was that the firm was intent on consolidating after its supersonic 40 per cent growth in personnel in 1986. Gutfreund also said that Salomon had set up more management committees, increased its number of managing directors and even promoted a former employee of McKinsey, a firm of management consultants, to chief financial officer to keep an eye on the firm's spiralling costs. Opined Gutfreund: 'Running Salomon is beyond the skill of any person.'

A mere three months after this presentation came news that showed that growing pains were far from over at Salomon. This was Gutfreund's sacking in July of Lou Ranieri, the firm's number three and the head of its biggest money earner, the mortgage-backed securities department. The development was a total shock. Ranieri was 'Mr Mortgage' on Wall Street and a one-company man through and through. Indeed his career was the stuff of Wall Street legend. He joined Salomon, aged nineteen, in the post room and worked his way right up to the top. He always liked to tell reporters the story of how, at the age of twenty, Salomon (which he liked to call 'the family') lent him money to pay $10,000 of medical bills.

The departure was hardly amicable. A stunned Ranieri was summoned to Salomon's lawyers' office and maintained silence after the announcement. A senior Salomon director made off-the-record comments to reporters to the effect that Ranieri's style was just too abrasive. That he was too much of a prima donna and was not prepared to surrender control of his own department to the firm's new formalized management style. Such explanations strained credibility a little, though there was genuine concern within Salomon that Ranieri was becoming too much of a law unto himself which is always a dangerous thing in investment banking. Still the reasons given for his abrupt departure offered a marvellous example of the pot calling the kettle black. Gutfreund and Ranieri had worked together for twenty years, a period when abrasiveness and 'street-smarts' were not only accepted qualities at Salomon but precisely what the firm was most famous for. Take those away and street-scrapper Salomon becomes just another run-of-the-mill investment bank.

In the wake of Ranieri's exit, trading of all debt securities was put under Craig Coates, former head of government bond trading and son-in-law of former American treasury secretary and ex-Salomon director William Simon. A towering presence on Salomon's giant trading floor, Coates does not appear a man to brook nonsense. Nor is Gutfreund. Outwardly smooth and soft spoken with, by Wall Street standards, an almost patrician manner, this unusual mix of ex-trader and English graduate once again, with Ranieri's abrupt departure, confirmed his reputation as one of Wall Street's toughest bosses.

However, there was worse to come, including an attempted takeover bid by corporate raider turned chairman of the Revlon Group, Ronald Perelman. By October the panic button had been pressed. Six consecutive declines in quarterly earnings forced Gutfreund to order an emergency, two-month-long strategic review, the first of its kind in the firm's history. The result was a dramatic volte face from the April meeting. Salomon announced that in a bid to control costs it was sacking 800 people, and most dramatically, quitting America's municipal bond market, the product area in which Gutfreund built his career. Salomon hoped to cut $150m. from expenses, then running at some $1.4bn. a year. Coming before the stock market crash, it was the first public retrenchment on Wall Street, though it was soon followed by nearly every other firm.

Even then Salomon's troubles were not over. There has since

been a continued departure of talent from the firm, including Kaufman and chief financial officer, Gerald Rosenfeld, among others. In February 1988 Salomon announced yet another reshuffle, creating four more vice-chairmen to make six in all. The move was interpreted as an attempt to appease warring factions within the firm to try and prevent a further exodus of talent. It only served to underline further the sense of mounting chaos, of a firm tearing itself apart. Gutfreund found himself facing growing pressure and personal criticism. To add salt to the wound he had to endure in January the embarrassment of a cover story in the glossy *New York Magazine* with the provocative headline 'Hard To Be Rich'. The article dwelt on the frantic socializing of Gutfreund and, more particularly, that of his second wife, Susan, and contained such details as how they spent a supposed $20m. decorating their Manhattan apartment. It was the worst kind of publicity for Salomon and was quite literally the talk of Wall Street.

There can be no doubt of the challenge facing Gutfreund and Salomon. That is to evolve from premier trading house to an all-rounder investment-cum-merchant-banking house, complete with a fee and principal business in M. & A. to buttress its trading activities. M. & A. has represented only 20 per cent of Salomon's revenues as compared with 50 per cent and more at, say, Morgan Stanley or First Boston.

Gutfreund always confessed to 'innate conservatism' about 'merchant banking' and said he was determined not to be rushed into a business he viewed with extreme caution. Yet his younger colleagues were constantly reminding him of the huge one-off fees being earned by rivals. That demanded a competitive response if Salomon was not to be left behind in terms of earnings' growth. Gutfreund must have finally caved in, for after the October 1987 crash it emerged that Salomon, the Johnny-come-lately in 'merchant banking', was exposed to the two biggest deals left overhanging the market. It and Goldman Sachs had $300m. each lent to Southland, a Texas convenience-store chain which was meant to be paid off through a junk-bond issue, and Salomon alone had another $450m. lent to Australian businessman Alan Bond to finance his purchase of America's Heileman Brewing. The temporary problem for Salomon was that in the immediate wake of the stock market crash the junk-bond market had seized up, which meant the Southland bridge loan could not be refinanced by the sale of junk bonds. The Southland bonds were finally sold a few weeks later but only after equity warrants were added to them.

So Gutfreund's worst fears seemed for a moment realized. His first concern had always been to preserve the credit rating which allowed Salomon to run its highly leveraged trading business. Now 'merchant banking' threatened that. With hindsight Gutfreund may end up wishing he had stuck to trading even if, as Pru-Bache predicts, bond-trading spreads go the way of corporate bond underwriting fees and shrink to near zero. That would mean Salomon ending up as a new kind of niche player, a global trading house. Interviewed in May 1987, that was not a prospect that seemed to worry Gutfreund. He said: 'If everybody wants to be merchant banks and tie their capital up, I think we would have a pleasant environment to trade it.'

Ultimately, talking to Gutfreund leaves the impression that he is deeply suspicious of too much elaboration in what is fundamentally not that complex a business. Technology has its place but it must be kept in perspective. This is clear from one of his favourite sayings: 'We are dealing in one commodity – money.' The plunge in the stock market will only have reinforced that suspicion and also his wariness of 'merchant banking'. This would not seem the time to be risking huge chunks of capital in takeovers, just as it is not the time to go expanding overseas offices. Rather, the name of the game has become survival. Salomon and Gutfreund may have learned that lesson too late.

MORGAN STANLEY

If Salomon was the bond trader trying to become an all-rounder investment bank, Morgan Stanley took the exact opposite course and, so far, with more success. Not too many years ago Morgan Stanley was Wall Street's most venerable institution with the pick of the *Fortune* 500 list of America's top companies. It also looked the most antiquated of the bulge-bracket firms. In a world where 'loyalty was one basis point', or one-hundredth of a percentage point, (to quote one of Wall Streeters' favourite clichés) Morgan Stanley was losing its way precisely because it lacked Salomon's trading capability, let alone its muscle. The firm's future was on the line. Hopefully no longer.

Back in 1972 there were fifteen people employed in Morgan Stanley's bond department. Now there are more than 800. Morgan Stanley may still make plenty of money from its M. & A. business, where it shares the biggest share of the market with First Boston and Goldman Sachs, but it now can make as much from trading.

A more formally structured and tightly managed organization than Salomon, Morgan Stanley has already had several years' experience in long-term 'planning'. In charge of strategic planning at the firm is Lewis Bernard. He became in 1973, at the age of thirty-one, the firm's youngest ever partner.

Bernard reckons that Morgan Stanley's biggest advantage in building a global trading business operation was that it came late to the business. That meant that it was not burdened either with bad habits or an obsolete infrastructure. The firm made one of its biggest bets in the area of systems' development. It invested in a fourth-generation computer program which developed a master program originally called TAPS (Trade Analysis Processing System) but now known as TRADEPRO.

Bernard describes TAPS as the spine from which the firm hangs its products. Its value is that it is a multi-currency, multi-product program which can be used to trade and settle securities in any market worldwide. This gives Morgan Stanley a common data-processing base, an advantage most of its competitors, at least for the moment, do not have. That is important because software is a major bottleneck to being able to trade efficiently in today's global market grid. The system also saves money.

A 1987 study by McKinsey, the management consultancy, estimated the costs of the electronics systems required by firms active in securities' trading. It broke them down into three areas. First, the back office which handles clearing and settlement of transactions and eats up 65 per cent of costs. Second, the trading-support systems on the trading floor which account for 25 per cent of costs. These tell the trader where he is rather than what to do (though predictably both American and Japanese firms are working on ways to apply artificial-intelligence technology to computerized arbitrage trading in a doomed bid to take the risk out of the markets). Third, is the money spent on what is known as 'analytics', carried out by Wall Street's community of 'rocket scientists'. This takes up only 10 per cent of costs though, being the research and development area of the securities business, it also offers the highest potential payback.

The attraction of a system like TRADEPRO is that it provides a uniform system covering both back office and trading floor while cutting out the flow of paper between the two. That leaves Morgan Stanley free to spend more money and apply more talent on proprietary R. & D. which is important because Wall Street is not only a short-term business in the trading sense. It also has to contend with short-term product cycles. A new kind of security can be quickly copied by competitors. To be six months late with a product has usually been too late. That has made the modern investment bank more like a collection of cottage industries, each working on its own product and with a constant need to erect new cottages.

If Morgan Stanley has embraced technology, it still recognizes that investment banking remains at heart a people business depending on brains to add value and hand-holding to preserve client relationships. (There will always be room for the good salesmen on Wall Street.) Nor, unlike a Salomon, is the firm trying to be the biggest as well as the best, if only because it lacks the capital clout, despite going public in 1986.

This makes it doubly important knowing what not to do, as well what to do. Hence Morgan Stanley's planning mechanism which is an attempt to try and formalize the never-ending process of generating new business ideas. A plan is submitted detailing the pros and cons of a new product: what the risks are, what hedging ability is needed, what distribution is required. This plan, if approved, becomes a budget. It forms a contract with the firm stipulating the resources needed, from the number of people right down to the amount of square feet of office space to be allocated.

The hoped-for ideal, if not the reality, is to fit this rigorous approach within the traditional investment-banking virtues of nimbleness and suppleness; the ability 'to turn on a dime' and seize market opportunities. The obvious problem for investment banks is not to lose such qualities during a period when they have grown from organizations employing a few hundred people to 5,000 and more. This is why Morgan Stanley is sceptical about size for its own sake. Bernard says: 'You cannot fall in love with your products. There is always a cycle. You have to be comfortable with change which large institutions are not.'

Still, if Morgan Stanley eschews size, it has made some pretty sizeable deals in 'merchant banking' where in the last two years it has been as aggressive as any Wall Street firm in investing its own equity. As at January 1988 the firm had a portfolio of stakes in forty-two companies, representing total sales of $12bn. For example, as a result of an L.B.O. Morgan Stanley owns 40 per cent of the now private Burlington Industries, America's biggest textile company. Five people now sit on Burlington's board, three of whom are Morgan Stanley investment bankers. This and other such deals represent big bets and, since employees still own 70 per cent of the firm's equity, Morgan Stanley is putting its own money on the line.

The coming bear market will put this business to the test. But in early 1988 Morgan Stanley was riding on the crest of the wave. As the most successful in avoiding financial debris during 1987, it was then commonly perceived as Wall Street's best managed major firm.

GOLDMAN SACHS

'We stand for a lot of corny things. We actually believe in this stuff.' The speaker is Roy Smith, a former partner at Goldman Sachs now turned professor. He was talking in the summer of 1986 when he was still at Goldman about the set of business principles which new employees are given when they join the investment bank. These stress team work at the expense of ego and other such laudable virtues.

Goldman's M.B.A. recruits, some forty of whom out of an annual intake of around 200 usually come from the same *alma mater*, Harvard, are only selected after an exhaustive interviewing process. An enormous amount of senior management time and effort is devoted to this recruitment process. It is not unknown for a new employee to be interviewed by as many as thirty-five people before receiving a job offer, which is probably more screening than is required to join most countries' secret services.

The reason for all this scrutiny is because Goldman wants to be sure that recruits are not only bright, but also that they will fit in. Aggressive loose cannons are discouraged at the firm, however brilliant the candidate. Smith's comment is to the point. 'We try to discourage the notion of individual superstars. They tend to go off into uncontrollable orbit.' So, on joining Goldman, recruits have to subordinate themselves to a defined corporate culture. Indeed, the firm likes to compare itself with Japanese companies. It seeks to hire people from college for life and claims to have the lowest staff turnover on Wall Street, some 2–3 per cent. Although they could earn higher salaries elsewhere, the best employees do not leave because of the lure of a private partnership. High flyers can become partners by their mid-thirties. Once there they can be assured of million-dollar-plus incomes and so multi-million-dollar wealth and, almost as important, arguably the highest status Wall Street has to offer.

However, this cosy system is under strain. Goldman may remain one of the leading firms in conventional corporate finance (if not in 'merchant banking') and also in equity trading. In recent years, however, the securities industry's explosive growth has forced it to dilute its tight-knit culture by hiring experienced Wall Street professionals in fast-expanding areas where it lacked existing in-house expertise, such as mortgage-backed securities.

Goldman's structure also made the firm slower to react to the need to expand its London and Tokyo offices to service the needs of twenty-four-hour financial markets and global investing, though it may not regret that so much post-19 October 1987. The reason was largely its partners' understandable reluctance to spend large amounts of their own money building up vast overseas operations in markets they were unfamiliar with. This would be fine, even sensible, so long as Goldman was happy to be a niche New York player. But it aspires to be a global one.

Hence the deal with Japan's Sumitomo, announced in August 1986. On the face of it Goldman got the best of both worlds: a 34 per cent or $500m. increase in its equity while forfeiting only 12.5 per cent of the profits, without any dilution of existing management control. This meant it could stay ahead of the likes of First Boston and Morgan Stanley in Wall Street's great capital race without having to float the company on the stock market, so retaining the treasured private partnership. This impression of a great deal for Goldman – gaining Sumitomo's capital while preserving its independence – was seemingly confirmed when America's Federal Reserve imposed in late 1986 surprisingly tough Glass-Steagall-type restrictions on the deal. By stopping any joint-venture tie-ups between Goldman and Sumitomo, a commercial bank, the Federal Reserve confirmed Goldman's independence. This, however, will prevent both partners from winning business from each other through the tie-up.

Longer term, Sumitomo is prepared to accept this arrangement, though it was unpleasantly surprised by the toughness of the federal ruling (which owed much to protectionist trade pressures in Congress). Doubtless it has taken the typically Japanese long-term view. Most Wall Streeters find it hard, if not impossible, to take such a long-term view. But the minority shareholding does threaten, however imperceptibly, Goldman's tradition of proud independence. The next time Goldman needs capital Sumitomo will be able to exert greater leverage when it comes to handing over the money, especially if the need occurs during a period when the investment-banking business is suffering. As Goldman's hard-headed financiers of all people should know, there is no such thing as a free lunch.

Meanwhile, Sumitomo could be forgiven for wondering if it has bought into quite the paragon of Wall Street virtue it thought it had. (Sumitomo only chose Goldman after hiring management consultant McKinsey and investment bank Lazard Frères to advise on the most suitable bulge-bracket firm to invest in.) For, if Goldman's boy-scout culture has come under strain because of the money industry's expansion and internationalization, it also faces a more alarming direct threat; its embarrassing embroilment in post-Boesky insider-trading scandals.

In an interview in his Old Bailey office in June 1986, Robert Conway, head of Goldman's London office, aired these thoughts: 'Insider trading is not a grey area. There is no sense in Goldman Sachs that that kind of area is acceptable. Our business is based on trust . . . I hope they shoot him. It takes years and years to build that trust and confidence with a client.' Conway was referring to Wall Street's first big insider-trading scandal in this bull market cycle when Dennis Levine, then of Drexel Burnham, pleaded guilty in June 1986 to accumulating $12.6m. from trading on inside information. Since then the scandal has moved on. Levine sneaked on Boesky who sneaked on Marty Seagal of Kidder Peabody, who in turn made allegations against two other investment bankers at Kidder Peabody and – most shockingly to the rest of Wall Street – Robert Freeman, a partner and head of risk arbitrage at Goldman Sachs. All three were arrested in their offices amid full attendant publicity (to Goldman's intense fury), and all three, for the first time in this spate of insider-trading cases, pleaded not guilty. In May 1987 the government, in the form of New York's politically ambitious and personally zealous district attorney, Rudolph Giuliani, dismissed the charges, saying that more evidence had been obtained and that it wanted to bring new and wider charges at a later date. The defence saw it differently. It argued that the prosecution realized belatedly its case was not as strong as it first thought.

Whatever the outcome (and the stock market crash may make prosecutors less aggressive about pursuing Wall Streeters for fear of further undermining confidence) there can be no doubt that the incident was very damaging to Goldman, given its school-prefect culture. For it highlighted the other less discussed aspect of that culture – making money, as much of it as possible. It was clear that Freeman's defence would rest first on character-assassinating

Siegal, a self-confessed felon, and second, on seeking to demons-trate that insider trading is precisely the grey area Conway denied it was. Already enough embarrassing information has surfaced through press stories leaking details of the government investigation to suggest that Freeman was swopping information with Siegal about deals and trading on the back of it, both on his own account and Goldman's. Even if no insider trading is ever proved in the legal sense, this looks dangerously close to the line, barely passing many in the money business's 'smell test' of what is acceptable behaviour.

To its credit Goldman has publicly stood by its man. However, a cynic might note that as a private partnership it had little choice. Otherwise Freeman could, if he so chose, plea bargain with the authorities and tell stories about others in the firm. But, more important, is the potential financial liability from the case in the form of law suits. Not being a public company, the partners' own capital is at stake. In all these insider-trading cases Wall Street firms face the possibility of being held liable to damages if it is deemed that they have been negligent in supervising employees and enforcing the required compliance procedures (which is one reason General Electric forced Kidder Peabody to do a deal with the government against the advice of the investment bank's own lawyer and pay a $25.3m. settlement in exchange for an agreement that no case would be bought against the firm). Nor, say legal experts, is it clear whether the Wall Street firms' insurance would cover them against such damages.

Goldman is, then, facing its biggest scare for a long time and at the hands of the federal government. Even if the case collapses and never comes back to court (and the insider-trading laws are somewhat murkier and less clear-cut than either S.E.C. enforce-ment officers or federal prosecutors would sometimes like to claim) nothing will ever be quite the same again at Goldman. Another indication that times were changing came in October 1987 when Goldman backed down from its long-standing policy of not sharing commercial paper deals with other firms, a market in which it used to be the leader. Until then Goldman had arrogantly gone on charging the highest fees in this market for short-term corporate financing, while ignoring the fact that the parcelling out of commercial paper deals between other firms was rife. The result was that it saw none of this joint business and was fast losing its market share.

With Wall Street now at the end of one of its longest booms and with every prospect of a deep and long downturn ahead, it is a fair bet that, by the time this year's crop of M.B.A.s would expect to become partners, Goldman will no longer be private, nor perhaps even independent. That, naturally, is a possibility no one at Goldman would ever admit to. In public, at least, the partnership principle is sacred (which does not stop the partners periodically debating the issue) as it once was at nearly every major Wall Street firm. Merrill Lynch was the first to go public in 1971 and Morgan Stanley the last, in 1986.

MERRILL LYNCH

Merrill Lynch is known only half affectionately as the Thundering Herd. This giant amalgam of retail broker, money manager, investment banker, and insurance broker suffers from an unfortunate reputation for pursuing fads. It focuses on a new business area, charges into it and then, as often as not, retreats as suddenly, often after losing a large sum of money. You can count on Merrill, Wall Streeters are fond of saying, 'to screw up in size'.

That is why 1987's huge trading loss was so galling. Merrill at last was beginning to be taken seriously as a bulge-bracket player, though some rival investment bankers still like to talk the firm down because it is run by 'stockbrokers'. The best response to that slur is to ask what is wrong with old-fashioned retail stockbroking. Merrill still makes more money from its retail side than from investment banking. This not only includes its 12,000 retail salesmen in America and 14,000 worldwide, but also the $165bn. in its all-purpose cash management accounts (CMAs) at the end of 1987. A Merrill Lynch invention and perhaps the most profitable, if not most glamorous, commercial idea in its recent history, the CMA combines a traditional brokerage account with many features of an ordinary bank account, including the ability to write cheques. Merrill also has a money management business which in 1987 provided fee income running at $500m. a year. That is steady cash flow compared with the risky way most investment bankers earn their money, trading securities or 'merchant banking'. It is also a cash stream the likes of which First Boston, Goldman Sachs, or Salomon do not enjoy.

Despite this, Merrill still labours under an inferiority complex. It wants to be taken seriously as an investment bank, to be perceived up there with the rest. This makes it a sucker for hiring investment bankers not on the road to the very top at their own firms for double and more their previous salary.

So, just as it charged into complex mortgage-backed securities with all guns blazing before recoiling after its huges loss (and for that matter into risk arbitrage before it withdrew abruptly post-Boesky, again nursing a loss), so it is now, alongside Morgan Stanley, the most aggressive Wall Street firm investing its own equity in L.B.O.s. That is why many on Wall Street are confidently waiting for a classic Merrill débâcle when the economy turns down and the firm is left holding sizeable stakes in heavily indebted companies it knows little about. The October 1987 stock market crash makes this even more likely.

Merrill Lynch's investment bankers (as opposed to its traders) were assured at the time of the $377m trading loss in 1987 that their bonuses that year would not be affected by the débâcle. Maybe. Certainly, Merrill needed to keep them happy. With many investment bankers earning basic salaries of 'just' $150,000 and less, bonuses are what make them millionaires quick. By some elaborate accounting, whereby it wrote itself a cheque out of reserves which most investment-banking analysts on Wall Street did not know existed, Merrill managed to reduce the hit into an after-tax loss of $145m.

Still, the whole episode only confirms the nub of Merrill's problem in investment banking – its lack of focus. The firm is a bureaucracy, which seeks to build a presence in every market and where managers pass responsibility up the line. Merrill suffers from too little cross-fertilization between business areas and job functions. Yet the key to success in modern investment banking consists of just such an integration between the various specialist areas – analysts, salesmen, and traders. If they had been talking to each other, it is hard to believe that loss could have been allowed to deteriorate during three weeks into a $377m. monster. In fact, Merrill is just the sort of bureaucracy other investment banks are trying to avoid becoming as they struggle with the consequences of too much growth.

On top of these problems is the underlying conflict between the firm's investment bankers, who view themselves as relative sophisticates, and Merrill's brokers, known half pejoratively by the investment bankers as 'stock jockeys'. Merrill is an unholy amalgam of traditional stockbrokers, who started their careers cold calling in a branch office and have worked their way up the organization, and senior investment bankers with long experience in the capital markets but perhaps with no instinctive loyalty to Merrill, save the number on the salary cheque and the largesse of the expense account.

By contrast, meet top executives at other bulge-bracket firms and they usually seem of a common type: lean, mean and hungry with a veneer of personable polish – classic investment bankers. That is even true of Shearson Lehman, an amalgam of retail broker Shearson, and wholesale investment bank Lehman Brothers, which at the beginning of 1988 bought faltering stockbroker E. F. Hutton. That made Shearson Lehman Hutton almost as big as Merrill and a direct threat to Merrill's long-held franchise as Wall Street's largest firm. Worse, Shearson is credited with being run by some of Wall Street's toughest, most cost-conscious hands-on managers. It is hard to see them suffering from the same lack of internal communication as Merrill did when it took more than three weeks before its furious chairman, William Schreyer, was informed of the trading disaster in a type of security he probably did not even know existed.

However, if Merrill has its problems, it is also an institution which, like McDonalds in fast food, enjoys a valuable retail franchise. That makes it less vulnerable to the cyclical booms and busts of the securities industry. When some of its more high-flying Wall Street competitors have been laid low in the looming credit crunch, there is a better than even chance that Merrill will still be doing business through its cash-management accounts. For when money leaves the stock market, it does not necessarily leave Merrill but rather goes into one of its money market funds or C.M.As. Keeping things simple is as good an idea in the money business as it is in any other. Many on Wall Street have forgotten that.

If all the Wall Street firms have their own peculiar characteristics, they have all had to cope with tremendous change. Tugged along by their swelling balance sheets during the 1980s, investment bankers have become hostages to the very deals they chased. They have kept on growing though they know that tomorrow's financial world will not be big enough for all of them. They do that because they want to wring every last cent out of the good times while they last. Now, when bad times are coming, as Salomon's example shows, they will ruthlessly cut bonuses, salaries, and personnel in a bid to bring costs down to match falling revenues. No one would, or should, ever assure an investment banker of job security.

All Things To All Men

The frenzied whirl of a financial centre like Wall Street can seem almost irrelevant to more detached players in the money jungle.

Dean LeBaron, founder, chairman and sole shareholder of the Boston-based money management company, Batterymarch, runs his firm in a way which makes much of Wall Street seem redundant. His company has for the past ten years used a computerized trading system. Batterymarch's money managers claim never to talk to brokers. Instead stockbrokers, be they based in New York, London, or Tokyo, have to log into the computer to check Batterymarch's buy and sell orders. They get the business if they can transact it at the lowest cost. If every institutional investor followed Batterymarch's example (they do not because they want their hands held or a broker to blame if an investment goes wrong) there would be far fewer jobs on Wall Street, or any other financial centre, bull market or bear market.

Walk into Batterymarch's office and it is like entering a semi-conductor facility. Little wonder LeBaron says: 'Wall Street does not not exist as a place. It is a cultural phenomenon; not a piece of real estate.' Morgan Stanley's Lewis Bernard, an unusually highbrow, reflective investment banker would, in the main, agree. He says: 'Wall Street is a misnomer. It is an enormous free flow of ideas and an enormous free flow of people.'

So there is more to the world of high finance than Wall Street or any other financial district. The reason such places still exist, is that financial people like to be clustered together, mainly because they like the camaraderie. Electronics means they do not need to be while (at least until recently) soaring property values and rents in the world's financial centres, meant they should not be.

But there are many things, it could be argued, that the big investment banks should not have been doing. The basic problem is that too many of them have been trying to do too much. Contrast how Wall Street has run its own affairs and how it has advised other industries to. Corporate restructuring became a fad in American business during the 1980s. It has also been used by the investment banking lobby to argue the merits of corporate raiders, hostile takeovers, L.B.O.s, and the other paraphernalia of modern corporate finance.

There have been inevitable excesses, as with any trend. Still, restructuring has made much of once fat and happy industrial America more efficient and more competitive, if also in many cases more in debt. Share-owning entrepreneurs will always make better managers than time-serving politicking corpocrats. But if restructuring, as advised by Wall Street, has generally been a good thing,

Wall Street itself has followed the exact opposite course. In contrast to the industrial conglomerates, which have spun off subsidiaries not in their core businesses, the investment banks have rushed into new businesses and new products, employing more and more people on more and more borrowed money. They were trying to be all things to all men and, increasingly, in all the world's markets.

This strategy was based on some absurdly optimistic assumptions. First, that the financial asset boom would continue when sluggish economies, soaring debt, and a dearth of new productive investment made clear that we were living in a classic speculative bubble and, second, that the financial markets would stay global and that protectionism or bear markets or exchange controls would not throw a spanner in the works.

Because both assumptions are far too optimistic, Wall Street will go through very hard times again. For it is guilty of believing its own rhetoric. The only question is whether it will make a soft landing or come down to earth with the hardest of bumps. Already the increasingly strident critics of contemporary Wall Street, the bores who had been complaining about the 'instant gratification' society and moaning about $500,000 a year twenty-eight-year-old yuppie investment bankers, have enjoyed their moment of glee. They have seen some of the youthful sheep, who rushed to 'The Street', end up on the street. There will be many, many more. Older hands realize this because they have seen it before; too many younger ones still do not.

Anybody who talked to young Wall Street investment bankers before the October 1987 crash could not but be amazed by their clone-like demeanour. They all seemed fresh-faced and eager-looking types, complete with no-nonsense tunnel vision. Just out of business school, and filled with the incomprehensible jargon of quantitative analysis, they seemed far removed from the dog-eats-dog jungle which is the reality of financial markets. They also compared unfavourably with the colourful, even sometimes eccentric, individuals running these firms, many of whom freely admit they would not have been hired if they had tried to join their firms today. They would not have fitted the perceived mould.

Even for the survivors of the coming crunch, the climate will be different. Tomorrow's big financial battalions will be more hierarchical, tightly managed institutions, more like a conventional commercial bank, and less like today's investment bank, and so less fun to work for. In this environment some of the best talent will move increasingly to the small firms which will concentrate on doing a few things well. There are already many of them and there will be many more. Perhaps today's best example is Lazard Frères. A sister bank of its Paris and London namesake, Lazard still makes a virtue of offering old-fashioned advisory investment banking. It has kept costs and headcount down and standards up throughout the 1980s, determined first not to put its own capital at risk and second, not to be seduced into pursuing size for its own sake. Yet under its famous post-war head, French-born André Meyer, Lazard was also taking stakes in companies twenty and more years ago, long before this generation learned the phrase 'merchant banking'. It just did not do it on today's hugely borrowed basis.

For the moment, however, the capital has been committed and the battle lines have been drawn. Most older hands were relieved to be out of the fray, even before the stock market took its record-breaking dive. One was Leon Levy, the former head of a successful, medium-sized New York investment bank, Oppenheimer, now active in his own private investment partnership named Odyssey. Speaking in May 1987, Levy remarked that he would not want to run an investment bank today 'because the whole forced necessity of doing things frightens me. You cannot afford to do nothing. But when things go wrong, they have a habit of going wrong everywhere.'

This was a remarkably prescient comment. The frightening thing is that the other two centres of the world's money jungle, London and Tokyo, still exhibit as great, if not greater symptoms of financial excess. And remember, global excesses breed global panics.

TOKYO

'Men, it has been well said, think in herds; it will be seen that they go mad in herds, while they only recover their senses slowly, and one by one.'

Charles Mackay, 1852

Land of the Rising Billionaires

It took a Japanese insurance company called Yasuda to pay $39m. in early 1987 for a Van Gogh painting to make the western world appreciate the extent to which that country was swimming in cash. The flow of money had been visible since 1983 to Wall Street investment bankers selling American treasury bonds to Japanese institutional investors. However, abstract talk about how the inscrutable orientals were financing America's huge budget deficit did not quite seize the popular imagination in the way paying that sum of money for a piece of canvas to hang on an insurance company's office wall did.

Not long after, America's *Forbes* magazine ran a cover story entitled 'The Land of the Rising Billionaires'. Not surprisingly, the magazine had no trouble finding twenty-two dollar billionaires while noting that there were many more. That was one more than the twenty-one American billionaires listed by *Forbes* the previous year in its annual feature on the 100 richest Americans, and that had included family units. Television then took up the topic. America's network T.V. show, *Lives of the Rich and Famous*, itself a monument to bad taste, crass materialism and fast money 1980s style, took a film crew to Japan and found a modestly sized Tokyo mansion worth a staggering $500m. That is equivalent to 30 to 40 times Japanese average wages.

Houses worth that much make no sense, however much the yen may have risen in value against the dollar in the past two years. These sort of media reports have exploded the myth perpetrated in the West by self-appointed Japan experts of a Confucian society toiling together for the good of their fellow-man. Japan's industrial bosses may eat hamburgers in the same canteen as their production-line workers but the country, like any other nation, has its wealthy elite. There may be nothing wrong with that. But what is frightening is that these excesses are also symptoms of a binge to end all twentieth-century binges.

The speculative frenzy has reached its most extreme expression in the Tokyo stock and property markets. As a bubble it compares in terms of overvaluations with some of the more extreme mass manias chronicled in history. Japan's peculiar brand of Tulipomania is golf club memberships. Memberships to the more exclusive clubs have sold for over $2m. Tokyo is a huge, densely packed city. So to Japan's *arriviste* stockbrokers, the ability to enjoy a round of golf represents the ultimate symbol of belonging.

Years of exporting success combined with the ingrained husbandry of its population, the biggest savers in the world, mean Japan enjoys a huge surplus with the rest of the world, and one which in recent years has been growing at the rate of $70bn. a year. At home Japan's gross domestic savings total Y100 trillion ($800bn.) per year, equal to 30 per cent of the country's nominal gross national product. This piling-up of cash on the sidelines has financed two developments, rampant speculation at home and a tidal wave of investment overseas. Japanese financial institutions, as the middle men channelling this liquidity, have so far profited from both trends. Neither can last. When the crash comes, and remarkably, considering its inflated levels, Tokyo's stock market managed to shrug off most of Wall Street's dramatic October crash, falling 'only' 20 per cent before recovering all its loss by the end of March 1988, the impact will be severe. It will be devastating not only for Japan but also, because Japan is the world's biggest creditor nation, for markets everywhere, asset values everywhere, and economies everywhere. Nor will the outcome bring much joy to the money men of Tokyo's financial district.

Japan's conservative monetary authorities are only too aware trouble lies ahead. An article in the *International Herald Tribune* on 30 June 1987 contained an interesting snippet. It quoted an anonymous Bank of Japan source as saying: 'We're afraid that some day the bubble will burst and that the deflationary impact on the economy will be disastrous.' The central bankers were right to be worried. By then, Japan's soaring markets and the strong yen had hit several landmarks which would have made any rational observer uncomfortable. First, the Tokyo stock market had overtaken New York's as the world's biggest. Second, the market value of all property in Japan was twice the value of all real estate in America, though Japan is less than four per cent of the land area of the United States. That means the unit value per square foot is fifty times greater in Japan than in America. Third, shares in the government-owned telephone company, Nippon Telegraph and Telephone (N.T.T.) were floated on the Tokyo stock market valued at a price earnings ratio of 250. P.E. ratios are the money industry's standard way of valuing shares and are calculated by dividing a company's earnings per share by its current share price. In America Wall Street peaked in August 1987 when the Dow Jones Industrial Average of leading blue-chip companies was trading on a P.E. ratio of 'just' 22. In terms of its stock market paper value, N.T.T. was three times the size of I.B.M. Back in the real world I.B.M. earned five times as much.

Japanese Methods of Investment

Where was the cash coming from to fuel this frenzy of speculation? First, from Japan's giant life insurance companies. The Japanese not only save more than any other nation, they are also more avid insurers of life. Japan's life assurance industry boasted total assets of Y71 trillion ($568bn.) at the end of October 1987. This is not only an embarrassment of riches. It is also much more than the Japanese government spends a year to run the country. New money coming into the life insurance companies averaged Y1.1 trillion ($8.8bn.) per month between April and October 1987. That is new money these institutions must invest.

Although until 1987 a rising percentage of this money was going abroad, the biggest chunk still has to find a resting place at home and much of that has gone into the local stock market. Committed to paying 7–8 per cent returns to their policy holders during a period when Japan's domestic bonds have been paying yields of 5 per cent at best, the life insurance companies were tempted to make up the extra by trading in and out of the stock market. They did it through what are known as *tokkin* accounts. Introduced in 1983, these are investment funds exempt from capital gains tax.

The lure of investing in *tokkin* accounts for the life companies is simple. It allows them to convert capital gains into income free of tax.

Another major source of cash flowing into the stock market and *tokkin* funds has come from manufacturing firms and other companies. Priced out of the export market by the stronger yen and faced until late 1987 with a sluggish economy at home, many Japanese companies invested their money in the local bond market and stock markets, both because they had nothing better to do with their mountain of cash, and also because they wanted to report the same profits by speculating at home that they could no longer make from selling goods abroad. This process became known as *zaitech*, which literally means financial engineering. Because *tokkin* dividends must be paid from real-life capital gains, this system encourages such frenzied trading.

The obvious danger is that the Tokyo market has been valuing companies partly on the basis of speculative earnings made in the market itself. When the stock market falls, this source of earnings will vanish. The first real shock, however, came not, as expected, in the stock market, but in the Japanese yen government bond market when Tateho Chemical owned up in August 1987 to losing Y20bn. speculating in the Japanese bond market. This effectively wiped out its net worth since the company only had total assets of Y16.5bn. Tateho's directors had literally bet the company, hoping to compensate for a steep drop in the firm's operating profit because of a slump in its core business of making electrofused magnesia for Japan's steel companies. Tateho probably speculated on bonds and bond futures thinking they were safer than shares. However, to the surprise of many, Japanese government bond yields nearly doubled in the second quarter of 1987 causing huge losses in bonds for investors as well as the Japanese brokers who, like their Wall Street investment-banking counterparts, tend to be net owners of pieces of paper. Tateho was the first public casualty of *zaitech*. It will not be the last.

So like the life insurers, companies have also put their spare cash into *tokkin* funds. *Tokkin* are managed by an external advisor, usually a Japanese stockbroker. Often this manager is a gunslinging youngster in his twenties, trading the account (and so generating commissions for his stockbroking firm) almost daily in whatever his firm's current hot share recommendations are. In London and New York and, for that matter, most of the world's major stock markets this practice, known as 'churning', is both illegal and generally shunned. In Japan, however, though technically illegal it remains standard practice. In January 1987 Nomura, Japan's biggest stockbroker, was judged to have betrayed a client's trust when two salesmen through unauthorized trades managed to lose more than Y50m. in a client's margin account. Nomura was ordered to pay back one third of the loss as damages. This, however, was the only case of churning ever brought and, significantly, the litigant was not Japanese.

The 'Chinese Walls' which are meant to exist in America and Britain to prevent conflicts of interest between the broking and money management sides of a securities company or investment bank are much less formalized in Japan where investment activities still tend to be seen as generating commissions for the brokers. In fact the young Japanese *tokkin* manager makes his New York or London investment banking or 'merchant banking' contemporary look like prudence personified.

In a rising market the *tokkin* formula has worked. *Tokkin* funds were Y12.6 trillion on 31 May 1986, and Yen 16.9 trillion at the end of 1987. So addictive did the habit become that many Japanese companies even borrowed money in London's Euromarkets to raise more cash to punt in the Tokyo stock market. Too often these companies were the least financially secure but, faced with slumping export sales and reluctant to lay off staff, they were desperate to maintain earnings of whatever quality.

So *tokkin* funds either come from companies' spare cash and are used as a way of converting capital gains to income tax free, or from the life insurance companies which want a 'guaranteed' return higher than that available to them on the money market. Added together and the *tokkin* phenomenon became one of the more extreme examples of 1980s financial-asset fever. The Japanese industrial miracle had turned into a casino den.

Whatever that might mean for the future of some Japanese companies, *tokkin* funds have been a bonanza for Japan's Big Four securities companies: (in order of size) Nomura, Daiwa, Nikko, and Yamaichi. For *tokkin* provided a continuous flow of liquidity to keep share prices going up, and so boosted the Japanese brokers' profits. In fact Nomura and the rest have in the past few years enjoyed what will probably prove an unrepeatable bonanza. There are several reasons for this. First, their Japanese clients, consisting of private investors, financial institutions, and industrial companies have in the past few years become the world's richest group of investors. Second, Tokyo remains the only one of the world's big three financial centres to still have fixed commissions for share and bond dealing. For a financial powerhouse like Nomura with approaching a 50 per cent share of the Tokyo stock market (including its subsidiaries) on a good day, this amounts to the nearest thing to a printing press in stockbroking. Nor do fixed commissions look likely to disappear for at least two years and probably five. Nor should Article 65 (Japan's version of Glass-Steagall) be dismantled before America's statute is. As in America, this forbids commercial banks from underwriting or dealing in securities and so protects Nomura and the others from competition from the likes of Dai-Ichi Kangyo Bank, Industrial Bank of Japan, and Sumitomo Bank. All this gives Nomura a huge cushion of profitability, which is why the company's stock market valuation at its peak was nearly $70 bn., more than the total capitalization of many nations' stock markets, including Australia's and West Germany's.

Nomura's power has indeed become formidable. Founded in 1925 as a spin-off from Daiwa Bank's bond department, in 1987 the stockbroker was the most profitable financial institution in the world. It reported pre-tax profits of Y495bn., or nearly $4bn., which means it also overtook for the first time such industrial giants as Tokyo Electric Power, and car manufacturer, Toyota. Nomura was helped by a 215 per cent increase in broking commissions to Y390bn. of which more than 60 per cent was earned in the home Tokyo market. All the Big Four Japanese brokers finished among the top ten Japanese corporate earners with Daiwa (no connection with Daiwa Bank) sixth at Y301bn., Nikko eighth at Y253bn. and Yamaichi ninth at Y233bn. A further indication of the dramatic shift in power among Japanese financial institutions in favour of the brokers, caused by the booming Tokyo market, is that only one bank, Fuji, made it into the top ten and only then at number ten.

So more than any other company Nomura has been the direct beneficiary of Japan's home-grown speculative bubble which is why astute investors perceived it a few years ago as the best play on the rising stock market and Japan's liquidity surge. The firm's share price appreciated 900 per cent during 1983–7 as its net profits increased more than fourfold. Equally, it will be the best play on selling Tokyo 'short' when the market finally collapses, which it assuredly will. Making nearly $4bn. with just 12,000 employees is both incredible and almost certainly unsustainable. Selling short is speculating that prices will fall. It is done by borrowing anonymously through a broker a share from another investor and selling it in anticipation of the price dropping. The aim is to buy it back later, hopefully at a lower price, returning the share to the original holder.

Nomura's protected profits at home have also given it leeway to spend lots of money building market share in London (successfully where it became the premier underwriter of eurobond issues in 1987) and New York (less so) without having to worry unduly about whether these overseas activities are profitable. That is the same familiar loss leader strategy once employed by the Japanese manufacturers in the electronics and motor industries.

The Japanese securities houses have enjoyed another advantage: the primitive nature of the local money management industry, their main institutional client base. As recently as 1986 an investment management industry, in the conventional western sense, scarcely existed in Japan. It is now developing fast as foreign and domestic money managers focus on the swelling cash hoard. However, the four big brokers still hold sway. They continue to wield huge influence over the market because the stocks they recommend go up in price as a result of the Japanese brokers' practice of 'ramping' stocks.

This is when Nomura (or one of the other brokers) target a certain share or sector and aggressively promote it through their salesforce. As a practice, it can be compared with the pool operations common on Wall Street during the 1920s. Shares are first accumulated, often in shadowy *tokkin* funds, and then the lantern is lit (*chochin o tsukeru*). This can be done by spreading rumours, misleading share dealing activity, planting stories in the press, and similar manipulative tactics until there is a big enough profit on the table to encourage the insiders to sell. In such ramps an obscure share can double or triple in a matter of weeks. Clearly, anyone who knows of the target of a ramp in advance can make a lot of money, especially a Nomura ramp. Because it is the biggest broker with the biggest distribution in terms of being able to push the targeted share through its 10,000 retail sales force, Nomura has the most muscle to exert in a ramp. Usually prior knowledge of one is confined to the broker and its favoured Japanese clients such as the big life insurers and companies whose *tokkin* accounts will be filled with the hot stock. However, occasionally Nomura or another Japanese broker may extend a helping hand to one of the increasing number of foreign, *geijin*, money managers based in Tokyo. They may be called up and told how a certain stock is definitely going up because it is being 'ramped' – the Japanese broker will often actually use the English word to make the point clear. The money manager, unless he is a masochist or unusually principled, will give the same broker an order to buy the shares for his funds and then go out and buy the warrants if there are any in issue for that company, (warrants are a more speculative way of buying shares) for his own personal account. He will do this despite the fact that the Japanese broker has given him no reason why the stock should go up in price. Sometimes it happens to be favourite of the moment. Sometimes it is because the broker, who also often acts as the investment banker to the particular company, knows something in advance in terms of forthcoming commercial developments which the market does not. The simple point is that past practice has demonstrated that it pays off to follow these tips.

This sort of activity would fail many people's 'smell test' in London or New York since it amounts to a form of insider trading. However, the Japanese see the matter differently. They dislike too rigorous a policing of their securities market. To date, there has never been a criminal prosecution for the offence of insider trading in Japan. This reflects a completely different cultural view of what is commercially and socially acceptable behaviour. In Japan, and for that matter the rest of Asia, insider trading, in the sense of buying a share of a company about which one has privileged information, is more or less common practice. It is also generally accepted, being viewed as one of the perks both of broking and of controlling a public company. Given this attitude, the Japanese mystification at the hue and cry over the Boesky scandal can be imagined. There is no word for 'corruption' in the Japanese language. The more the American firms become a major presence in Tokyo, the more this will cause a strain with the Japanese in their home financial market, especially since the S.E.C. is already talking of trying to enforce worldwide regulation of what are now twenty-four-hour global financial markets. In an attempt to ease such concerns Japan's Ministry of Finance in 1988 was drafting new anti-insider-trading legislation. This is expected to plug one major loophole where company executives and shareholders with more than 10 per cent of a company need not report sales of their shares. Still the legislation will not curb the common practice whereby information is exchanged within the many groups of companies which have interlocking shareholdings. These groups usually include major institutional investors such as the banks and life insurance companies.

The large-scale presence of a Salomon, Morgan Stanley or

Goldman Sachs in Tokyo analysing, selling and trading Japanese shares is a comparatively recent phenomenon, only some three or four years old. They are trying to research Japanese companies and to recommend shares based on 'fundamentals', not as the Japanese brokers still often do, on the basis of forthcoming ramps, which, incidentally, the foreign brokers are usually the last to learn about.

American investment bankers, newly arrived in Tokyo, often express amazement if not outright shock at the customs of a local stock market which is, after all, now bigger than their own. This springs from the strong legalistic strain of the American mind, which is both a little naive and also starkly didactic. To make lots of money is good; to break the law is bad. Boesky, an American self-made hero one minute, became an outcast the next. That obsession with insider trading stems from a legitimate desire to get rid of 'cheats' and perpetuate that peculiarly American myth of the level playing field.

The major British and Swiss stockbroking firms, banks, and specialist investment management firms, by contrast, have tended to adopt an altogether more worldly, if cynical, approach. Because they have been investing in Tokyo and other Asian financial markets much longer (in many cases twenty years and longer) they are much more attuned to the art of adapting and profiting from local ways of doing business. This requires not imposing one's own ideas of right and wrong on a foreign culture. It is not yet clear how well the Americans will be able to make that mental leap, though by employing increasing numbers of Japanese, they are clearly addressing the issue. Meanwhile the Tokyo stock market will remain for the time being a 'rotational' market where stocks and sectors go in and out of fashion in the short term depending on which area Nomura and the rest is pushing that month. Longer term share prices have to come into line with fundamentals, even in Japan, which is where the foreigners may have the advantage.

This cosy arrangement for the big Japanese brokers is coming under strain from the 'buy side' of Japan's money industry. The institutional investors, who are the brokers' clients, are beginning to demand a different kind of service. Overflowing with money and besieged by American, British, and Swiss firms eager to manage their billions, Japanese institutions are learning fast about what western investment techniques have to offer. They are also beginning to realize that the type of vat-churning 'management' practised by the Japanese brokers' *tokkin* managers is not acceptable, which is why they are giving foreign money managers an increasing amount of *tokkin* money to invest for them. At the end of 1986 over $16bn. of Japanese money was already being managed by non-Japanese money managers. This is either *tokkin* money or an international investment fund sold by the Japanese broker to its retail clients but invested by foreigners in markets outside Japan. These were proving popular, at least until the October 1987 crash, showing that international investment could be sold at the retail level, even in a country where it was an unfamiliar concept. Morgan Grenfell, a London merchant bank, is one of the biggest players in this market. In 1987 it was managing some $1.2bn. from Tokyo and nearly all of it is retail money, sold through the Japanese brokers' network of retail salesmen, many of whom are women. In Japan shares are sold door to door like double glazing or encyclopedias are in the West. The broker charges a 5 per cent front-end load-purchase fee on the sale, and Morgan Grenfell earns a mangement fee. This is the best it can hope for. It cannot sell the funds itself not only because it has no distribution network but also because only Japanese securities firms are allowed to sell such investment trusts.

The longer the Tokyo stock market manages to defy gravity, and it has only become riskier as a result of other markets' steep decline, the more attention will focus on the excesses. But until now *tokkin* money has been good news for everyone. It has helped provide the liquidity to keep share prices going up, has added to the Japanese brokers' earnings and has helped to pay the inflated overheads of foreign money managers' Tokyo offices. But as a source of earnings on which to base a business it is of the riskiest kind. *Tokkin* money is icecube money; and it can melt easily. It will disappear as quickly as it appeared for two contrasting reasons. Either the Japanese economy will recover and industrial companies will start investing their money in their own businesses again. (This was already happening during 1987 and into 1988 as the domestic economy picked up steam and the inflow of money into *tokkin* accounts slowed.) Or company earnings will decline, leaving the companies with less money to play the market and so removing the liquidity which is fuelling it. Both trends will ultimately be bad for the stock market.

However, the authorities seem determined to keep the *tokkin* fever going for as long as they can, since they realize it is an important prop for the stock market. That was why in January 1988 the Ministry of Finance postponed for a year new accounting rules on *tokkin* funds. The new rules would have required that *tokkin* funds value their shares at either the market price or the purchase price, whichever was lower. This prompted fears that the funds would sell shares to realize gains before the new rules went into effect on 1 April 1988. That sell-off had indeed begun in December when *tokkin* assets fell by Y89bn. in one month. Worries were then growing that this comparative trickle would turn into a flood.

Certainly the market celebrated the authorities' convenient change of mind. Tokyo's benchmark Nikkei Index rose 5.6 per cent the day of the announcement, its second largest daily gain ever. Investors also liked the Ministry of Finance's second decision in January 1988 to let insurance companies invest a maximum 5 per cent, instead of 3 per cent as before, of their assets in *tokkin* funds in the stock market for short-term gains. That added about another Y1.4 trillion of new money that could go into the market. These two announcements encouraged foreign investors to start buying Tokyo shares again, however inflated the price. In October and November they had accounted for 22 per cent of net selling. In January, fed up with waiting for the crash, foreigners capitulated and became net buyers again.

Pension Funds

Still *tokkin* funds remain short-term money. The real plum in Japan's nascent money management industry is not today's hot area, *tokkin* accounts, but the pension funds, the capitalist world's largest under-exploited financial asset pool. Indeed, the deregulation of the management of Japanese pensions funds will in a sense be Tokyo's equivalent of London's Big Bang, though in Tokyo's case detonation is still some time away, though pension deregulation is currently being debated in the Japanese diet.

The opening salvoes in the battle to come over Japan's pensions funds were fired in 1983 when Nomura and Morgan Guaranty, the American commercial bank whose holding company is J. P. Morgan, applied to Japan's Ministry of Finance to set up a money management joint venture. After much wrangling the application was eventually turned down by the ministry, partly because of worries that Nomura was becoming too dominant a force in the market but mainly because it raised the hackles of vested interests, namely the trust banks and life insurance companies which currently enjoy the exclusive right to manage pension fund money. For though the original application had not specifically mentioned pension funds, Nomura's intention was to use Morgan's name and expertise to position itself in the campaign to manage pension fund money. As for Morgan, it was so keen to get its foot in the proverbial Tokyo door that it was prepared to compromise on its instinctive snobbish hostility to any form of joint venture.

The seventeen trust banks (including nine recently established foreign trust banks) and twenty-one life insurance companies together with one retail bank, Daiwa Bank, currently preside over the lucrative pension business. It is a fantastic growth area. Pension funds are swelling fast in Japan. Yet the way they are managed remains unsophisticated in the extreme with lacklustre investment returns. This has prompted competitors, locked-out of the business, to claim they could do a much better job. The companies themselves are, if only gradually, becoming aware of their future funding requirements and so growing more concerned about the quality of investment performance. They should be. Japan's faces the world's worst ageing population problem. Tomorrow's workers will have to bear an unenviable burden paying the pensions of today's workforce.

This problem is not yet pressing. Most company pension plans remain 'young' with contributions far exceeding pay-outs. That is one reason they are growing so fast. During the past ten years Japan's corporate pension funds grew at a compounded average annual rate of 23 per cent to Y19.54 trillion as at 31 March 1986. Assuming a relatively conservative 15 per cent annual growth rate, this figure will reach Y77 trillion or over $600bn. by 1996. It is this huge amount of cash over which money managers everywhere are salivating.

The arcane way in which these pension funds are currently managed justifies this interest. Japan's Pension Fund Association, which has led a campaign to get a more active performance measurement, estimates that in 1985 some 90 per cent of Japan's pension funds reported an investment return of between 9.28 and 9.7 per cent. All the funds were not invested in the same shares, however. Rather, as in any good cartel, the return is rigged to meet an agreed-upon rate. This is only possible because of Japan's 'book-value' system of accounting. A pension fund's investment performance is calculated by book value, that is what the fund paid for a share or bond, not on its current market value. All unrealized gains and, more importantly, losses are simply ignored. The total investment returns, in the sense of what the securities can be sold for, which is how any individual would measure his portfolio, is considered irrelevant. In the case of pension funds managed by the life insurance companies, which have a more than 35 per cent share of this market, all pension funds are pooled into a single, vast account, making it even harder for the client companies to demand accountability for the money manager's actions.

These primitive pension arrangements contrast with the sophistication of the same Japanese companies' manufacturing prowess. It is only considered acceptable because the pension business is still not regarded as important by the bosses of Japanese industry. As in America or Britain twenty years ago, the man responsible for supervising the pension fund tends to be a minion in the accounts department. The issue will probably only come to a head when the ratio of contributions to pay-outs becomes less favourable. Meanwhile, to question in any way a company's ability to fund its pension commitments, is viewed as that worst of Japanese corporate sins – disloyalty.

If the pension accounting system is primitive to western eyes, the investment practice is also extremely conservative. The average Japanese pension is invested 55 per cent in Japanese bonds, 17 per cent in Japanese equities, 10 per cent in foreign securities (nearly all bonds), and 11 per cent in long-term loans. They could be more aggressive if they wanted. Government regulations allow up to 30 per cent of a fund to be invested in shares. But because of the effective cartel, there is no incentive to be more adventurous or enterprising. And given the precipitous slide in world stock markets in October 1987 the pension funds may be glad they were run so sleepily.

Although competing financial institutions locked out of this business are doing their best to make pension fund management a live issue in Japan, there will be no radical change until legislation dismantles the present system. That will take time. Pension funds are an extremely sensitive subject because the trust banks and life insurance companies are large shareholders in many of the big industrial companies. This system reflects the period when the financial institutions dominated Japan and companies were dependent on them for financing. The result is a labyrinthine network of interlocking cross-shareholdings. Anthony Rowley in his book *Asian Stockmarkets: The Inside Story* records that a popular view in Tokyo is that around 50 per cent of the shares in issue on the Tokyo Stock Exchange are cross-holdings. Some estimates put the figure even higher. The set of circumstances that gave rise to this system no longer applies because companies do not depend on the banks for financing. Indeed large companies now raise most of their external financing through equity and equity-linked bond issues, which is itself a reflection of the stock market's high valuation. That means there is less reason for the pension cartel to remain. Still the entrenched interests in a traditional country like Japan should ensure it will take a few years, not months, to wither. As an executive at Sumitomo Trust in Tokyo commented: 'We hope it will last for ever. The reality is not so optimistic.' The best bet in Tokyo is, with the pension law due for amendment in 1988, Japan's 'city' banks (the country's national retail banks) will probably be allowed into the business though the Japanese brokers' money management subsidiaries and foreign firms may have to wait longer.

The pension issue is important in Japan not only because of the sheer amount of money at stake, but also because the present, sleepy system highlights some of the inconsistencies of Japan's financial bubble. For the ultra-cautious, if not downright lazy, way pension funds are managed offers a stark contrast with the *tokkin*-fuelled stock market fever. This reflects the contradictions of Japan's still tightly regulated financial structure. On the one hand, pension funds are inadequately managed to suit the interests of a sleepy cartel. On the other, companies' spare cash is risked recklessly in short-term gambling. Japan's financial system, therefore, suffers from the worst of both worlds, too much caution and too much risk. With such unsophisticated customers as their main institutional clients, it is no wonder that the Japanese brokers have concentrated more on ramping shares than analysing companies. Their clients have not demanded a better service. In the money business you often get what you deserve.

Japanese Investment Overseas

The lack of Japanese investment expertise, combined with the questionable practices of the country's stockbroking fraternity, has also proved a liability in recent years when it comes to venturing into overseas markets as investors. The Japanese have been reluctant to send their money abroad but the sheer size of their capital surplus has forced them to. So far their investment decisions do not look too clever. Indeed, the Japanese have fast earned the unfortunate reputation (in Wall Street at least) of the suckers who are always on hand to pay 'top dollar' at the peak of a market, be it American bonds, shares, or Manhattan or Los Angeles office blocks. This contrasts with the awesome reputation in America and Europe of Japan's successful manufacturing exporters. The worry is that the cash accumulated from twenty years of successful exporting will be dissipated, not in wild living, nor in building of mega white elephant projects which is how Saudi Arabia used up much of its 1970s OPEC oil bonanza, but rather lost in a stock market and property crash at home and in a massive depreciation through dollar devaluation of the large holdings of dollar paper securities, most of them I.O.U.s issued by an already heavily indebted American government, the world's biggest debtor.

Indeed, the Japanese today are like the British in the 1870s and the Americans in the 1950s. They enjoy a vast capital surplus with the rest of the world. Only part of that money can be spent building factories overseas. The rest has to go into financial assets. Hence the increasingly urgent task for the Japanese of learning the modern techniques of investing in strange foreign markets. That urgency is compounded by one often ignored fact. The Japanese are being forced to assume tremendous currency risks. This contrasts with the experience of their once wealthy British and American predecessors. When these countries ran big surpluses they were investing their money in essentially sterling and dollar worlds. Not so the Japanese. Each time they invest money overseas they take a foreign-exchange risk, there being no substantial investment outlets in offshore yen. They suffer then from the straitjacket of having to live in a dollar world while wearing yen clothes.

The dilemma this poses is enormous. It is also without precedent in recent financial history. At no time since the Industrial Revolution has a country had to assume such foreign-exchange risks with such a large body of the assets from which it hopes to derive its future prosperity. By contrast, Britain simply created a sterling area in its colonies around the globe, while America established the Eurodollar world in which its multinational companies operated.

The Japanese may then have lots of money, but they also have lots to worry about. Until 1987 the Japanese put most of their current account surplus into American treasury bonds. The amounts were huge and bear spelling out. According to Salomon Brothers' estimates, Japan's net, long-term capital outflow in 1986 exceeded $130bn., of which 70 per cent was spent on adding to existing foreign (mainly dollar) bond holdings. This sum amounted to more than the 1986 current account surplus of $86bn. The extra cash was raised by borrowing short-term in the Eurodollar market. In the first ten months of 1986 Japanese institutions borrowed net $50bn. offshore in this way.

The Japanese were doubling the number of pieces of foreign paper they bought every year to the delight of financial middle men everywhere. The outflow began in earnest in 1983. At the beginning of 1987 Japan's external investments were greater than OPEC's ever were in the 1970s and they may grow further. Salomon estimates that Japan's long-term external assets will exceed $500bn. by the end of 1987 and $700bn by 1990. OPEC's peaked at $380bn. in 1983. However, there are clear signs that the pattern of buying has shifted. Net buying of foreign currency bonds reached a record of $93bn. in 1986, according to Japanese official statistics. That probably marked a peak in the rate of growth of foreign bond holdings. The reason is that the Japanese have being losing far too much money.

Japan's twenty-four life insurance companies, for example, have traditionally not liked to hedge against currency risk. The unfortunate result is that, because of the yen's sharp rise, they suffered in 1985–6 estimated unrealized currency losses on their dollar bond holdings of some Y3–4 trillion. In the financial year ended March 31 1987 alone the life insurers lost a total of Yen 2.24 trillion, while the top seven companies wrote off Yen 1.7 trillion between them, three times more than the previous year. Clearly these were huge losses.

The Japanese seem to have finally had enough in the spring of 1987. Until March of that year the net Japanese net monthly buying of dollar bonds was running at several billion dollars, when it suddenly dropped to a comparatively paltry $3bn. The cause was mounting paper losses. The Japanese had bought thirty-year treasury bonds three months earlier at a yield of 7.1 per cent. Those yields had jumped within three months to over 8.5 per cent and higher, meaning a capital loss of nearly 15 per cent. That combined with a more than 10 per cent decline in the dollar during the same period meant the Japanese had lost 25 per cent of their investment on paper in just three months in supposedly safe bonds. Despite this unhappy experience, the Japanese bought more bonds than generally expected in the August 1987 auction and again soon found themselves suffering big capital and currency losses as the dollar fell again and U.S. treasury bond yields hit a twenty-month high of nearly 10.5 per cent in October. Indeed, it was that sharp rise in interest rates which proved the killer body blow to the stock market.

Losing money in bonds, the Japanese have responded by increased buying of other kinds of dollar assets, especially American shares and property. They did this even though Wall Street was well into the fifth year of its bull market in stocks and American commercial property prices were softening in response to growing vacancy rates. Net Japanese buying of American shares jumped to $7bn. in 1986. It more than doubled again in 1987, as the increased buying unhappily coincided with the top of the market. Since October 1987, however, Japanese purchases of American shares have virtually dried up. They even became net sellers.

So far there is no shortage of cash to fund this continuing commitment to dollar investments. The annual coupon income from Japanese foreign bond holdings runs at some $15–20bn. This alone provided enough cash to pay for the shift towards buying shares without requiring any new cash, let alone any sales of bonds. But if their cash flow is still enormous, the Japanese have realized that they have no option but to make some hard investment choices. They cannot, as they once naively hoped, just buy treasury bonds and forget about them since the dollar cannot be relied upon on to hold its value while interest rates will remain volatile, causing the risk of capital losses. So far the main consequence of Japanese buying of American government paper, apart from the currency losses they have suffered, has been to encourage America's governors to let the country go deeper into debt, making it a better than even bet that the long-term direction of the dollar will be sharply down. This is not an attractive prospect, either for American tourists venturing abroad or for Japanese holders of dollar paper, a fact which is slowly but surely sinking into the Japanese psyche.

Their concern is that they will be left holding, in yen terms, near worthless paper. That risk would only change if and when the U.S. Treasury switches at its quarterly refundings to auctioning yen rather than dollar treasury bonds. That day still seems some way off, which is why America still enjoys the considerable luxury of borrowing its own currency, the same paper its government prints. It is an indulgence, however, which may prove its undoing. Both America and the rest of the world will rue the day that market discipline was not enforced earlier on Washington's great paper chase.

The Japanese Approach to Investing

Suffocating in this unfamiliar dollar world, the Japanese have needed investment acumen and they have needed it fast. The trust banks and life companies hoped to learn the business of international equity investment by piggy-backing. All the major life companies have set up offshore subsidiaries, mostly in Luxembourg. These usually apportioned a modest amount of money, say $50m., to a foreign money manager. In return Japanese trainees were placed with the investment company to learn the money managers' secrets. The long-term goal is to bring the management of these subsidiaries' funds back in-house and then substantially increase their size.

There is a problem, however, with this copy-cat approach. Investing is not like making widgets. It does not lend itself to mere copying. Money management demands intuitive, individualistic decision-making skills. These are not the qualities normally associated with the traditional Japanese strengths of painstaking consensus building. Where will the Japanese find their 'contrarians', those perverse betters against the prevailing trend who can make some of the best investors? To the westerner that sounds like a contradiction in terms. The Japanese realize they have a problem in this area. That is why they are anxious to take the human element as far as possible out of investment by exploring more mechanistic approaches to investing currently being dreamed up by Wall Street's 'quant' community through the use of stock index futures and other, so-called 'derivative securities'. Ultimately the Japanese will be disappointed in this quest. All the mechanical devices in the world can, at best, only be an aid, at worst a hindrance. In the October 1987 crash the Chicago futures markets failed to perform the arbitrage and hedging function they are supposed to because of turmoil on the floor of the New York Stock Exchange. You cannot hedge in the futures market when you do not know the price in the cash market. The Japanese will find they can never remove the risk and emotion from investing. Markets are made up of human beings and hence emotions. They consist of alternating bouts of greed, fear, and sheer boredom. And risk is risk.

If these generalizations about the Japanese character seem specious, one should add that the Japanese themselves are aware of a problem. In a speech in New York in April 1987 Michiya Matsukawa, chairman of the Nikko Research Institute and a former senior Ministry of Finance official, described the herd-like mentality of Japanese investors. A passage from his speech merits quoting at length:

> In conclusion I should make a short comment on the behaviour of average Japanese people. In Japan everybody is looking around and watching similar types of persons . . . In Japan, if one of them does something, then the others will follow. Even though it is risky, they will never be blamed as they did the same as the officers in a different company in a different position. This means, if one or two life insurance companies buy a large amount of U.S. treasury bonds, then the other insurance companies may not do the same. But once no one is forthcoming with a large amount of orders, then all will take a similar attitude and no one will come to the market.

In other words Japanese investors, like Japanese citizens, do not like to stand apart from the crowd. That means that the stream of liquidity, which is still keeping the Tokyo stock market going, could be turned off at any time. The crash of October 1987 saw the hose turned off foreign stock markets and pointed back at Tokyo. That will and has propped up sentiment for a time in Tokyo. By May 1988 Tokyo's Nikkei Index had rallied back to reach a new all time high of over 28,000. This astonishing performance was in defiance of the world's other markets, nearly all of which have failed so far to follow Tokyo's lead.

The rise may not have been totally unconnected with the fact that on 1 April 1988 the Japanese government scrapped a tax break for small savers known as *maruyu*. At the end of September 1987 some Y300 trillion or $2.4 trillion out of Japan's total savings of Y637 trillion was in accounts benefiting from this tax break, mostly held at Japan's huge postal savings banks and other commercial banks. Japan's stockbrokers were naturally hoping that some of this enormous sum of money would go into their investment trusts, the Japanese equivalent of Britain's unit trusts and America's mutual funds, and hence into the stock market.

So the Tokyo market continued to rise on great-fool-theory liquidity arguments. The fact remains that, when they finally leave the party, Japan's investors will all stampede for the exit together, which is a scary thought. What event could precipitate this is anyone's guess, though several spring to mind. One such is a decline in Japan's property market, which is closely interconnected with both the Tokyo stock market and the local banking system.

One reason Tokyo property values have reached such dizzy levels is that there are so few transactions. That is not so surprising when you consider that there is a 80 per cent capital gains tax on any Japanese property sold within ten years of purchase. Seeing the value of their investment soar but not able to cash in on it without giving the government most of the money, Japan's property owners have done the next best thing and borrowed from the bank 100 per cent of the appraised value of their property. Often this money is then put to work in the stock market. Likewise, aspiring home owners in Japan have become so concerned that they will soon never be able to afford a home within two or three hours' commuting distance from Tokyo, so dramatically have prices risen, that the banks have started offering them two-generational mortages spanning sixty years. Father is therefore condemning son to pay off a loan for a house or flat bought at the top of perhaps the biggest property boom this century. At the centre of such practices is the belief shared by both property buyers and the banks that property values can only go up. In a country where Draconian zoning laws mean that only 2.95 per cent of the land surface of the country is zoned for residential use, this is patently absurd.

But the real reason why Japan faces a looming credit crisis is the exposure of its biggest banks to the property market. A December 1987 study by the Washington Econometrics Forecasting Services points out that if real estate in Japan were suddenly revalued back to the levels which prevailed in 1984, it would result in a loss of wealth in Japan exceeding $3 trillion. That is a decline in collateral which even Japan's big banks would have trouble stomaching, and they are the world's biggest. Of the world's ten largest companies eight are Japanese and six of these Japanese banks. The very size of the Japanese banks means that a credit crisis in Japan caused by a crash in property values there would have deflationary consequences throughout the world. It could certainly precipitate a wholesale liquidation of Japanese assets overseas, including American treasury bonds, perhaps causing a sharp upward spike in dollar interest rates. Compounding the danger, Japanese banks hold a far greater percentage of their depositors' funds in shares than do America's banks. So a property crash would feed directly into a stock market crash, or vice versa. That is why it is not absurd to contemplate a 90 per cent decline in Japan's shares and property values.

A crash in Tokyo could even be precipitated by a severe earthquake in Tokyo. The last big quake there was in 1923 and another one is now due. There are small rumblings all the time in Tokyo. Such a natural disaster would cause the insurance companies to sell large amounts of paper securities to meet the enormous claims which would be generated. Indeed, one traditional reason Japanese insurance companies have assets invested abroad is to hedge against the earthquake risk. They are directed to do so by the Ministry of Finance. An earthquake would also force companies to take money out of financial assets and plough it back into rebuilding Tokyo, a city whose history is that of a series of destructions and reconstructions in which the catalyst is nearly always the same, an earthquake (a fact which makes present property values in Tokyo look even more insane). The clear risk of a major natural disaster in Tokyo is cited just as an illustration of how vulnerable Japan's liquidity bubble is to shock events, natural or man-made, outside the politicians' and Nomura's control.

Another cause for concern is that the Japanese have not experienced a severe bear market in their recent history. They avoided the worst effects of the Depression which engulfed America and Europe in the 1930s while their stock market has been essentially climbing since the 1960s. There are not the same recent bear-market memories in the local culture. That is dangerous since it means more greed and less fear when markets get absurdly overblown as they have been in Japan for at least two years, this cycle's supreme example of financial asset inflation.

Moreover, the Japanese seem dangerously complacent, if not downright arrogant. They are confident in their ability to keep the stock market bubble going and to postpone the inevitable day of reckoning. Thus, the response to the Wall Street crash was a determined attempt to prevent full-scale panic with the Big Four brokers buying shares after some nudging by the Ministry of Finance. The market was helped by Tokyo Stock Exchange rules which suspend dealings in a share if sellers exceed buyers by a ratio of ten to one. That was why on 20 October 1987, the day after Wall Street's record-breaking fall, volume in Tokyo was one tenth of the average daily trading volume of recent months. There were plenty of sellers but few buyers. The result was that the Tokyo market fell 'only' 15 per cent and then recovered half of that fall the next day. This is not bad considering that Tokyo was already by a long way the most expensive stock market in the world before other markets began plunging. Does this reflect impressive Japanese confidence in their own market or rank manipulation? The answer is a bit of both.

Tokyo's resilience, however, brings to mind a worrying historical parallel. Sixty years ago America was the dominant economic power but a secondary player in dictating the world's political order compared with Britain and other European powers. Today Japan is the dominant economic power but still a relative political eunuch compared with America in view of its meagre defence capability and (aside from former prime minister Yasuro Nakasone) self-deprecating politicians. It was then America, following the October 1929 Wall Street Crash, which led the world into the 1930s Depression. The interesting point, though, is that Wall Street crashed some nine months after London peaked in January 1929.

Could the same pattern be repeated with this time, Tokyo being New York and New York London? One factor which could bring an end to the Tokyo party is the pressure the lower dollar and so higher yen is putting on Japan's exporters. Another fear is a revival of protectionist forces accompanied by a contraction in world trade.

Certainly a lower dollar was one at least temporary consequence of the Wall Street crash. For faced with a choice in a presidential election year of correcting its trade deficit through recession and higher dollar interest rates or dollar devaluation, the Americans would be tempted to opt for the latter. By the end of October 1987 it was clear this was what was happening. Indeed, treasury secretary James Baker told the world so.

The problem for the Japanese is that the dollar will stay weak so long as America's trade deficit continues to grow, thereby making it harder for them to export. Yet if America's trade deficit starts improving and the dollar rallies as a result, as was beginning to happen in the first quarter of 1988, that will reflect a slowdown in America's economy and in its consumption of imports, which in turn will be bad for Japan's exports. Either way after so many years of plenty Japan faces the prospect of the shrinking of its biggest export market, as America finally starts correcting its huge trade imbalance. And yet it was the growth of Japan's trade surplus which tracked the soaring value of its stock and property markets.

Whatever the exact outcome, it is hard to disagree with the conclusion of Mark Faber, a Swiss-born economic historian turned stockbroker who runs Drexel Burnham's office in Hong Kong and has years of experience investing in Asian financial markets. He wrote in an investment report in 1987:

> Every country goes in its development through at least one major financial boom and bust period. The railroads in the UK around 1857, the Vienna stock and property market boom of 1873, the USA in 1927–9, Hong Kong in 1972–3. Japan is the next country in line.

Nor would it be so surprising to see Japan's trade surplus vanish far more quickly than conventional wisdom now suggests, just as OPEC's did. Faber calls a Japanese trade deficit 'a distinct possibility five years from now'.

Indeed, the most interesting question is not if this impending crash in Japan will happen, nor even perhaps when. Rather it is how the Japanese will react to the financial débâcle in their home markets. The likelihood is not that well. Since the Japanese tend to move in the same direction all at once, they tend to overdo everything, be it selling cars to Americans or ramping their companies' shares out of sight. They do not know when to stop, nor are they good at coping with failure. So precisely because Japan is such a group culture, there is a clear risk they will be collectively stunned by unpleasant shocks to the system. These traits could breed mass panic, the worst reaction to financial as well as natural disasters. A crash in the Tokyo stock market could affect the psychology of the whole country, especially as more and more small investors have caught the bug of speculating in shares. Asked how he thought Nomura would react to a precipitous crash in its home market, an American who worked with Nomura for several years in New York replied: 'I think they would be stunned like when you run up and hit someone with a lemon pie. They would probably panic and then try to generate sales commissions on the downside. I don't think they can control the market. If they lose the public's confidence, it will be all over.'

If, so far, the Japanese have shown impressive control in averting panic in their own stock market (even if it was partly by rank manipulation), compared with the freefalls witnessed in New York, London, and just about every other market around the globe, believers in the powers of markets to correct excesses must reckon that Japan's speculative bubble will burst. The point is that the longer the suspension of reality, the bigger the bloodbath. Such a crash would have global consequences. It would constrain the largest source of savings to the world economy causing a drop in asset values in every market where the Japanese have been paying top dollar.

Doubtless the Japanese will pick themselves up after the initial trauma of the crash and rebuild their industrial and this time probably military complex, in as impressively a disciplined manner as they rebuilt following Hiroshima and the Second World War. On the outcome of that will depend whether Japan replaces America as the world's political as well as economic superpower. First, however, Japan must weather that financial storm.

LONDON

'The City of London is now faced with a vast surplus of firms, capital, office space, computer space and, above all, absurdly over-priced individuals, all committed to speculative markets which in volume terms can support only a fraction of these resources.'
International Currency Review. 1986.

To the casual observer the City of London suddenly became a topic of conversation during the countdown to Big Bang in the mid-1980s. Suddenly everyone became aware of the unprecedented sums being paid to buy up London stockbroking firms as the world's top financial institutions sought to position themselves in the third leg of the global twenty-four-hour financial market. This was partly just luck, a question of time zones. London dealers talk to Tokyo when they arrive at the office and New York before they leave to go home. The City is the chain that links the world's financial markets together, be it trading foreign exchange, gold, treasury bonds, or shares of the world's leading companies. This happy position led to substantial million-pound-plus payments for senior partners of stockbroking firms, though the so-called 'marzipan set' (up-and-coming brokers just below partner level) were less fortunate, seeing their firms sold from under them before they had a chance to own a share in the equity.

However, Big Bang was always as much about hype as reality. The actual event merely concerned the introduction of negotiated commissions in Britain's comparatively unimportant stock market and government bond (gilt-edged stock) market, and allowing outsiders to buy London Stock Exchange member firms. This meant not only that banks could buy brokers, but also a lot more cut-throat competition in Britain's domestic markets. The days of cosy fixed commissions and long, liquid City lunches were over. Henceforth it would be a fight for survival. The number of primary dealers (market makers) in gilts, for example, suddenly jumped from three to twenty-seven, a fact which made most observers wonder why many new entrants were bothering with the gilts market at all.

What all the fanfare ignored was that London was already a leading financial centre regardless of Big Bang. And this had nothing to do with its domestic markets. Numerous banks had maintained big operations in London for twenty and more years, even though they had little to do with the local stock market or bond market. The reason was first the foreign-exchange market, where London remains the world's largest centre trading around $90bn. a day and second, the Eurobond market.

The Eurobond Market

The Eurobond phenomenon has helped entice more than 550 banks and brokers from abroad and made London the dominant centre it still is in world debt markets, dwarfing its domestic market activities. In 1986 the Eurobond market raised some $180bn. in new debt issues. Compare that with the total of £9.2bn. raised in the London stock market the same year. Britain may have had socialist governments during the post-1945 period but no politician was silly enough to interfere with this offshore bonanza which has helped London retain its status as a top financial centre long after economic decline had reduced Britain to a second-class power.

London won the opportunity to become the centre of offshore finance because of misguided regulation in America. The key event occurred in 1963 when President John Kennedy introduced a tax on foreign bond issues in the domestic dollar market. Then in 1968 legislation stopped American companies from financing overseas investment in their domestic market. The consequence was a loss of business for Wall Street, especially as American banks enjoyed all manner of freedoms operating in London that Glass-Steagall denied them back home. They were also attracted to London as an offshore centre both because it had the history, communications and general infrastructure of an international financial centre and, at least as important, spoke English.

The Euromarket grew with America's trade deficit and the resulting proliferation of dollars outside the United States, was

fuelled both by the investment of American multinationals overseas and the Vietnam War. Because it was an offshore market
there was no central bank regulation, there being no international
central bank. That meant the banks faced no reserve requirements
and so were free to lend as aggressively as they liked. By the early
1970s for every dollar the big American banks lent at home, they
were lending six or seven offshore.

Accordingly, the market exploded. As at 31 March 1987 the
offshore Eurocurrency deposit market totalled $3.85 trillion, some
70 per cent of which was in Eurodollars. A Euro-deposit is a
deposit held at an offshore bank. This was money outside the
world's national banking system. (A Eurocurrency is money held
outside the country it comes from, be it a dollar, yen or D-Mark.)
Two-thirds of that figure represents transactions between banks.
But even the remaining $1 trillion-plus is hardly puny. As Jeffry
Frieden observes in his book *Banking on the World*: 'The market's
trillion dollars could buy every manufacturing corporation in the
United States, as well as the livestock, crops, buildings and
machinery on all American farms.'

If the Euromarket is huge, its very size is also what' makes the
City of London so vulnerable should the mountain of debt issued
there ever implode through a financial panic triggered by some
kind of banking collapse or default. For the Euromarket is nothing
but a function of available credit. The City of London has certainly
enjoyed a secular as opposed to cyclical boom. For more than
twenty years the Eurobond market demonstrated all the classic
virtues of a free market as capital was moved quickly and
efficiently via electronic communications from lender to borrower
across national boundaries. Just as in any other successful market
however, this very success bred its own excesses, in this case excess
capacity with too many participants chasing deals and wafer thin
profit margins, if any.

By 1987 the strains were obvious not only in dwindling profits for
the market's financial middle men, many of whom seemed only
too prepared to bring bond issues to market at a loss in order to
keep their firms ranking in the league table of lead managers of
new issues, but also in declining activity. After two decades of
virtually untramelled growth the international debt market started
slowing down. Eurobond new issue volume dropped 23 per cent in
1987 from $184bn. to $143bn. Behind these figures lay growing
suspicions among bond investors about the liquidity of the market.
A bond market without liquidity is not much use to any investor

since a bond that cannot be sold in the secondary market has to be held until maturity, making it more like an ordinary loan.

The middle men in the Eurobond market, a category which includes American, European, and Japanese commercial banks as well as the world's investment banks and securities firms, had responded to competition by creating ever more exotic products to steal an advantage on the competition. As on Wall Street some of these new securities proved too complicated for their own good, especially when there were few genuine investors interested in buying them. Indeed, many bond investors have begun to show greater appreciation for the merits of boring old government bonds which, at least, can always be sold. When people grow more cautious in their outlook, an offshore and unregulated market conducted purely over the telephone where there is no central bank to act as lender of last resort, and no government to bail out bust banks, can suddenly seem rather less attractive. The result is that both bond investors and depositors start withdrawing their money.

These lurking dangers are not widely appreciated outside the money business itself though their consequences may one day be felt at a far broader level, just as those who thought in October 1987 that the stock market crash did not affect them just because they did not own shares at the time are in for a rude awakening. The Eurobond market is perhaps the most important and under-reported phenomenon in the money business. It is not much written about save in trade journals such as the ultra-glossy publishing success story *Euromoney*, which, in a sign of the times, has recently suffered a sharp fall in advertising revenues. This lack of press attention is because the Eurobond market seems a rather esoteric affair, an entirely abstract marketplace with no central exchange or trading floor, though in practice some 70 per cent of the people in it are located in London. It is far easier for journalists to write about 'Big Bang'.

Yet this market is used by government, supra-national organizations, companies, and banks from all over the world to raise money outside their home markets. The Eurobond market's attractions have traditionally been twofold. First, being largely unregulated, there are limited disclosure requirements for issuers while competition means transaction costs are low. Second, there is the crucial point of anonymity. Eurobonds are bearer bonds so they can be owned anonymously by private investors. There is also no withholding tax on interest payments. This makes Eurobonds the perfect vehicle for the Swiss banking system and the other offshore vehicles which specialize in keeping private capital outside the hands of the taxman. That is why the Swiss banks have always been among the top Eurobond players. The joint venture between a leading Swiss bank and Wall Street investment bank, Credit Suisse First Boston (C.S.F.B.), was top of the league table of lead managers of new issues throughout the 1980s until it was ousted by Japan's Nomura in 1987. The Swiss have traditionally been able to issue bonds, confident they can distribute them among their network of private banking clients. So the secrecy factor was part and parcel of the growth of the Eurobond market, though in recent years the importance of the retail investor has dwindled.

This forced issuing houses, as they strove to move up the league tables, to resort to launching issues which on occasion they have had to keep on their own books because no one wanted to buy them. The unfortunate consequence is that frenzied competition to issue paper has led to a proliferation of debt, often despite the lack of genuine buyers for the bonds.

So the Eurobond market has been showing clear signs of strain. Given the looming debt contraction facing the world the question is less whether the market has seen its best days (it surely has) but whether it can survive in its present freewheeling, unregulated form. Its demise would certainly threaten London's status as a financial centre to equal New York and Tokyo. The Eurobond market is perhaps the key symbol of the post-war era of untrammelled debt creation. The concern is that during periods of financial panic offshore financial centres will lose money fastest as capital returns home seeking safety first. The ability to borrow would then dry up as deposits flee the offshore banking system. With no regulatory system in place and no central bank in charge, it would be that much harder for the authorities to respond quickly to a crisis.

A harbinger of what may be to come occurred in the Euro-markets in late 1986. It concerned a hybrid security known as a perpetual floating rate note, a typical example of the kind of complex product created by the money industry's self-described breed of 'financial engineers'. Because perpetuals are never repaid by the borrower but rather go on for ever paying interest (hence the name), the value of these undated securities hinges on the fact that they pay higher interest rates than conventional floating rate notes (F.R.N.s), a favourite Eurobond instrument. The attraction of perpetuals to the issuers, which were mainly banks, was that it let them borrow money without ever having to worry about paying it back. That is why they rushed to issue some $18bn.-worth of perpetuals in a very short time prior to the market's collapse. Most of this paper was bought by Japanese banks which liked these securities because their regulators let them count perpetuals as part of their primary capital. Indeed, the product was designed with this specific group of investors in mind. That was its undoing. It needed only a rumour that Japan's Ministry of Finance was about to define its primary capital requirements more strictly to expose the perpetual market as the liquidity trap it was. Prices plunged in December 1986 and genuine investors in these exotic instruments vanished as the Japanese banks tried to sell. Within months the perpetual market was all but extinct. The Japanese banks, which were estimated to be left holding some $12bn.-worth of perpetuals, were hurt the most, losing an estimated $1.5bn., though several lead underwriters were also caught holding paper they could only sell for bargain-basement prices.

This débâcle may not have been front-page news but its implications were dramatic. For the first time in the history of Eurobonds demand for a product dried up and a market perished. A product which was created by clever middle men to cater for the specific needs of certain issuers and investors alike collapsed when those criteria were no longer met. That is why it was misguided to lay all the blame on the fifty or so firms which made a market in perpetuals, most of whom suddenly abandoned their commitment to the market and stopped answering the telephone. The real drama lay in the fact that suddenly no one wanted to buy a particular product. Trading in Eurobonds would never seem quite the same again. The experience is also one reason why investors are increasingly only interested in ordinary vanilla Eurobonds issued by major names in large, say, $300m.-plus issues. They are prepared to pay a premium for this kind of paper (in the sense of receiving a lower yield) because they want to be sure they can always sell the bond. So the Eurobond market is increasingly closed to lower rated borrowers, which is another way of saying it is shrinking.

The signs of investor concern continue to grow. In 1987 it extended from perpetuals to the much larger $150bn. – F.R.N. market. F.R.N.s have been the most actively traded part of the Eurobond market during the 1980s. As the interest rate paid to the investor fluctuates with market rates F.R.N.s have proved an attractive hedge to the bond investor against the ever lurking menace of rising interest rates. The 1980s have seen mostly falling interest rates but investors wanted F.R.N.s, remembering the losses suffered on fixed-interest securities during the inflationary 1970s. The problem was that the F.R.N. market was suffering from a glut of issues because of the Eurobond market's favourite practice of underwriting issues at a loss. Some of these issues carried an interest rate coupon less than could be earned in comparative short-term debt instruments.

The result was that major buyers such as the Japanese, who had been buying more than 50 per cent of all F.R.N.s, began to withdraw from the market. Then in early 1987 investors became worried about F.R.N.s issued by the big bank creditors to the Third World. These worries were triggered by renewed concern about Third World debt because of Brazil's decision to stop paying interest payments on its bank debt and spread to the rest of the F.R.N. market, again emphasizing the lack of a solid investor base underpinning it. Since then the market has adjusted by pricing the bonds at a decent enough yield to lure back buyers. Still damage has been done to the market's reputation, as is clear from the figures. The volume of new F.R.N. issues dropped 80 per cent from £50bn. in 1986 to just £11bn. in 1987.

While they were prepared to admit to the difficulties which faced the Eurobond market during 1986–7, many Eurobuffs comforted themselves that they had discovered a new growth area which would compensate for the maturity of the bond business. This was Euro-equities, and again the business was based in London. Euro-equities are shares issued by companies away from their home stock exchanges. This new product took off both because of the worldwide bull market in shares and the renewed interest in international equity investment. The annual value of new Euro-equity issues trebled in three years to reach nearly $18bn. in 1987. However, that was the cyclical peak. Since 19 October new issue activity has dried up while secondary trading volume has dwindled. Still London is likely to remain the world centre for telephone-and-screen trading of international shares so long as there are investors who want to buy equities outside their home country.

So the Euromarkets are in a bind. The Eurobond sector suffers all the characteristics of a mature industry while there are fundamental question marks over the lack of liquidity in the market save for the most blue chip of issues. Also, a promising newcomer in Euro-equities has been struck down by the force of the world stock market crash just when it was gathering momentum. Given the severity of the worldwide crash in share values Euro-equities are unlikely to revive in popularity soon.

None of this is good news for the numerous financial institutions which are active in the Euromarkets, especially as many of these same firms used the occasion of Big Bang to expand the size of their London operations. It was always a matter of wonder why many of these firms bothered with Eurobonds at all since they certainly did not make any money from them. The explanation always given was the macho one that firms needed to show their face in Europe if they wanted to be viewed as international players. Such a rationale begins to look a litle thin when the losses mount up. That was why layoffs had already begun in the Eurobond market even before the stock market crash precipitated wholesale retrenchment throughout the City with every prospect of more to come.

The key participants in the Eurobond market can be divided into three main groups. They are the American investment banks, the universal banks, and the Japanese securities firms. Of the three, the Japanese firms have made by far the biggest gains in recent years, partly because they have been happy to use their huge profits at home to buy market share, causing competitors to accuse them of 'dumping' financial services, and partly because they have tremendous placing power both through their institutional clients and their thousands of retail clients in Japan. The Japanese firms enjoyed great success with equity-linked yen bonds issued mostly by Japanese companies. These bonds had equity warrants attached to them giving the investor a speculative bet on the company's share price. That proved popular during a period when the Tokyo stock market has been so strong.

The Japanese have also been helped by the growth in the Euro-yen sector which increased in popularity as the currency appreciated. The yen sector accounted for 15 per cent of the new issue market in 1987 compared with just 3 per cent in 1984. By contrast the dollar sector has declined in importance as investors preferred to buy Eurobonds in other currencies. This has not been good for the American investment banks. For it is their experience in the domestic dollar bond market which gives them a natural advantage issuing Euro-dollars. If Morgan Stanley advises General Motors on a domestic bond issue on Wall Street, it also has a good chance of getting the business when G.M. issues a Eurobond in London. Its expertise is dollars.

The third category is the universal banks. Here the principal players are C.S.F.B., Swiss Bank Corporation, and Deutschbank.

A 1987 study of the Eurobond market conducted by the MAC Group, a management consultant, points out that these banks' traditional strength is that they have been able to sell their own bond issues in-house to their retail clients whose portfolios they manage. The MAC study lists three key advantages shared by the universal banks. First, they can often sell bonds at lower yields than would be acceptable to institutional investors. This is because the individual investor, especially in Switzerland, is more concerned with capital preservation than yield. Second, they can underwrite a bond with enormous confidence in their ability to distribute it. Because many of the portfolios managed by these banks are discretionary the banks can buy their own issues for their customers without them even knowing it. Third, distribution can be more profitable because the Swiss banks can charge additional commissions from selling bonds to their own retail customers. Combined, these benefits show the underlying profitability of the Swiss banking system. They also demonstrate why giving a Swiss bank discretion to manage an investment account can be an expensive pastime.

These three groups are the strongest competitors in the Eurobond market. There are then the various niche players like Baring Brothers, which only deals in Euro-sterling bonds; Hambro, another London merchant bank which specializes in Australian and New Zealand Eurodollar issues; and Woody Gundy, which, not surprisingly for a leading Canadian securities firm, handles Canadian dollar Euro-issues.

The odd men out in this list are the big American commercial banks. Nearly all of them have a presence in the Eurobond market but they have not become dominant forces in underwriting and distribution. The exception is J.P. Morgan, which has long been as strong as any of the Wall Street investment banks in Europe. The other commercial banks have tended to use the Eurobond market as a way of gaining experience in the securities business in an environment free of Glass-Steagall-type restrictions. However, their activity has not been very profitable. By early 1987 Bank of America, Chase Manhattan, and Chemical Bank had all publicly dismissed Eurobond specialists.

Aside from niche roles, the London merchant banks have also been conspiciously absent from the Eurobond league tables. They have neither the capital strength nor the distribution muscle to compete with the giants. Nor have they relished the risks which need to be taken. As the MAC study commented: 'The potential for losses in the eurobond business is high relative to the profits some of the merchant banks generate. A loss of $5–10m. in Eurobond trading is quite damaging to a firm making $40–50m. in pre-tax profits.'

The main exception to this rule is S. G. Warburg, Britain's most successful securities firm. This is appropriate since Warburg's founder, Sigmund Warburg, a refugee from Nazi Germany in the 1930s, is generally credited with inventing the Eurobond market in 1963 when his firm managed a $15m. bond raised by Autostrade, the company which runs Italy's motorways. However, even Warburg has in recent years shied away from the increasingly kamikaze loss-leader mentality to be found in the Eurobond market. Its reluctance to bid for new issues at a loss caused it to fall from fourth place in the lead manager league table in 1982 to nineteenth in 1986.

The Big Bang

The separation of the Eurobond market from Britain's domestic capital markets has been almost complete. The two have different sets of players. If London's prime role in the world money business is linking borrowers from all continents with investors from all continents via the Euromarkets, the impact of Big Bang fell in the domestic arena. Fixed commissions were not only abandoned in the stock market but foreign banks and securities companies, as well as British banks, were allowed to buy stakes in London Stock Exchange member firms. The old City separation between merchant bank, stock broker, and jobber (the name given to the London market maker in share prices) vanished. The brave new world promised by Big Bang was to be that of the integrated securities firm, combining market making, stockbroking, corporate finance, merger and acquisitions, and money management. London was to become more like Wall Street and its merchant banks and stockbrokers were to be glued together and recast in the mould of America's investment banks.

The countdown to Big Bang caused a bidding war for London's major stockbroking firms, most of whom, being brokers, sold themselves shrewdly. Hundreds of millions of pounds was spent on buying stockbrokers, despite the harsh fact that the assets of these companies, namely the people in them, could only too easily walk straight out of the door. The Americans and Japanese also threw resources into London. They saw the City as the laboratory of the global financial market where, because of deregulation, they could compete on a level playing field. Salaries soared and executive head hunters had a field day as anyone with any experience whatsoever saw his market value soar while the money industry prepared for the City's new era.

The frenzied preparations for Big Bang were punctuated by the announcement of a succession of deals as banks bought into brokers. This spawned some interesting combinations in the adventure to build an investment bank from scratch. But there were also those few City firms which elected to stay independent, and those major foreign players which decided to resist the rush to buy, preferring to wait for the only too predictable shake-out. None of these alternative courses of action promised success. Nor did they guarantee failure. There have been examples of both. Warburg chose to put aside its natural dislike for taking large risks and took the plunge to become a full-scale player. Helped by its local knowledge it bought what many regarded as the pick of the City bunch. Its shopping list included stockbroker Rowe & Pitman (the royal family's broker); Mullens, the top gilts broker; and Akroyd & Smithers, one of the three jobbing firms which mattered in the pre-Big Bang City. By contrast, Morgan Grenfell, Warburg's chief rival for the position of London's premier merchant bank, elected not to buy any major stockbroking firm (Rowe & Pitman offered itself first to Morgan Grenfell) but rather chose to build its operation bottom-up by hiring individuals rather than buying a stockbroking company.

Of Britain's four main clearing banks, only Lloyds elected not to join in the buying spree. In June 1987 it showed its suspicion of the securities business by pulling out of both Eurobonds and gilts after its investment bank had lost £20m. in the first half of that year. Barclays was the most aggressive, buying a leading stockbroker, De Zoete & Bevan, and a leading jobbing firm, Wedd Durlacher, to form Barclays De Zoete Wedd (B.Z.W.). (The third major jobbing firm, Smith Newcourt, elected to stay independent though it sold a minority stake to merchant bank N. M. Rothschild.) Midland bought a top stockbroker, Greenwell, and a merchant bank, Samuel Montagu. National Westminster adopted a more low-cost route to building an investment bank by buying a small stockbroker and jobber to incorporate in its merchant banking subsidiary, County NatWest. The plan was then to build this essentially modest operation from ground-up.

Setting up these securities businesses from scratch did not come cheaply. In 1986 these four British clearing banks lost or wrote-off against reserves £162m. due to start-up costs in the securities business. More losses followed in 1987. B.Z.W., for example, as probably London's biggest equity market maker, lost an estimated £50m. in the October crash. Despite the size of the loss, however, it is to date the most likely candidate among the clearers to prosper as a full-scale investment bank. And, like Warburg, it followed a policy of buying leading established firms. Big Bang may have been a case of getting what you paid for.

Some top City stockbroking firms decided to sell themselves to foreigners, sometimes just because they were the highest bidder, sometimes because it was hoped that geographical distance would result in more hands-off management. City stockbrokers have always had a healthy suspicion of the bureaucracy associated with being owned by a commercial bank. Banks, it was felt, did not understand the business. The deals proliferated. Among the more important, Vickers da Costa and Scrimgeour Kemp-Gee were bought by Citicorp. Simon and Coates, and Laurie Millbank by Chase Manhattan, Hoare Govett by Los Angeles-based Security Pacific, James Capel by the Hong Kong and Shanghai Bank, and Phillips & Drew by the Union Bank of Switzerland.

But if the commercial banks were active, Shearson Lehman was the only major Wall Street investment bank to buy a London stockbroker when it purchased Messels. The other Wall Street firms preferrred to build up their London offices by aggressive hiring. The same approach was followed by the Japanese Big Four securities firms. It was these Americans and Japanese who were most instrumental in bidding up City salaries. There was general outrage in low-salary Britain when it was learned that Goldman Sachs was touring Oxford and Cambridge universities offering twenty-one-year-old university graduates the unheard of starting salary of £25,000 a year.

Of those City firms that elected to remain independent, by far the most important was Cazenove, London's most blue-chip as well as most discreet stockbroker. Cazenove's prime expertise is in corporate finance rather than more mundane stockbroking. It specializes in advising companies on how to raise money from the stock market or how to price a takeover. Under London's peculiar system known as pre-emption rights there has to be a rights issue whenever a company issues shares, which means that existing shareholders get the first right of refusal to take up any share issue. This prevents use of the common Wall Street practice, the 'bought deal', where the investment bank will bid for the whole of a share issue at a very thin profit margin with a view to selling it all on. Under the London system size and capital become less important than being able to place an issue with enough friendly institutions and compliant private clients, the Cazenove art. This is one reason the Wall Street firms have not yet established the presence in London's domestic market they hoped to. Even so, as a defensive measure to prepare itself for Big Bang, Cazenove did establish an underwriting syndicate with a selection of its most loyal institutional investors. So far at least the firm seems to be prospering despite being the City's only surviving major partnership.

Many of the London merchant banks also elected not to become involved in the pre-Big Bang auction, which in their case meant not paying top-of-the-market prices for stockbroking firms or not being bought out by bigger banks. Their preferred course was continued independence, even if that meant remaining small and marginal. Such historic names as Baring Brothers, Hambro, Lazard, and N. M. Rothschild all decided to stay independent and, hopefully, exclusive.

Less than eighteen months after Big Bang it was already possible to draw some tentative conclusions on the winners and losers. Problems were already surfacing in the City even before the October 1987 stock market crash, during which London share prices fell further than in New York or Tokyo. The débâcle served to underline one harsh fact: that trading volumes in London would never be big enough to justify the huge overheads built up in the countdown to Big Bang. The crash also undermined the confidence of the many bumptious market makers who had become increasingly cocky about their ability to make money trading shares for their firms' own account in London's new, all-electronic Stock Exchange. For Big Bang not only meant the end of jobbers, but it also marked the advent of an all-electronic trading system whereby prices were agreed over the phone and in front of a screen and where the floor of the London Stock Exchange was reduced to an historic relic. With firms losing tens of millions of pounds in the crash the number of genuine market makers declined sharply as did the size of the positions securities firms were prepared to hold.

Still, there will be survivors. Warburg looks to have established itself as the British investment bank with the best chance of making the grade internationally. Even its strength, however, hinges mainly on its domestic British business. A British securities firm does not have the large domestic market nor the long corporate client list to feed off which its American and Japanese counterparts can rely on. Nor does it have the franchise enjoyed by the Swiss, namely the secretive investor. The British have to be that much more creative to earn a buck.

With its Goldman Sachs-like team culture and its dislike of star individuals, Warburg emerged from the crash with an estimated £20m. loss from equity trading but with its reputation and finances intact. The same cannot be said for Morgan Grenfell, once its chief rival among the merchant banks. This firm has suffered a succession of setbacks. Most serious was its involvement in the Guinness affair, the British offshoot of the Boesky scandal. Morgan Grenfell's aggressive M. & A. team was accused of masterminding an illegal share support operation during a tightly contested, hostile takeover. Various parties were paid to buy the shares of Distillers, a drinks company, in the ultimately successful attempt by Guinness to buy that firm. Morgan Grenfell's chairman was forced to resign as a result of the scandal following Bank of England prodding, as has the chairman of Guinness and Morgan Grenfell's senior M. & A. advisor, both of whom face criminal charges. The only reason the British authorities ever tumbled to this scandal was because Ivan Boesky played a part in the support operation and disclosed his knowledge to the American authorities who promptly passed the information on. The Boesky curse had, therefore, stretched 3000 miles across the Atlantic. Cynics can only wonder how many other British takeover battles were won by similar dirty tactics.

However, Guinness was not Morgan Grenfell's only problem. Its decision not to buy a major stockbroking firm had left it woefully short of much-needed distribution skills. That was one reason why, with its morale still badly shaken by Guinness, the merchant bank was keen in 1987 to pursue merger talks with Hoare Govett, a top London broker. Senior managers at the two firms hoped to create a full-scale British investment bank. The problem was that both sides preferred to ignore one technical detail: Hoare Govett was already owned by Security Pacific.

Security Pacific was the first commercial bank to buy into a London stockbroker back in 1982 when it purchased around 30 per cent of Hoare. Hoare, for its part, was among the first of the London brokers to realize deregulation was coming and to prepare accordingly. Its concern was to sell itself to a bank which would leave it alone as far as possible to run its affairs. One of the main reasons Hoare Govett's top managers selected Security Pacific as a buyer was precisely because it was based in far-off Los Angeles. The rationale was that the 'laid-back southern Californians', as the Hoare men rather patronizingly liked to refer to them, were as likely as any owner to leave the firm alone. This proved true for a long time and Hoare Govett enjoyed one of the longest honeymoons of pre-Big Bang marriages. When it inevitably ended, the rupture was swift. Security Pacific became upset when it discovered that discussions with Morgan Grenfell had reached a developed stage almost behind its back, an example of two British firms who knew each other acting as if the American party scarcely mattered.

In fact, there was never much chance of a deal. With Morgan Grenfell not wanting to give up majority control and Security Pacific not wanting to see its investment in Hoare Govett reduced to a minority holding in a securities subsidiary, the talks broke down. Security Pacific then lost little time in bringing Hoare more firmly under its control. Within a matter of weeks three of Hoare's leading managers who had been pushing for the Morgan Grenfell tie-up had resigned, including Hoare's chief executive.

Security Pacific had used the opportunity of the stock market crash to throw its weight around. A clause in the original management contract stated that if Hoare ever lost more than £5m. in a single month, the whole arrangement would be up for renegotiation. That figure was easily torpedoed in October 1987 when Hoare lost some £40m. on market making and various underwritings. Security Pacific waded in, effectively ending any lingering sense of independence at the stockbroker.

Doubtless there were those at Hoare who, with hindsight, regretted that they had not remained independent longer so they could have merged with Morgan Grenfell. Still the episode shows how easily things can go wrong in the money business. Hoare Govett is now in danger of falling apart. For, as the example of Salomon on Wall Street shows, a securities company is only a collection of people. Managed without a firm sense of direction, the firm can quickly unravel if morale is lost. Since the talks broke down with Morgan Grenfell there has already been an exodus of talent.

Big Bang has already seen the demise of a once prominent broker. This was Greenwell, which shrank to a shadow of its former self under Midland's ownership. In late 1987 Midland pulled out of institutional equity broking altogether at a cost of £46m., having already earlier closed its equity market-making business. That left Midland and the once proud Greenwell active only in gilts. Only a few months earlier Morgan Stanley had offered to buy Greenwell's already troubled equity side from Midland. The bank had foolishly turned down the offer.

Another example of changing fortunes in the post-Big Bang flux is that of Edinburgh-based stockbroker Wood Mackenzie. It was originally bought by the merchant bank, Hill Samuel, which wanted to build a Warburg-style investment bank. However, it did not have the capital to make the grade and ended up selling itself to the Trustee Savings Bank, Britain's sixth largest retail bank centred mainly in the north of England, a particularly galling fate for some of Hill Samuel's more snobbish merchant bankers. Wood Mackenzie was then nearly bought by both U.B.S. and J. P. Morgan. It was finally purchased by National Westminster's County NatWest in early 1988, when the parent bank decided it could do with some disciplined Scots to help run its securities operations. For County NatWest had been running amok in the markets. It managed to lose £116m. in 1987, a loss which resulted in the resignation of both its chairman and chief executive. That was quite a feat as County was not a big market maker in equities like B.Z.W. or Warburg. Nearly £50m. of the loss stemmed from underwriting in September 1987 a £837m. rights issue by the employment agency Blue Arrow, which was raising the money to finance its acquisition of Manpower, an American firm. In what can only be described as an aggressive punt, Country NatWest ended up owning 9.5 per cent of Blue Arrow's equity, an investment which looked like a foolhardy gamble when the London market crashed the following month.

So the turmoil in the City has continued as the underlying business deteriorates. More broking firms will go to the wall as trading volumes shrink. Compounding the gloom, there is the aggravation of the clash of cultures which occurs at both the American and Japanese firms. This is more surprising in the American firms. The Americans and British may speak the same language but there is a huge difference in management styles. These things can matter in a people business like the money industry. Anecdotes abound in the post-Big Bang City of these cultural clashes. They will go from the funny to the unpleasant as business deteriorates and tempers shorten. Take Messels where Shearson Lehman's aggressive, cost-cutting culture has grated on many British employees' nerves. When Shearson summarily sacked 105 people in its London office in 1987, it chose to make the announcement over the firm's loudspeaker, seemingly confirming every cliché about Wall Street's hire-and-fire management style. Likewise Salomon sacked over 300 people in London in October in almost as peremptory a manner.

In general, British employees tend to make fun of the investment banking stereotypes cultivated by their American bosses. There is general mourning for the loss of what the British are fond of calling 'characters'. For their part, the Americans have little tolerance for what they call 'eccentrics'. These subtle but real differences in outlook have also stopped the Americans making as much headway as they had hoped in British M. & A. British companies are more comfortable using their traditional British merchant bankers and stockbrokers. There can also be a failure of communication. Americans like to spell everything out, a trait the British describe as stating the obvious. For their part, the British tend to assume tacit mutual understanding where no such comprehension exists.

How naive Americans can be outside their own home market became only too clear with the B.P. fiasco. Four big Wall Street investment banks, Goldman Sachs, Morgan Stanley, Shearson Lehman, and Salomon Brothers, committed a significant chunk of their capital to underwrite a large portion of this privatization issue several weeks before it was due to start trading in the market. Unfortunately for them, that interlude coincided with the October 1987 stock market crash. Distracted by as dramatic events back home on Wall Street, these investment banks blandly assumed that the British government, as the seller of the shares, would cancel the issue in view of the adverse market conditions. They could not have been more wrong. When, a matter of days before the deadline, it dawned on the Wall Street firms that the British government was going ahead regardless, there was a frantic behind-the-scenes lobbying effort to have the issue cancelled, including direct appeals to the Bank of England. Predictably, there was much self-serving talk about the danger of upsetting further already nervous markets.

The Wall Street firms failed to realize they were up against the free-market instincts of Margaret Thatcher's government and, in particular, Nigel Lawson, her Chancellor of the Exchequer. His unimpeachable logic was that the precise reason the investment banks were paid underwriting fees was to assume the risk of taking a share issue on to their own books. That was what underwriting fees were all about.

Instead the Wall Street firms found themselves in the unaccustomed position of having their cause supported by Britain's opposition Labour party. It wanted the B.P. issue cancelled so that small investors would not lose money. Not many years earlier the Labour party had been threatening compulsorily to buy back privatization shares at a below-market price. Now, so successful had privatization been politically, that Labour had abandoned that unpopular policy at the height of the bull market. In retrospect this was a classic signal that the privatization bandwagon was about to run off the track, taking the bull market with it. When the British Labour Party decides it is a good thing to own shares, you know it has to be time to sell.

So the B.P. issue gave Lawson the amusing opportunity to taunt the Labour Party in Parliament for being 'friends of Goldman Sachs'. It also cost the Wall Street firms a lot of money because Lawson went ahead with the sale. He did not regard it as his fault that the investment banks, in their eagerness to do a privatization deal, did not follow the British practice of sub-underwriting the risk by pre-selling most of their allotted shares. Nor was he concerned if B.P. was reluctant (as it was) to see the issue flop for fear it would damage the company's name in the financial markets. After all, the seller was the British government and its interest was to get the best price for the tax payer. It had done this by pricing the issue before the crash.

The sledgehammer pressure from Wall Street did reap some dividends, however. At the last minute Lawson agreed to a significant compromise where a floor was put under the B.P. share price. The Bank of England would act as the buyer of last resort of B.P. shares at a pre-determined floor price. Even with this help the four Wall Street firms lost between them pre-tax some $300m., their biggest single loss in the crash. It would have been even worse without the Bank of England's intervention. So B.P. was a salutary reminder to Wall Street of the risks of operating in markets they knew less about than they thought they did. It also made many senior executives back in New York ask themselves just why they had been so aggressive putting money and troops into London and chasing business there. They were fast realizing that there were neither the trading volumes nor the deals in Britain's domestic markets to justify all this expense.

In fact Big Bang was increasingly proving a big non-event save to those stockbrokers who had made millions out of it by selling their firms. While the prospects for a protracted bear market made it likely that the rush to cut costs had only just begun. Nor, as it contemplated retrenchment in its ludicrously overstaffed domestic capital markets, could the City of London hope for much relief from its other major investment in paper prosperity, Eurobonds. A beneficiary of financial fever, this was perhaps the money business's prime example of too many players competing for too few crumbs. A shake-out in the international debt business was inevitable even before world stock markets crashed, compounding the pain and so hastening the inevitable surgery.

The only question now is whether it will be a cyclical hiccup where the weakest withdraw and the survivors emerge stronger and with more of the business, or whether the whole edifice of offshore debt finance is threatened by systemic economic contraction. For a depression usually starts when the weaker links of the financial structure start falling. A case can be made that the unregulated Euromarkets are *the* weak link in the modern money world's chain because there is no lender of last resort and therefore no one authority responsible either to Eurobank's deposits or indeed Eurobanks themselves. That is why the Euromarkets would be the most vulnerable to a financial panic. If so, then the City of London could be in for wrenching times. For a town that has been 'riding so high on the hog' for so long, that may not be so surprising.

INVESTING

'Everybody does well in a bull market. But don't confuse a bull market for brains.'
Jimmy Rodgers, investor turned professor, 1986

The Competitive Performance Game

John Maynard Keynes is this century's most famous economist. He was also a Bohemian-living aesthete who happened to make a fortune in his spare time speculating in currencies from his bedside. Keynes liked to compare investment to a game of musical chairs. The point at issue was not to be left standing when the music stopped.

Money managers are continually caught up in this competitive 'performance' game. They look to make incremental returns to beat the commonly followed indices of the market, be it America's Standard & Poors 500 or Tokyo's Nikkei. If they fail to beat the indices, as America's professional money managers as a group underperformed the S. & P. 500 for the past five years, then they risk losing their clients' business. So, despite the only slightly unfair grey, boring image of the money manager, the business of investing is both competitive and changing. Competitive because each manager is marked on his performance and because investing by its very nature is a perpetual tug of war between buyer and seller. Changing because the markets never stand still.

Money managers are the 'buy side' of the securities industry. On the 'sell side' are the swarms of middle men. These are the stockbrokers and bond salesmen for whom the money managers are the clients to be lunched, dined, and generally courted, and the traders who 'make the markets' for the money managers to buy and sell into. If brokers are forever on the telephone, usually

99

wasting a money manager's time, one eye on the computer screen and one eye on the order sheet, the traders are constantly absorbed by the screen, their world consisting of one basis point (one-hundredth of a percentage point) moves in the price of a bond. 'Meetings' are held constantly in the form of two-word conversations shouted across the trading floor. In this mesmerized world tunnel vision is in; lateral thinking is out. A trader would not recognize an event 'out there', by which he means the real world away from this screen, if it came up and hit him in the face.

Money management is at the other end of this financial spectrum. Money managers have to take a view on the 'big picture' as well as the minutiae of a company's financial statements. They usually buy a share with the aim of holding it for at least a few months, not minutes. Whether they are managing a pension fund, a unit trust, mutual fund, or a private portfolio their business can be broken down into two kinds of two decisions. These are known in industry jargon as 'asset allocation' and 'stock picking'. Asset allocation is the strategic decision of where to invest the money; which instrument, be it in bonds, shares, precious metals, or cash; which sector, say technology or heavy industry and, in the case of the swelling ranks of global investors, which country and currency. Stock picking is, as the name implies, deciding what share to buy. The money manager can either generate his own ideas in old-fashioned ways like visiting a company and reading balance sheets or through computer screening which helps highlight anomalies between values. Best of all he can combine the two or, less impressively, he can opt out altogether by buying stock index contracts where he is simply investing in the index.

As clients, money managers are at the receiving end of a never-ending flow of stockbrokers' research, much of which ends up in the office rubbish bin. Here the professional's task is to discriminate. He will always be mindful that, unless he is an important, and so privileged, client, he will receive a stock recommendation from a broker at the same time as all the broker's other clients. That is why the best money managers never rely purely on outsiders' research though they will always have their few favourite brokers who give them the best service both in terms of executing their orders and keeping them informed and whose telephone calls they make a point of answering.

If money managers use computers increasingly as an aid, they are not yet their servant. The money manager will use a screen to check prices but unlike a broker or trader he is not chained to the tyranny of the screen unless, of course, he has taken too big a gamble and cannot afford not to know what is going on minute by minute. When that happens money managers are probably losing money. In general though it is a more leisurely pursuit. Compare that with a youthful trader of the German stock market working in New York. Encountered one night in an Upper East Side Manhattan bar mumbling into his beer about 'windows of opportunity', it was 10 p.m. and just five hours before he was due to get up to start his commute to work from Long Island. How long can anyone stay sane surviving that kind of punishing routine?

Money managers avoid those kinds of pressures. In fact the best ones enjoy the option of working from their homes. Because there are so many brokers interested in keeping them up to date on market developments and because of electronic communications, it matters hardly at all where money managers are based. Centres include not only the three major financial ones but also more specialist centres such as Boston, Edinburgh, Honk Kong, Geneva, and Zurich. John Templeton, perhaps the world's most famous money manager and still active in his seventies, is based in the Bahamas though the rest of his firm works out of nearby Fort Lauderdale, Florida.

Nor does it cost much to set up as a money manager. The only real expenses are computers (which get cheaper all the time), office space, and secretaries. Money managers do not need the huge amounts of capital required by the big New York investment banks and the ambitious London merchant banks to offset the risks of trading losses. All they need to get started is an initial $100m. or so to manage. Because the entry costs are so low, established money managers are·constantly leaving big organizations and setting up their own specialist 'boutiques', usually taking a few colleagues and some of their old firms' clients' money with them. It is this entrepreneurial side to the business which explains why at the time of the October 1987 crash there were some 1,500 serious firms managing money in America.

Amazingly, money managers prospered during the 1980s, despite the fact that so many of them underperformed the index. They got away with this because financial asset inflation, in the form of rising bond and share prices, created a false prosperity for many money management firms. As they charge fees on a percentage of assets managed, their fee income rose with the markets and the increase in the amount of money they managed, though many firms were not winning any new accounts and some were losing them. This good fortune explained the gathering rush to float money management firms on the New York and London stock markets in the last years of the bull market. Investors were awarding money management firms a significantly higher rating than an investment bank, merchant bank, or old-fashioned stockbroker. That was because it had proved a steadier earner which did not require large chunks of capital to be constantly leveraged and risked many times over in the financial markets. Generally London merchant banks have been more astute in retaining their money management activities than New York's wholesale investment banks, many of whom are not even in the business. The fact is that money management is less boom and bust than most areas of the money business and so a worthwhile revenue earner. That does not mean it is not also a casualty of bear markets, only that it is a little easier to stay in business during downturns.

So money managers in bull markets can make lots of money even when they underperform the market. Yet if, to borrow Keynes' analogue, it is in money managers' interest to keep the music playing, like an overworked disc jockey, they have been forced to change records at an increasingly frantic pace.

The reason is performance measurement. In America managers of pension funds and mutual funds have long been measured by their quarterly investment performance. In Britain, the next most sophisticated market, they have begun to be. In Japan and Switzerland, this competitive game has barely begun despite the huge amounts of capital managed in both countries. Japan's financial institutions may be the world's wealthiest but they are inexperienced international equity investors in a business where long-standing relationships remain the deciding factor in why a particular financial institution gets a company's pension fund to manage.

As for the Swiss, they instinctively remain deeply suspicious of the whole trend towards performance measurement. The appeal of Switzerland as a capital haven is not only secrecy but also a tradition of capital preservation which does not concentrate on outperforming the competition. You do not pay the Swiss banks their very expensive fees to outperform a particular stock market index. You pay them to hang on to your money and keep it out of the hands of the taxman.

Competitive performance measurement, however, does have a certain logic. It makes money managers accountable for their actions. Otherwise they could literally go to sleep replete after their brokers' lunches with never a thought for the morrow, which was the old way of doing things. But despite the benefits of competition, the consequences of quarterly measurement provoke growing controversy. The reason is that the system puts money managers under the gun, tempting them to invest in an increasingly short-term and so, reckless, manner. This not only increases the volatility of financial markets. It also increases risk. The $2.4 trillion of pension fund money, which was being managed around the globe before world stock markets crashed, was meant to pay the long-term liabilities of pension plans. The purpose is supposed to be investing on a five-,ten-,or twenty-year view depending on the age of the pension plan. It should have nothing to do with three-monthly investment contests. With the downturn now here, beneficiaries of pension plans will gradually wake up to how their future security has been squandered in an irresponsible paper chase. When they do there will be an all too predictable hue and cry, though by then much of the damage may have been done.

For pension funds have been run increasingly in just such a cavalier manner during the bull market. Money has been constantly shifted to flavour-of-the-month sectors or markets. It is as if investors everywhere have caught the Japanese appetite for 'rotating' stock markets. Common sense as well as history suggest that short-term investing is usually bad investing (unless the investor is acting on good and, therefore, probably inside information). Each time a switch is made it increases the chances of the money manager making a mistake. This high turnover only has the merit of generating more commissions for brokers which is why, of course, they encourage it.

The real skill in investing is picking the long-term trend and sticking with it, not trying to be clever and profit from every little wrinkle in the market. One of the classic ways to invest is finding long-term growth companies before take-off. Any investor who stuck over the long haul with an I.B.M. in America or a Hanson Trust in Britain and took up every share issue made fantastic gains. But that would have meant resisting the always easy temptation of trading in and out or trying to guess the market's next move up or down.

Most money managers will admit to the increased risks that come with more short-term trading, which is why they will deny they invest in such a manner. The problem is that competitive pressures are always intervening. And the more volatility in the market, the more there is the temptation to try and turn a quick 10 per cent going 'in and out', egged on by the persuasive broker. That temptation only increases after a few bad quarters.

Despite this you will not find the best money managers moaning about performance. They recognize it as a fact of life which will not go away. Clients naturally want to know what is happening to their money and quarterly measurement gives them that service. Most firms which manage pension funds say they are given at least three years to prove if they are any good. Certainly, no one is sacked because of just one bad quarter.

Performance measurement may also be here to stay because it has become the *raison d'être* for a whole profession which has grown up almost from scratch in the past fifteen years. This is the pension fund consultant, an example of the money industry's natural talent of breeding layer upon layer of advisor, each of whom charges a fee. Many of these consultants are professional salesmen, former stockbrokers who spotted a niche and exploited it. They saw the opportunity to advise companies on the management of their fast growing pension assets. Trustees of pension funds welcomed the consultants' arrival on their doorstep. Legally liable for imprudent investments, they want someone to blame when things go wrong as they now have.

Consultants began by offering performance measurement services. This evolved from a crude comparison of one manager with another to an elaborate discipline complete with the usual pseudo-scientific jargon. From measuring performance consultants have expanded their role to defining and labelling money managers' investment styles. From there it was but a short step to consultants usurping the role of the money manager and making decisions themselves on asset allocation. This effectively deprives the money manager of half his job reducing him to a mere stock picker. This process has gone furthest in America where it is common practice for money managers to be awarded specialist mandates, for example to manage a high technology or Japanese portfolio.

All this has made the consultants increasingly important to the, usually tacit, irritation of money managers. The consultants' self-interest in fragmenting and complicating the business has also resulted in a concoction of largely meaningless labels to describe various investment styles. Consultants talk half seriously (depending on whether they have a sense of humour) about 'growth' investors, 'value' investors, 'contrarians', 'sector rotators', 'market timers', and numerous others. The truth is that all money managers try to do the same thing. That is to buy shares or bonds which they think will rise in price. But they go along with the consultants' labelling because it suits their commercial interests. The consultants have the ear of the pension fund trustees and it is their advice which usually decides which money managers get the account.

The consultants also understand the trustees' needs. These worthies are less interested in last year's performance than in hiring managers with consistency of investment style. Hence the need for inventing labels. A record of super high returns way above the index suggests an excessively risky approach. What pension fund trustees are really concerned about is protecting themselves from law suits from out-of-pocket beneficiaries. The consultants understand this and so let them sleep easier at night.

If labelling has become mostly a nonsense, specialist investment mandates, like bespoke tailoring, can make sense. Different firms and managers have different areas of expertise which are worth tapping. Before the introduction of specialist mandates each firm would award general mandates to, say, six different money management firms. Each would then broadly duplicate the same portfolio. This was both inefficient and costly. However, from that logical starting point, the labelling of money managers has reached a degree of over-elaboration which confuses rather than clarifies. What on earth is a sector rotator? That can conceivably only have meaning in Japan in the sense of someone who is in on every ramp in the Tokyo market. And no consultant is going to advise a pension fund to hire an insider trader!

The labelling can be dangerous as well as comical since it forces money managers to fit themselves into a fictitious straitjacket in the hope of obtaining accounts. It also breeds an illusory scientific gloss to a business which remains decidedly an art, a hybrid of the intuitive and the judgemental. The lip service paid to labels has been totally discredited by the 1987 crash when the only thing that mattered was being in cash. Batterymarch's LeBaron says: 'The labels were created to market a product. Otherwise they are meaningless.' Still, the Batterymarch boss is pro-consultants. 'They make clients feel more comfortable about what they were going to do anyway.'

Indexation, 'Passive' Investing

If consultants are a headache which must be tolerated, a more serious problem for 'active' money managers during the bull market was the surge in the popularity of indexation, otherwise known as 'passive' investing. In an indexed fund money is literally invested in the shares which make up the index. The investor is assured his performance will, as near as damn it, equal the index's. When indexation first appeared on the scene more than ten years ago, it was regarded as unAmerican, a cop out. T-shirts were printed depicting George Washington pointing his finger and declaring, 'Indexation Is Bad For You'. The problem for the macho world of 'active' money managers is that the history of the 1980s bull market provided a powerful argument for indexation. It showed that the index consistently outperformed more than 50 per cent of money managers, though it rarely made it into the top 25 per cent. However, with the S. & P. up nearly 40 per cent in the first seven months of 1987 and the index stocks stronger than the broader market, some 75 per cent of active managers were underperforming just prior to the crash.

To many, risk-averse pension funds consistently better than average performance seemed extremely attractive. Indexation offered them two other benefits. First, it does not cost much because 'passive' managers charge much lower fees since they are only being paid to mimic the index. (There is also less spent on broking commissions.) Second, indexing is a practical way to manage unwieldy multi-billion dollar portfolios. An increasing popular strategy has been to index a large chunk of a pension portfolio, say 50 or 75 per cent, and let the rest be invested more aggressively.

If indexation is not brand new (it was pioneered by San Francisco-based commercial bank Wells Fargo in the mid 1970s), it exploded in the last years of the bull market. As at 31 May 1987 $123.6bn. invested in American equities was indexed compared with just $9bn. in 1980. That money was mostly indexed to the S. & P.500 but in second and third waves of the same fad, bond indexing and international equity indexing were also fast catching on. Bond and international indexing grew for the same reasons. Money managers were underperforming in a rising market. More than 80 per cent of bond managers underperformed Salomon Brothers' bond index in the five years to 1986 which corresponded with the explosive bull market in bonds. That is one reason presumably why the New York Retirement System sank $17bn.-odd into bond indexing in late 1986 (after the bond market had peaked), virtually doubling in one stroke the amount of money in bond index funds.

Indexation poses a direct threat not only to the way all money managers (and indirectly stockbrokers) make their living but also to their claim that they can do better than the market. That they recognize this is a threat is clear from the many supposedly 'active' managers who in practice were increasingly happy to mimic the index as the bull market dragged on lest they underperformed it too badly. This meant that they would buy a share just because it was a component of the index, regardless of what they thought of the company as an investment. Thus, when British Telecom was floated on the London market in 1981 institutional investors scrambled to buy the shares not wanting to be underweight in a new component of the index. But, more ludicrously, they did the same thing with another government-owned telecommunications company, Japan's N.T.T., despite the huge valuation put on that company.

Ultimately if this trend continued, the *reductio ad absurdum* would be reached and the index would become the market. This is what Morgan Stanley's splendidly iconoclastic investment guru, Barton Biggs, meant when he lambasted indexation as 'investment socialism'. Will this ever happen? It is unlikely. The craze for indexation has probably peaked with the stock market. In a period of financial asset inflation, such as the 1980s, it is not surprising that investing in an index consisting of such assets should be so popular. The same would have applied to investing in an oil index in 1974. The acid test comes when stock markets fall. Will pension funds still want to be invested in a falling index when they are losing money? Or will they want the manager who made the right decision beforehand, namely to sell shares and raise cash? At that point the issue becomes capital preservation not comparative performance against a particular index. Kurt Meyer, head of institutional investment at Switzerland's U.B.S. sums up the indexation problem neatly. Interviewed in Zurich in October 1986, he said: 'I think indexation will be a disaster one day. It's an easy way out.' A year later he was proved right.

Indexation's appeal also reflects a craving for mechanical formulae designed to reduce if not eliminate risk, which is why the Japanese are interested in it. Unfortunately in investing there is no such thing unless this also means completely eliminating reward, the perfect hedge. That is an age-old lesson which has had to be relearned by this generation of computer whiz kids. For the indexing boom has been helped on its way by Wall Street's 'quants'. They have applied techniques gleaned from statistics, computing science, pure mathematics, and sundry other disciplines far removed from stockbroking or investment to almost every aspect of the securities business. These boffins know everything about manipulating numbers with statistical formulae and 'derivative' securities (options and futures). Usually they know next to nothing about the 'market' itself or what lies behind the numbers they are manipulating. 'Quants' (their background is in quantitative disciplines) have used their sampling techniques to construct synthetic index-weighted portfolios.

Portfolio Insurance

One product dreamed up by 'quants' and proving attractive until the crash to both pensions funds and the Japanese was the comfortingly named portfolio insurance. As the label suggests, this was another seductive mechanical formula designed to appeal to institutional investors looking for ways to eliminate risk. The idea was that a pension fund not wishing to stomach more than a certain fall in the value of its portfolio over a particular period of time could protect itself against the risk of a falling market by foregoing a certain amount of the gain should prices rise. With many trustees understandably anxious to lock in gains scored by Wall Street's five-year-long bull market this was a product whose time had come; which is why portfolio insurance grew from just $4bn. at the end of 1985 to an estimated $80 bn. before the product was discredited in October 1987.

How did it work? Say a pension fund wants to ensure that its $100m. worth of shares will have the same value in twelve months' time. Using options and futures, the quants will construct a portfolio 61 per cent invested in shares and 39 per cent in cash. If shares subsequently fall the amount of new cash in the portfolio is continuously increased so that, if the stock market has fallen 15 per cent after six months, the amount of cash on the sidelines earning interest will have risen to 97 per cent of the total portfolio, with shares accounting for just 3 per cent. In this way the minimum value of $100m. is maintained through the interest earned on the increased amount of cash. To reverse the example, if share prices rise, the number of shares in the portfolio is increased proportionately.

One feature of portfolio insurance is that it forces a pension fund to sell shares (in practice stock index futures) after the market has begun falling (and buy them after the market has started rising). In practice this means selling stock index futures at a discount to the underlying value of the shares. (A stock index future, which first appeared in Chicago's futures markets in 1982, is simply an agreement to buy a portfolio of all the shares that make up the index at a certain price at a fixed date in the future.) These contracts are bought from portfolio insurers by so-called program traders, otherwise known as index arbitraguers. They try to arbitrage the usually small differences between the value of the stock index futures contract and that of the underlying shares. Because program traders buy stock index futures cheaply from the portfolio insurers (i.e. at a discount to the shares) they calculate that they can make money by immediately selling the more valuable shares in the 'cash' market (i.e. the ordinary stock market as opposed to the futures market). Their profit is the discount at which they bought the stock index future.

Academics warned that this process of portfolio insurers triggering program trades, which in turn trigger more portfolio insurance sales, could in theory go on for ever, fuelling a one-way downward market, an alarming thought. This is only partly what happened during Wall Street's record-breaking fall. However, it would be wrong to blame program trading in the sense of index arbitrage for the crash, as many have tried to do on the grounds that computers always make an easy target. In fact the 500-point wipe-out on 19 October was so savage that the computers were for the most part left on the sidelines. Conditions were so chaotic that index arbitrage could not be executed. At one stage the S. & P. 500 stock index futures contract stood at an unprecedented 23 per cent discount to the cash market. Yet arbitrageurs did not step forward to sell the underlying shares and buy the futures and pocket the huge discount. They did not because they could not be sure at what price they could sell the shares on the floor of the New York Stock Exchange. Its specialist system, where the task of making a price in each share is assigned to a single market maker or 'specialist' had broken down, there being no trading at all in several shares. Program traders as well as individual investors were intimidated out of the market because of the sheer confusion. And so the vital link between the cash and futures markets became unhinged. For it is index arbitrage which keeps the two markets in line.

However, portfolio insurance was a problem, as was demonstrated by the official report of the Brady commission on the stock market crash. During the débâcle portfolio insurance proved the false comfort its critics had always claimed it was. Everybody rushed to sell at the same time, just as if a fire broke out at a crowded nightclub and everyone stampeded for the same exit. That meant that portfolio insurance-triggered sales of stock index futures were executed (if they could be executed at all) at an increasingly deep discount to a cash market which was not trading. The Brady report identified portfolio insurance as responsible for the sale of $20–30bn. – worth of shares between 14–20 October, the period when the fall in share prices was picking up momentum. It reported that before the start of trading on 19 October portfolio insurers still faced a huge overhang of selling, ordered for them by the mechanical formulae they were slavishly following. The report says: 'Their models dictated that, at a minimum, $12bn. of equities should already have been sold. Less than $4bn. had in fact been sold.' Out of a total sales on the New York Stock Exchange that day when the Dow fell more than 500 points, selling by three portfolio insurers alone made up nearly $2bn. In the Chicago futures markets portfolio insurers sold the equivalent of $4bn. of shares or 40 per cent of futures volume.

If this all sounds more like science fiction than investing that is precisely the point. Portfolio insurance and program trading are examples of how institutional investing in America, at least, had gone high-tech. London and Tokyo were following fast prior to the crash. A period of sober reflection will now follow.

So the days of calling up a friendly broker and hearing the latest rumour were fast disappearing. But was this progress? The problem has been that in their fascination for what can be done with the seemingly endless spin-off products that could be developed using options and futures, many on Wall Street had forgotten that many of these toys had only temporary value. They were most effective when only a few investors used them. Thus when portfolio insurance was limited to only a few players it was easy to implement the trades. In that sense the money business is like the computer business. Product cycles grow ever shorter. Financial fever was stretched to its logical limits during the bull market through the application of 'quant' techniques. That was fine only so long as it was remembered that at heart all markets trade on emotion and not the microchip.

This is a lesson investors will have to relearn. As America's stock market soared ever higher during 1987 with the Dow on its seemingly inexorable path to and through 3,000, many market observers comforted themselves with the notion that the market could not be nearing a top because the 'general public' was not yet

in the market. What these observers forgot was that the small
investor was now in the market but in mutual funds not individual
shares. At the peak of the market in September there were 791
equity funds in America with assets totalling $233.4bn. and 884
bond funds with assets of $287.6bn.

One reason the small investor was put off owning shares
directly, preferring to put his savings in a mutual fund or unit trust
was because he had long ago been intimidated by what was going
on in the stock market. Faced with the new computerized trading
techniques he did not understand, he felt uncomfortable and
rightly so. Because of the increased use of stock index futures and
the like major stock markets were trading more like traditional
commodity markets, which are renowned for their volatility and
sharp, V-shaped tops and bottoms. Baskets of shares were
increasingly being traded like sugar or potatoes. In April 1987, a
First Boston technical analyst, Jo Generalis wrote almost prophe-
tically in a market report:

> The increasing use of futures and associated derivative securities is
> beginning to gradually mesmerise many of the financial markets'
> traditional participants; subsequently it will immobilise and, even-
> tually, may eliminate them. We believe this process will take
> another 12–15 months to complete.

He was, like most of Wall Street's bears, wrong on the timing.
They were expecting the stock market to crash in 1988 not 1987.
They were also mostly expecting Tokyo to go first, conveniently
giving everyone a sell signal. Markets have a habit of playing tricks
on even the best prepared plans.

Blinded by science, investors at the height of the market were
increasingly opting out of these 'commoditized' stock markets,
leaving the field to indexers, program traders, portfolio insurers,
and the like. That paved the way for a débâcle in the sense of a
one-way falling market with even more dire results than if all New
York cabbies were long of General Motors shares and decided
to sell on the same day, the characteristic of a classic market
top.

International Investment

Investing on Wall Street may have become increasingly high-tech
but money managers could still employ more traditional methods
investing in overseas markets. It was during this bull market that

the American institutions made their first large-scale commitment to overseas investing. Wall Street may have been sophisticated in home-grown techniques but it was a mere sibling when it came to investing outside the home country.

From 1945 on America's multinationals were happy to spend money building factories throughout the dollar world. But it took them another thirty years even to contemplate investing their pension funds outside America. The novice picked up the habit fast. In the six years up until 1986 American pension fund money invested overseas jumped from virtually zero to over $50bn. With their tradition of foreign investing, the money management firms based in London and Edinburgh enjoyed a distinct advantage in competing for these accounts. The British have been investing overseas since the nineteenth century and London remains the centre of international money management. American Express, Citicorp, and J. P. Morgan all run their international investment from London where an estimated $650bn. was being managed prior to the October 1987 crash.

International investing was justified by Americans for the same reason it has long been by the British. It diversifies risk. The dollar was no longer king pin. Nor was Wall Street so dominant in terms of global stock market capitalization.

Statistics only tell part of the story, though. International investing could also be fun. A few years ago 'modern portfolio theory' was all the rage in American academic circles. It postulated the so-called 'efficient market' market theory which asserted that there was no such thing as an unexploited opportunity to make money from investment because the market immediately discounted all information. Money managers always dismissed this dogma as just another attempt by academics to turn the fun of investing into a dismal science. They also said it flew in the face of practical experience that some people make money in markets and others do not.

Still, America's stock market is undoubtedly the most efficient because it is the most comprehensively researched. Portfolio theory really falls on its face in these foreign markets. They can be highly inefficient in pricing securities, which means that if the risks may be greater so are the rewards. The greater the scarcity of information, the greater the divergence in quoted securities from their true values. Take some examples, first of a stock, and then of a whole market. Philippine Long Distance Telephone, that country's equivalent to A.T. & T., British Telecom, or N.T.T.

rose from under $2 just prior to the ousting of former Philippine dictator Ferdinand Marcos in early 1986 to a peak of $40 in mid 1987 before crashing again. Yet even at its peak the share still traded on a P.E. of only 6 compared with N.T.T.'s 250-odd. Such a move meant fantastic percentage gains for money managers who knew the company was sound and were prepared to take a view on the political situation. Likewise Brazil's Bovespa Index doubled in dollar value in the four weeks following the country's currency reform in February 1986. (When was the last time the Dow Jones doubled in a month?) It subsequently shed all those gains and much more by the time the fundamentally flawed Cruzado Plan went up in smoke in early 1987, so at the time of writing Brazilian shares were again among the cheapest in the world, even by post-crash standards.

Bahamas-based Templeton, a veteran of global investing, is never one to miss a bargain. He threw $1m. of his own money into the Argentina stock market in 1985 when he noticed the capitalization of the entire stock market was worth a mere $750m. His view was simply that all the country's publicly quoted companies had to be worth more than that. Sure enough he soon exited with a trading profit. Jimmy Rodgers, another international investment adventurer turned professor at New York's Columbia University put some money in the long-dormant Portuguese stock market in 1986. His correct reasoning was that with Portugal entering the European Economic Community and orthodox capitalist economic policies being pursued, the stock market had to rise, just as virtually every other European market had doubled or better in the preceeding two years, from Sweden to West Germany to France to Italy to Spain.

International investing also offers the opportunity to get in on the ground floor of a country's development. Japan was still a comparatively small market in the 1960s. It has now overtaken Wall Street. International money managers have since been busy looking for the new Japan. Some think they have found it in South Korea. For years money managers had been visiting Seoul, licking their lips at what to their minds were greatly undervalued companies busy working another Asian export-led economic miracle. They were frustrated though because the local government forbade them from investing in the market. They still cannot do so save through specially created funds such as the Korea Fund which is managed by the New York investment firm, Scudder Stevens & Clark and quoted on the New York Stock Exchange. It was a huge hit, causing a rush of 'country funds' to be sold as an easy way to invest in a particular country. In July 1987, despite anti-government riots on the streets of Seoul, the same month the fund was trading at an astonishing 120 per cent premium to the value of the shares in it. There are two reasons for this. First, unlike most country funds, investors have no other way of buying Korean shares other than through the Korea Fund. Second, the country's stock market has been a top performer while investors were correctly convinced that the Korean currency, the won, would rise in value against the dollar. However, when the euphoria dies down and, more important, when the market is opened up to foreigners, that premium should vanish overnight. Most closed-end funds such as the Korea Fund, where the number of shares is fixed, sell at a discount sometimes as great as 30 per cent.

The greater risks and rewards, combined with the added currency risk, mean that international investing is not for the unsophisticated. This needed to be remembered in the increasingly frantic 1980s game of financial pinball where orders to buy and sell flew between Sydney and Milan, Hong Kong and Zurich, New York and Tokyo, London and Kuala Lumpur. There is also political risk. So far politicians in developing countries have been competing to attract the world's portfolio capital. That has meant a bonfire of withholding taxes, exchange controls, and the like as more and more developing countries from South Korea to Chile took steps to open up their stock markets. This had the potential to breed a virtuous circle as more money went into shares, the risk capital of the world. Contrast that with what happened in the 1970s. The boom and bust in sovereign lending to the Third World, financed by commercial bankers' recycling of petro dollars, ending up in capital-flight Swiss bank accounts or, at best as in Brazil, in monster white elephant projects. Now at least some of that debt is being converted to equity as bankers realize this offers the best, if not the only, hope of their ever getting their money back. In one of the biggest moves to date Citicorp announced in August 1987 that it planned to swap some $500m. of its Argentine debt for equity investments in that country's domestic industries.

International investing has then the potential to be perhaps the most positive outcome of financial fever providing it survives cyclical dips. But will it? October's panic was noteworthy for the way stock markets slumped across the globe. Global greed bred global panic. In these circumstances what is the charm of diversification? Worse, in the smaller foreign markets it was often literally impossible for big institutional investors to get out in size without accepting a price way below the market. Also, as a result of the crash, there is the risk that governments are more likely to lose their only recently ignited enthusiasm for stock markets and conclude that they were just the casinos they always suspected they were. That could mean the re-introduction of exchange controls and the like.

Despite these all too obvious cyclical risks, most money men were confident during the 1980s that the new fashion for global investing would not wither with a market bust. The other view was put by Jeremy Paulson-Ellis, chairman of London-based stockbroker Vickers da Costa, a subsidiary of Citicorp, at a London conference on this very subject.

> Are political leaders really ready as yet to accept the free flow of funds across borders? I see the answer as No. Governments may inspire such a course for a short term, but when an industry is in trouble and investors are investing in overseas competitors there is a great temptation to restrict the flow of funds – and this will always stop a truly international market developing.

That cautionary note should have been borne in mind in the recent euphoria. The 1980s fad for global investing has not abolished the age-old principle of national self-interest. Nor has it altered the fact that in uncertain times capital has a habit of returning home fast.

Australasia and Hong Kong

Speculative mania was not just confined to the tripod of global finance, New York, Tokyo, and London. It spread to virtually every capitalist country where stockbrokers were tolerated, helped by financial deregulation and the enhanced appetite among American, European, and Japanese investors for foreign shares. Stockbrokers and money managers travelled the world first class, touting their wares and looking for the next hot exotic investment.

Two classic celebrations of global finance, or rather the top of the market, occurred in New York in October 1987. First, Mackintosh Hampson Hoare Govett, one of Australia's top stockbroking firms, held a lavish conference to sell the merits of

Aussie shares. Enlisted in their cause was none other than Australia's Labor Prime Minister and former trade unionist, Bob Hawke. Via a telephone link-up with Down Under, Hawke answered money managers' questions on the merits of investing in Australia, a stock market which had risen nearly 500 per cent in the previous five years and is generally regarded as one of the financial world's more frenzied casinos.

So here was the country's political leader shamelessly touting stocks. Within weeks the Australian market had plummeted nearly 40 per cent. As for the host, Mackintosh Hampson Hoare Govett, it was doubtless relieved it had floated its own company's shares on the stock market only a few months earlier.

The severity of the crash was not coincidental. Australasia had enjoyed as exaggerated a bout of financial asset fever as anywhere during the 1980s. Indeed, it might be called an example of financial deregulation gone mad. In both Australia and New Zealand the stock market soared and stock market operators flourished while debt levels rose out of all proportion to the size of the economies. Australia's gross external debt (government and private sector) is nearly 38 per cent of the country's gross national product compared with 13 per cent in America. In New Zealand it is 70 per cent. These debt levels are only possible because both countries have kept the confidence of foreign creditors. Comfortable with their white skins, knowledge of the English language and general Anglo-Saxon airs and graces, bond investors have been happy to buy these countries' bonds, especially since they have consistently offered interest-rate coupons well into double figures. Australia and New Zealand have also had nominally socialist governments which keenly promoted financial deregulation. In both cases the deregulation occurred in financial markets whose stock markets already had well-earned reputations as casinos. In New Zealand there was the added problem of peculiarly lax accounting standards. The boom-and-bust sequence has been correspondingly severe. Australia was down 40 per cent from top to bottom as at February 1988, and New Zealand down 55 per cent; both far larger falls than yet seen in London, New York, or Tokyo. Once high-flying individuals also lost huge amounts of money by local standards. Australia's share-dealing entrepreneur, Robert Holmes A. Court, suffered paper losses of about A.$800m., or U.S.$550m. in the crash which caught him long of assets and short of cash flow. In New Zealand Sir Francis Renouf, the founder of the country's first merchant bank, reportedly lost more than 90 per cent of his estimated N.Z.$250m. or U.S.$150m. fortune.

The second top-of-the-market celebration was a jamboree arranged by the Hong Kong Stock Exchange at New York's World Trade Center, again in October 1987. Hong Kong has always had a spectacularly volatile market where both greed and fear run rampant. A tiny area of land with a politically uncertain future, the normal emotions of any marketplace are compressed in Hong Kong in a pressure cooker atmosphere. Hong Kong had already found time for one boom and bust in the early 1980s. During 1984 when worries about Hong Kong's political future under Chinese ownership were at their greatest, the Hang Seng Index sank under 800, well below its 1981 high of over 1800, as most pundits wrote off the territory's future.

All too predictably to those familiar with Hong Kong's predilection for exaggerated boom-and-bust cycles, within four years the market was again riding high. The Hang Seng had reached 4,000, a gain of well over 400 per cent, when Hong Kong Stock Exchange chairman, Ronald Li, visited New York. His hard sell was suitably brazen. Li, clearly informed of the post-Boesky environment in America, went out of his way to reassure his audience that there was no insider trading in Hong Kong, a comment which can only be described as comic. The local attitude was better expressed in 1986 when Hong Kong's biggest property tycoon, Li Ka-shing, was found by a panel appointed by Hong Kong's British colonial government to be 'culpable for insider trading'. Li is a director of the Hong Kong and Shanghai Bank, which is known as 'The Bank' throughout the colony, while companies he controls account for around 20 per cent of the capitalization of the Hang Seng Index. Predictably, no action was taken against this fattest of the local Chinese fat cats. Nor was there any real public demand that anything should be done. Rather the locals' reaction was rather that of an embarrassed yawn.

Within weeks of Ronald Li's New York presentation the growing confidence in Hong Kong's Stock Market had been dissipated. For the stock market was closed, apparently at Ronald Li's own initiative, when Hong Kong woke up the day after 19 October, or Black Monday on Wall Street. The reason given was to prevent default by punters who owned too many stock index contracts as a bet on a rising Hang Seng Index. When the market eventually reopened after a four-day closure, the Hang Seng plunged 35 per cent in a day, causing defaults on the Hong Kong Futures Exchange of some HK$1.8bn. ($230m.) The market would have fallen even futher the next day had it not been for a coordinated buying operation launched by the Hong Kong Bank and the Beijing-owned Bank of China.

That Hong Kong's stock market was the only one to close during the worldwide crash was the worst of publicity. It infuriated foreign money managers who found themselves locked into the market. And it revived suspicions that Hong Kong was a 'Mickey Mouse' market where you could not trust the locals. Finally it made a mockery of Hong Kong's hard-won reputation as one of the few places which still practised solid *laissez-faire* principles. Surely Hong Kong, with its long history of surviving panics, was the last place to close down in just such a panic.

However, there was worse to come. A few weeks later Ronald Li, the man blamed for the closure and for allegedly trying to bail out some of his cronies, was later arrested and charged under Hong Kong's bribery ordinance, accused of accepting payments in return for influencing the timing of new share issues. For Ronald Li, who in the weeks before the crash had been a sponsor of a new issue to float Club Volvo, a luxury girlie escort club owned by Beijing interests, it was a devastating loss of face. For Hong Kong it was a cathartic chance to put its house in order.

These examples show that financial fever was not confined to the three centres of global finance. The boom-and-bust sequence has been repeated in virtually every country where shares are publicly traded. Everywhere wealth grew on paper and everywhere paper wealth vanished overnight. In general the smaller and more illiquid the market, the quicker the vanishing act.

The Money Managers

Who are these money managers and what makes them tick? Ordinary ones tend to be mediocre as in any trade, and merely follow the herd. The good ones are probably the money world's biggest prima donnas. Highly individualistic, they live off their wits, sharing a common addiction to moving markets. There follows three examples: a veteran who craves value; an enthusiast who paints from the broadest canvas; and an amateur philosopher turned professional investor who applied the dialectic to investing.

JOHN TEMPLETON

A visit to John Templeton in his Bahamas home is almost like a pilgrimage. Now in his early seventies, Templeton has become the clichéd legend in his own lifetime, partly because of his outstanding long-term record, partly because of his disciplined contrarian approach to investing which he pursued long before it became the fashion it is today, and partly because he was about the first American to do serious global investing.

Personally, Templeton exudes an earthy common sense. A religious and straightforward man, he is essentially modest about everything save his investment abilities. His home in the Bahamas' Layford Key Club may be splendid but it is not ostentatious. He would claim that it helps him maintain perspective from the frenzy of Wall Street or other financial centres. It is certainly a million miles away from the hype and temporary enthusiasms of such places. Here is a man who eschews fashion. Templeton is best known as the most stubborn of 'contrarians', which means doing the opposite of what others are doing without ever being perverse for its own sake. The objective is bargain-hunting: to find value. 'We want to buy things which are thoroughly unpopular,' he said in an interview at his home in September 1986. That philosophy demands a great deal of patience. Templeton has it. He holds a share on average for six years. The industry norm is more like six months and shortening. This policy requires gutsy decision making. 'The only time you can get things at real bargain prices is when other people are selling because they see a bad outlook. It requires a lot of patience,' he says.

Templeton's critics like to scoff at his short-term performance. And unarguably the 'long-term' is made up of a series of short terms. It is true enough that investors in Templeton's funds have suffered the bumpiest of rides. In 1963, for example, Templeton finished last in the performance tables, a fact which would not have enamoured him to pension fund consultants. In 1985–7 his funds suffered badly from being virtually out of the high-flying Japanese market – Templeton basically sold Tokyo five years ago. In 1973 his flagship Templeton Growth Fund had 52 per cent of its assets in Japan; in 1981 4 per cent, and in 1986 only 2 per cent. As seen from his Bahamas hideaway, Templeton has wanted nothing to do with the highest share valuations in the world. He simply declined to come to the party, or rather as one of the earliest investors in Japan, he decided to leave before midnight, long before the other revellers became dangerously intoxicated.

Templeton does not care that in index terms Japan is too big for his competitors to ignore. For his uniqueness is that he is prepared to make major bets away from the commonly followed indices and does not panic when he finds himself way out of line with prevailing fads. Rather, he welcomes it since he is not in the business of trying to profit from temporary enthusiasms. He defends his record, as does his promotional literature, by pointing to the performance of the Templeton Growth Fund. Launched in 1954, it had risen 4,586 per cent by April 1986 compared with a 359 per cent rise in the Dow Jones.

If value is Templeton's yardstick, he shrewdly has no rigid set of rules for successful investing. He cites only three essentials; common sense, an international outlook, and flexibility. On the last point he likes to quote his favourite homespun philosopher, Thomas Eddison: 'If there is anything you are doing the same way you were doing twenty years ago then there must be a better way of doing it.' His point is that all investment techniques become obsolete once they grow too popular. This is a peculiarity of the investment business. For if you merely ape what the competition does, you cannot hope to do better.

From a historical perspective Templeton appears something of a supreme optimist, a position he has maintained after the October, 1987, crash. He believes that equities will continue to outperform all other forms of investment. And he also believes (this borders on a crusade for him) that the number of people owning shares will continue to rise. 'We are witnessing a major permanent change in the fact that it will be normal for most families to own shares. The common sense thing for them is to buy shares through unit trusts.'

This visionary approach separates Templeton from most other investors who tend to be cynics at heart seeing themselves profiting from the ever repeated boom-and-bust cycles of human folly. Templeton is far too experienced an investor to deny the existence of such cycles, though he does not like to dwell on their darker side. He believes instead in being positive and maintains an unashamed confidence in progress, which is one reason why he is prepared to put money in the stock markets of developing countries. The cult of share ownership, he contends, has only just begun. 'Socialism is history. Socialism is largely over in terms of evolution.'

Religious crackpot or political nut? It would be only too easy to dismiss Templeton as out of touch with political reality. The problem is that Templeton has proved himself an astute investor in markets across the globe, and international investing is all about distinguishing between perceptions and reality, political as

well as economic. Templeton is also a keen and frequent travel-
ler who is renowned for his international network of contacts.
That Templeton is so positive is refreshing. But it should be
noted that being positive is something of a fetish for him. It has
also never stopped him selling shares which he regards as fully
valued.

RICHARD THORNTON

If Templeton is the dry calculator of value, Richard Thornton is a
natural enthusiast and an intuitive investor. Thornton co-founded
the London-based G.T. Management and built it into a top
independent money management firm with an expertise in international investing. Ousted by his fellow directors a few years ago in
what amounted to a palace coup, Thornton took some young
employees with him and set up Thornton Management, which he
was due to take public last October. He was five days late, though
apparently Thornton had managed to pre-place 10 per cent of his
company with institutional investors prior to the flotation. The
Wall Street crash has probably ended any hopes for now of a public
flotation.

Thornton made his name investing in the Far East stock markets
of Japan, Hong Kong, Malaysia, and Singapore. He was one of the
first foreign investors in the Tokyo market in the early 1960s, while
G.T. was one of the first money managers to open an office in
Hong Kong. The British colony's communications, tax structure,
and international outlook have always made it an ideal place from
which to manage money.

Thornton remains as enthusiastic as ever though this time in a
more bearish mood. Interviewed in the summer of 1986, he
worried about what he saw as long-term deflationary trends which
were pushing the world economy inexorably into a downward
spiral. Unlike Templeton who has a 'bottom-up' bias, looking at
companies before countries, Thornton tends to be 'top down',
placing countries before companies. He looks at trends in liquidity, claiming, 'Stock markets have never been anything but
liquidity driven.' To Thornton, the 1980s liquidity glut was a sure
sign that people did not know what to do with their money so they
spent it on shares (which was good for his and other money
managers' business of selling unit trusts or mutual funds). The
stock market, as the first credit instrument into which spare cash
flows, was the natural beneficiary. The key question then become

how long that excess liquidity would keep fuelling share prices. Liquidity may keep shares rising for longer than many people think possible, witness Japan. But ultimately all liquidity arguments for buying shares rest on the greater fool theory, that there is another sucker around to sell the overvalued paper to.

The same view was aired bluntly by Morgan Stanley's Biggs in an interview with America's premier weekly investment newspaper, *Barrons,* in the issue dated 20 October 1986.

> BARRONS: What is bullish about low growth?
> BIGGS: Liquidity. You can have a replay of the Japanese market next year in Europe. You had very low growth in Japan, and very high liquidity and the market going through the roof.
> BARRONS: There's no reason to put your money into building something, so you might as well buy stocks?
> BIGGS: Well that's what this bull market is more or less all about.

Thornton would have agreed with such a frank admission of what propelled share prices ever upward during the 1980s. However, it was never highlighted in his or any other money manager's promotional literature or, for that matter, the numerous prospectuses of the many money management firms which in recent years sensibly rushed to go public as the ultimate beneficiaries of financial asset fever.

As a Far East buff it is perhaps not surprising that Thornton expects a re-ordering of the post-1945 economic order. The world is in the throes of the emergence of the yen as the dominant global currency. How long today's liquidity game lasts, he contends, will depend on how long the Japanese are prepared to go on spending their $70bn.-odd of surplus cash a year on buying depreciating dollars to finance American consumption. At some stage in the game, he argues, they will no longer be prepared 'to sacrifice themselves on the altar of American spending'. That will produce the demand for a better store of value in which to express Japanese liquidity.

The only way out of this downward spiral, says Thornton, is to fix the yen against gold at the equivalent of, say, $800 an ounce, a level gold last reached at its euphoric peak in 1980. Thornton says: 'If you want to reflate the world you have to hoist the price of gold. You can't produce a gold glut.' Is there any chance of this happening soon? He thinks not. 'We are a million miles away from this point. That is why it is going to be so dire.' He believes that we will soon see the emergence of isolationist policies to compare with those which followed the First World War and led to the Great Depression. Then the revaluation of gold did not occur until 1933.

GEORGE SOROS

A third professional investor is Hungarian-born George Soros. New York-based Soros is probably the wealthiest of the three having made tens of millions of dollars from his offshore Quantum Fund which claims the best investment record ever. A sum of $100,000 invested in January 1969 had grown to nearly $23.4m by the end of 1986. The Quantum Fund's annual report stated: 'No fund anywhere in the world has shown anything approaching this performance.' This was truly making money out of money.

Soros himself has for most of his career been acutely shy of publicity. He was also known as having an awkward personality. There is an apocryphal story of how once, visiting London, he rang up his favourite broker in British government bonds, better known as gilt-edge securities, to check on the market. The happy salesman was eager to meet his long-standing client and asked him to dinner. 'Why spoil a good relationship?' came the cryptic reply. In 1987 Soros almost became a media figure, however, with the publication of his book *The Alchemy of Finance*, revealingly subtitled 'Reading the mind of the market'. Such was his growing fame that he even met premier Deng Xiao Ping on a visit to China and his book has been translated into Chinese and Russian.

In an interview Soros is hard to pin down. His mind is like quicksilver, darting from one thought to another. That also seems to be how he invests. Soros' book is no crude how-to-get-rich thesis. It is rather a philosophic tract in which he puts forward his theory of 'reflexivity'. Soros argues not only that market values are always distorted ('economic theory attempts the impossible by introducing the assumption of rational behaviour') but also that those distortions can affect, in the case of shares, the companies themselves. The relationship is 'reflexive' because it is like a two-way mirror. Regardless of whether this is just a profound way of stating the obvious, or genuine insight, no one can deny that it has helped Soros in acquiring his reputation as an uncanny reader of the markets who, in Biggs' phrase, 'transmutes events into profits'. His strengths are his flexibility, his continued reassessment of how he sees things and his readiness always to change his mind. The result is a constantly shifting, intuitive, if not instinctive, response to the ebbs and flows of the markets. His friend Barton Biggs wrote in a review of his book:

> As an investor, George is incredibly flexible and willing to change his mind if the market appears to be going against him. One of his great strengths is that he has no pride of position. Does this come from reflexivity or by observing his father change safe houses on intuition when the Gestapo was chasing his family in Budapest during World War II?

What about Soros' world view? We are in what he calls a 'twilight zone'.

> Until now the authorities have been able to prevent a bust. We find ourselves in a twilight zone where the 'normal' process of credit expansion culminated long ago but the 'normal' process of credit contraction has been prevented by the authorities. We are in uncharted territory because the actions of the authorities have no precedent.

Soros also observes that this could be the declining phase of a larger cycle, while admitting that though there is a general awareness of a long fifty-to-sixty-year cycle which he shares, it has never been 'scientifically' explained. He writes:

> The fact that we are in the declining phase of the larger cycle is usually left out of the account. I contend that all previous recessions since the end of World War II occurred while credit was expanding, while the one we may or may not be facing would occur when borrowing capacity in the real economy is contracting. This creates a situation that has no precedent in recent history.'

All this rather begs one key question. Does the delay engineered by the authorities (by what Soros calls 'artificial means') only mean an even bigger bust further down this uncharted road? Interviewed in the spring of 1987 Soros was still hedging his bets. 'The correspondence with 1929 is amazing. It is not to be disregarded. I am reasonably convinced that the denouement is not going to be the same. It is a thesis which will be proven wrong.' But disturbing him was that nagging doubt. 'You have not allowed the credit cycle to play out.'

At that point in early 1987 Soros was concentrating his investments on what he then viewed as the most interesting area, stocks. By contrast, bonds and currencies were no longer attractive. In 1985 Quantum made more than a 100 per cent return, thanks mainly to betting heavily against the dollar. When he is convinced a big move lies ahead, Soros is not afraid to gear up. The annual report stated: 'At the peak of our engagement in currencies our short position in the dollar was nearly twice our equity.' Soros is also completely flexible. He will go wherever he sees the best risk-reward ratio, be it in the cash or future markets, on the long or short side, in stocks, bonds, or currencies. He is also prepared to plough into foreign markets in size. He has bought up so many shares in Finland's stock market that brokers joked about how that small market had become his private fiefdom. An exaggeration may be. Still at 31 December 1986 the Quantum fund held $147.4m. worth of Finnish stocks, considerably more than its holdings in the much larger West German, Japanese, or British stock markets. In 1987 Soros weighed into Thailand. He bought a portfolio valued at over $60m. from the Thai government. This consisted of shares bought by the government almost ten years earlier in a buying operation designed to stem panic selling during a stock market crash in Bangkok.

When the bust came in October 1987, Soros was unhappily caught cruelly exposed. Not even he was immune from hubris as the markets again proved a great leveller. The publication of his book had spawned extensive media attention, including a September cover story in America's *Fortune* magazine. This hitherto low-profile financier suddenly became public property, appearing like countless other pundits on T.V. screens. It was not a well-timed entrance. In the *Fortune* article Soros predicted a crash in Tokyo while explaining how much higher American shares could go, the fashionable view at the time. The article ended with the following comment: 'The American market has only recently got carried away, and it can still correct these excesses in a mild orderly fashion.' A month later the Dow was down 36 per cent from its top in a matter of weeks while Tokyo was still riding comparatively high. Soros was not spared the consequences losing, according to a *Barrons* article dated 2 November 1987, some $840m. in less than two weeks, mainly from betting on S. & P. stock index futures. Soros reportedly doubled up on his stock position by buying some 5,000 S. & P. futures contracts, representing an exposure of $1.1bn., on 21 October, two days after the crash. When the market opened strongly he apparently changed his mind, or as Barrons put it 'panicked' and sold the whole lot, causing a downward spiral in the price.

Punditry can be a dangerous affliction. Soros must have wished he had stuck to his previous posture of near zero exposure. In the money business a high profile, like a big ego, can be a dangerous thing.

WAVES AND CYCLES

'Do not buck the trend; it is too pervasive.
Simply understand it and then flow with it to
profitable investing.'

Douglas Kirkland, 1985

The capitalist world in the first nine months of 1987 was a confusing place. Booming financial markets, sluggish economies, severe trade imbalances and overhanging everything, a scary layer of debt. What did it all mean?

Most people working in the money industry did not know and did not even pretend to know, save for one thing, that there was lots of money around and it was flowing into the world's financial markets. This 'liquidity' was bidding up the price of financial assets but not the price of goods. So long as this continued, why worry?

Such was the orthodox rationale of continuing paper prosperity found in New York, London, and Tokyo. It was not hard to see why. Only the most perverse of stock pedlars would have warned publicly against such a lucrative trend. But if the trend was established, an explanation beyond greater-fool liquidity theory was not. The nagging worry in the pit of the stomach persisted that the financial markets were flying a kite far removed from the stark realities. And that one day the kite would be buried and, with it, many people's hopes, dreams and aspirations. Those concerns were confirmed for some by the October 1987 crash. As governments and senior figures in the money industry sought to talk up the market and avert panic, to others the precipitous falls in stock markets everywhere only confirmed what they had long feared; that the world was heading for a debt deflation and slump-like depression.

127

The Elliot Wave Theory

To understand why, it is necessary to explain the renewed interest in wave and cyclical investment theories which gathered pace as the bull market grew increasingly extreme. This interest was greatest in America, home at least until 1986 of the world's largest stock market and still capitalism's biggest playground. An investment sub-culture has existed for years in America, independent of the deal makers and fixers on Wall Street. It is centred on the world of freelance investment newsletter writers, many of them refugees from Wall Street. They earn their living forecasting short- and long-term market moves, and their staple income is the money people pay to subscribe to their newsletters. They are known as 'market timers'.

Investment newsletter writers have always been made fun of by the established Wall Street firms. They suffered earlier this decade from the publicity-seeking antics of Joseph Granville, the man who forecast the start of a huge bear market in 1981. He could not have been more wrong, though he is still in business. There has since been the rise and partial fall of a new star, Robert Prechter, who in January 1987 succeeded in making the covers of both *Barrons* and *Fortune*. Despite all the hype, Prechter was not a brash showman. Rather, he was personally a modest man who understood the need for publicity while trying, though ultimately unsuccessfully, not to be consumed by it. Visitors had to seek him out at his lakeside retreat in rural Georgia, two hours' drive from Atlanta.

Prechter made his name from market timing. Investment newsletter writers are now measured by independent advisory services in a bid to monitor the inevitably exaggerated performance claims. Market timers, like politicians, are experts at talking up their own case. Prechter headed the Florida-based *Timer Digests*' list for the four years up until and including 1986. His success in the stock market (if less so in the bond and gold markets) focused attention on the arcane discipline he uses to predict the markets – the Elliot wave theory. This is a 'technical' (i.e. not based on economic or corporate fundamentals) way of predicting market moves, developed by a retired Californian accountant in the 1930s. Ralph Elliot came to his conclusions empirically by exhaustive studies of stock market charts, hourly, daily, monthly.

For Prechter, a Yale graduate in psychology and a former technical analyst at Merrill Lynch, the stock market is the best measure of mass psychology at work. He likens it to a thermometer which registers changes in the level of social optimism and pessimism. It is these changes in mass psychology, he argues, which cause changes in 'fundamental' events, not the other way round. Precisely because he does not want to be personally influenced by this mass psychology during stock market trading hours, Prechter follows the tape, which shows the minute-by-minute stock prices on America's Financial News Network with the volume permanently turned down.

Elliot wave theory teaches that the market moves in a predictable pattern. This pattern is derived from an inspection of charts and mathematical relationships known to exist in the universe, based on the Fibonacci series of numbers, an infinite series in which each member is the sum of the previous two. Such is his confidence in the tenets formulated by Elliot, that Prechter had been waiting for the 1980s explosive bull market ever since 1975. It was then that he recognized the market would 'soon' be entering what is known in Elliot wave-speak as the 'fifth wave' of the bullish five-wave trend which began in 1932. If Elliot wave theory seems arcane, it is also complex. Simplified to its most extreme, it says that each upwave in the market is characterized by three upward movements and two down (and each downwave by two down and one up). The final fifth upwave of that big upward move from 1932 began in August 1982 when the Dow Jones broke through 800. It was by 1987 extremely advanced. The only question was how advanced?

Prechter's long-standing prediction was that the Dow would peak within 200 points of 3,686, probably in late 1988. It should be noted that Elliot wave theory only predicts price movements. It says nothing about timing. To forecast timing Prechter relies on cycle theory as well as what he calls 'momentum' and 'sentiment' indicators. Momentum is looking at the way the market is trading. A market rallying in high trading volume is bullish. Conversely, a market rising in weak, thin volume is unconvincing and so probably bearish. Sentiment is measuring what other speculators/investors are doing. This can be gauged from various indicators such as the put/call ratio, which shows what view people are taking in the options markets. Thus if 95 per cent of option investors are buying 'call' options on gold (bets that the price of gold will go up in the next three to six months as opposed to 'puts' which is a bet that prices will fall) that means that nearly all the participants in the market are 100 per cent bullish on gold. To Prechter, that is a clear danger sign, signalling that euphoria is overblown, investors are too greedy, and that prices are likely to fall sharply when these expectations are disappointed. However, cycles, momentum and sentiment are only complements to the all-important Elliot wave discipline. For that gives the long-term trend in respect of price movements. The market timer's art then lies in interpreting the waves from the practical point of view of making short-term market forecasts. Prechter like many market timers runs a daily telephone hot line where subscribers can phone up for the latest market view.

If all this sounds like gobbledegook, sceptics should note that the study of charts has long played a part in forecasting financial markets. Money manager George Soros does not scorn charts, commenting: 'They show the rhythm of the market. As such they are relevant.' Most stockbroking firms employ what are called 'chartists' in Britain and 'technical analysts' in America. Scoffers should be aware that Prechter had been predicting a Dow at over 3,000 since 1982 (when the level of disbelief was that much higher since the Dow was then hovering around the 800 level), and that in between times he had made some well-publicized correct, short-term calls as well as some wrong ones. This is why most technical analysts on Wall Street were receiving his newsletter, even though they may not have personally subscribed to Elliot wave theory.

Indeed the man and his message had by 1987 become an important theme of the 1980s bull market. This was Prechter's undoing. Wall Street professionals talked about the market in terms of whether they accepted or rejected the overall Prechter thesis while the market twitched at every rumour of his latest forecast. When that happens prophecies have a habit of becoming self-fulfilling. Prechter was attracting attention both because of the accuracy of his predictions to date and because of the scale of the bull market he was predicting. This climaxed when he issued a strong buy recommendation on 31 December 1986, predicting the Dow would rise by at least 700 points that year. It hit his 'minimum' target in August. That New Year's Eve prediction coincided with Wall Street's explosive rally at the start of the year, and the man and the message became front-page news.

But far more interesting was what Elliot wave and Prechter said about what happens after the climactic peak. This naturally was forgotten when the Dow appeared in hindsight to have peaked at 2,700 last August, nearly 1,000 points short of Prechter's target, and subsequently crashed. Faced with a barrage of 255 media requests for interviews, the guru went temporarily underground.

He was being blamed unfairly for precipitating the collapse. In fact, he had called only for a correction two weeks before Black Monday when the Dow plunged over 500 points. Clearly the subsequent collapse proved more than a bull market correction. That was obvious to Prechter as well. From listening to his hot-line messages to clients, it became clear to those familiar with Elliot wave jargon that he was telling them the stock market was now in a bear market and that the collapse would be deflationary. At his first public appearance after the crash at a conference of invest-ment newsletter writers in New Orleans in November 1987, Prechter offered one crumb of comfort, saying that financial collapse was then still some time away. He told his faithful followers: 'You have a year to get your life in order and your debt out of the way.'

All along Prechter had been less happy to talk about what happened after the top preferring, for obvious reasons, to stress the gains that could be made in this 'bull market of a lifetime'. This made commercial sense. Americans are natural optimists and Prechter was running a business. He should also be credited for predicting in 1982, as early as most, a long-term bull market. That was the same year that Mexico nearly defaulted and prophets of gloom were two a penny.

His gathering fame served Prechter well. During 1986 the number of his subscribers jumped from 3,000 to 15,000, each paying $233 a year. So from the newsletter alone Prechter was earning a handsome income of $3.5m., which compares favourably with most of Wall Street's top-salaried chiefs. That figure does not include income from the hot line, for which subscribers pay an extra $377. Yet despite that growth in circulation Prechter never raised the subscription price following his newsletter's launch in 1977, which at least shows that he is not greedy.

Indeed, talking to Prechter earlier in 1987, it became clear that, having achieved financial security, his main ambition was to predict the top of the bull market, advise his subscribers to sell and then get out of the business. Unfortunately the market did not allow him that luxury.

Prechter's desire to quit the guru business is natural given the scale of the disaster ahead which he predicts. According to his interpretation of the Elliot wave theory, the world is heading for a depression even deeper and longer lasting than that of the 1930s. The Dow, he says, will collapse way below the 1,000 level – his long-term projection for the Dow is a mere 70. The havoc will be even worse in the 'debt' (bond) markets where even blue-chip corporate issuers will default.

Lapsing into what he terms 'non-Elliot speculation' Prechter predicts that the political response in America to deflation will be to inflate: 'They will keep printing money until the dollar is destroyed as a currency.' And perhaps most alarming, he adds: 'Stock market crashes are followed by depressions, which are followed by war. The negative psychology has to find an outlet and wars are one of the outlets.'

With these Armageddon-type views it is perhaps not surprising that the talk in the fringe world of market timers in early 1987 was that Prechter had been buying property in Australia, though why he should perceive Australia as the best hedge against social, political and financial chaos is perhaps less clear. Still, when it comes to hedging against the risk of such calamities, an individual can only try his best. Nothing is foolproof, which is why some more paranoid survivalist-kit individuals do not even trust storing gold in a bank's safety deposit box. Prechter tells the story of a Jew who fled Germany in the 1930s and took the ultimate precaution before leaving of burying his gold hoard. He returned after the war to dig up his gold – two miles from the East German border.

The Kondratieff Wave

Prechter's view of the world may come from studying stock market charts. But his conclusions are similar to those observers who study the long economic wave, otherwise known as the Kondratieff wave. This is a phenomenon which tends to be take more seriously by investors like George Soros than economists, the vast majority of whom denounce it. What is it? In 1922 Nikolai Kondratieff, a Russian government official, published an essay entitled 'Long Economic Cycles'. His conclusion was that there was a long-term business cycle of prosperity and depression spanning forty-five to sixty years. Like other cycles in nature (high and low tide, summer and winter, life and death) this was subject to the same immutable laws of natural ebb and flow.

Kondratieff was sent off to Siberia for his pains, doubtless viewed by contemporaries as a subversive crank. But his work not only angered the Soviet authorities, who did not like their subjects to think for themselves, it has ever since been anathema to most orthodox economists. They view the economy as essentially in equilibrium, subject to fine tuning and rational management.

Kondratieff's basic and unflattering message was that most of what they say and do is irrelevant.

It is true that there is no statistically verifiable evidence for a Kondratieff cycle. This is because threadbare statistics only go back to 1789. It is also true that Kondratieff never postulated an exact cycle in terms of number of years. What he did say was that the long wave averaged fifty-four years, or a period between forty-five and sixty years. This lack of statistical proof does not necessarily mean the whole concept is bunk, just that it cannot be statistically proven. Anyway, the claimed importance of the Kondratieff wave in investment terms lies in what it says about recognizing the long-term trend, so helping the investor to hang on to his money, not in pinpointing precise dates or timing.

The essence of long-wave theory is that the world economy passes through upswing, crisis, and depression. There have been various attempts to say what causes this. The German economist, Joseph Schumpeter, the doyen of business-cycle theorists, ascribed it to technological innovations, called the 'displacement theory' in economic textbooks. The classic example is railroads in America last century. (The amount of railtrack in America almost doubled from 34,000 miles in 1865 to 65,000 miles in 1873, giving a tremendous, once-of-a-kind boost to the economy.) In recent years Professor Jay Forrestor of the Massachusetts Institute of Technology (M.I.T) has concluded that it is the rise and fall of capital investment. Significantly, Forrester's 'Systems Dynamics Group' works out of M.I.T.'s Sloan School of Management, not the economics faculty, and its work is categorically rejected by most establishment and academic economists. Speaking to a Washington conference in late 1984, the professor made his own view clear: 'The economic long wave, which is also called the Kondratieff cycle, is a major rise and fall of economic activity that spans forty-five to sixty years between peaks. The wave is a much larger and more important business disturbance than the business cycle.'

Such a view leads to some pretty shattering conclusions about the relevance of most contemporary political and economic debate. Forrester, who like Prechter, believes we are about to enter another economic downturn akin to the 1930s, has reached his conclusions through studying computer models of his own group's design. Unlike most econometric models which use macro-economic data, this is bottom-up, feeding in the operating policies and decisions taken by companies, financial institutions, and governments. That means it seeks to measure what managers do in their practical, everyday world, not aggregate economic behaviour. Note also that Forrester was not looking for a long wave when he began studying the model more than ten years ago. Rather, the evidence convinced him of it.

For non-academics dubious about the value of any 'model', an Arizona-based money manager Douglas Kirkland, has produced an easily understandable – and in my view, most convincing because most common-sense – definition of what causes the long cycle. That is simply the accumulation and then destruction of debt. In his remarkably lucid book *Power Cycles*, Kirkland has chronicled the three and a half Kondratieff cycles which he reckons the world has lived through since 1789, and examined the history of and implications for various areas of investment: stock markets, debt markets, property, and gold. The overall message makes arresting reading for anyone thoughtful enough to have been perplexed by the seemingly contradictory 1980s mix of raging debt and roaring stock markets. Certainly the stock market crash would have come as less of a surprise.

Believers break down the Kondratieff wave into three parts. First, the growth phase of twenty to thirty years. This is divided into a cautious phase lasting about ten years (this time round say 1946–58), followed by an increasingly euphoric phase (1958–73). It is a period of strong economic growth punctuated by mild recessions. General affluence also encourages a climate of growing political and social 'liberalism' (to use the American not the British meaning of the word). Then comes a severe 'post-war recession' (late 1973–early 1975), albeit a short, sharp one. This is when governments first try to bring rising inflation (in this case Vietnam War/Eurodollar-fuelled inflation) under control.

This marks the end of the growth phase and paves the way for the 'plateau' period, which usually runs for some ten years. It also indicates the start of the 'downwave'. According to Kondratieff devotees, the world has been nearing the end of the plateau of this long cycle during the 1980s. The plateau is characterized by economic slack, low growth, high unemployment, low inflation and booming financial markets; there being no incentive to plough money into 'real' investment – the 1980s condition. It is also a period of growing political and social conservatism.

At the end of the plateau the economy slides into the depression phase which removes all the excesses accumulated during the growth and plateau periods. What triggers this slide into depression is a crash in the financial markets. This is a time of self-feeding deflation and economic contraction followed, unlike the 'post-war' short, sharp shock, by a long-protracted slump. Economic distortions have to be purged from the system before sustained growth can once again proceed. And the bigger those distortions the more severe and longer drawn out the subsequent purging.

What unnerved believers in Kondratieff's theories was that the crash in the stock market in October 1987 marked a clear signal that we were sliding into just such a depression. Such a view clearly flies in the face of the post-1945 maxim that there will never be another depression because governments 'will not allow it', first because they will go on spending money and second, because central bankers will go on printing it; a view which, to Kondratieff devotees, displays a touching faith in muddling through, the ability of politicians to continue fixing deals and so control destiny.

Avoiding a Deflationary Depression

Before looking at the remarkable similarity to date between the passage of the 1920s and 1980s it is worth examining why consensus opinion is so convinced that central bankers today can avoid another deflationary depression. This view was articulated by Paine Webber's Thomas Doerflinger in a 1987 article provocatively entitled 'Where the "Long Wave" Theory Crashes'. Doerflinger wrote: 'An essential ingredient of this (bearish) scenario, as in the Great Depressions of the 1840s and 1930s, would be monumental errors by economic leaders, especially central bankers.'

This assumes that last time round it was essentially the central bankers' fault. The basis of this theory was propounded by the monetarist school of economists under Professor Milton Friedman of the University of Chicago. They argue that depressions, including the 1930s version, have always been accompanied by a sharp decline in the money supply and, therefore, that the central bankers were to blame for not printing enough money. The connection between depression and contracting money supplies may be true but the monetarists have not proved cause and effect. Indeed, Friedman and the rest are wrong to heap all the blame on the Federal Reserve which was just as anxious to avoid depression as this generation is. Just as Alan Greenspan's Federal Reserve temporarily injected liquidity into the system immediately following the October 1987 crash, so the 1929 Fed at once eased monetary policy following the October 1929 stock market crash. The problem was that the pumping of liquidity did not work because the contraction in the money supply was caused by the onset of a deflationary mentality and not the other way round. For when financial panic occurs, it rapidly degenerates into debt liquidation and destruction of wealth. The problem is not that debtors run out of money (a central bank acting as 'lender of last resort' can always keep bailing them out by printing money) but rather that lenders lose confidence and stop lending and even demand their money back. There is a stampede for cash. This is why during the 1929–33 period the total money supply was contracting while the currency percentage of the money supply was rising. That suggests a liquidation of debt and a corresponding rise in cash holdings.

What causes this onset of a depression mentality and rush for liquidity? James Dale Davidson in his Strategic Investment newsletter argues that it is usually some kind of unpleasant surprise.

> A shock, such as a major debt default, protectionism, currency weakness or even a fraud, demonstrates the overvaluation of financial assets. As financial assets tumble in value, wealth shrivels and collateral in the banking system is impaired.

Davidson also points out two other basic problems with the keep-on-printing-money argument. First, the printing press has been around since medieval times, so why have there been so many economic contractions since then? Governments, if given the choice, will always favour more inflation which initially makes people feel better off than deflation which leaves everyone poorer. Second, there is an arithmetical limit to how long debt can go on accumulating which makes liquidation and default inevitable. A borrower can double his debt service – interest payment – costs from 10 to 20 per cent of his income with only a little pain, and even double them again from 20 to 40 per cent. But no one can spend more than 100 per cent of his income servicing old bills. Such is the logical limit of indebtedness. The practical limit is, of course, well below that, a fact which anyone trying to service mortgage payments amounting to more than 50 per cent of their income can appreciate.

The degree of current complacency both about the authorities' ability to print their way out and the unlikelihood of deflation, was well summed up by another investment newsletter, the *Kondratieff Wave Analyst*. Its publisher Donald Hoppe wrote in June, 1986:

> It is quite possible that even though the Fed makes money freely available to the banking system, a combination of defaults and a

reluctance to borrow by consumers, investors and business people will cause a general contraction in the money supply, just as it did in the 1930s. The fact that it has become an article of faith with today's bankers, economists and the Wall Street crowd that simply keeping the money supply expanding is the secret of perpetual prosperity is in itself a warning. We could be in a dangerous situation in that, once again, the 'lender of last resort' might be undone by a collapse in borrowing. Remember, what everyone knows is not worth knowing, and if the crowd now believes in the money-supply connection, one can almost be certain that it is a fallacy.

So if today's interdependent world – the other side of the 'global-finance' coin – is indeed sliding off the Kondratieff plateau into the abyss global trading and the Reuters screen will make it much harder for the authorities to control mass liquidations when they occur short of the extreme act of closing down all the world's financial markets, cash and futures.

The Precedents of the 1920s

The most worrying symptoms are the uncanny historical precedents with the 1920s. Indeed the two decades have mirrored each other so closely that it worries long-wave devotees. Fate, they reckon, must be storing up some diabolical surprise, the point being that history never repeats itself quite so exactly. That surprise may simply be that this time the slump will be that much worse.

Kondratieff noted that the first symptom of a downwave was a depression in agriculture. Agriculture peaked in 1920 (nine years before the 1929 Wall Street crash) and again in 1980. Property peaked in 1925 (in the middle of the plateau) and is once again softening in America. The pattern is the same. Property is weak first in the periphery areas and then gradually eats into the centre. The last area to turn down is property in the financial centres which remains strong with the stock market until the end. (New York's Empire State Building was under construction in 1929.)

Like the 1980s, the 1920s were a period of growing stock market fever which climaxed in general euphoria. In the 1920s punters bought shares on margin. In the 1980s they bought stock index futures contracts. Both periods also saw inflation in the value of stock market seats. In 1929 a seat on the New York Stock Exchange sold for $500,000. It took another forty years to beat that record though seats sold for over $1m. before the October 1987 crash, and in Tokyo for $7m.

What about the bond market? Back in the 1920s American interest rates bottomed and the bond market peaked in January 1928. This time round the American bond market peaked in April 1986 when the Dow still traded well below 2,000. The largest part of the great stock market rally, which occurred in 1928 and 1929, took place in the face of four increases in America's discount rate. The same happened this time round when the Dow exploded from under 2,000 to over 2,700 in the first eight months of 1987 in the face of rising interest rates.

There is another common feature with the 1920s. Foreign stock markets peaked in January 1929, nine months before Wall Street, as foreign capital flooded into America, viewed then as now as the capitalist world's safe haven. The fashionable view among long-wave devotees until October 1987 was that this would be repeated, meaning America would end the 1980s bull market as the world's best performing stock market, having been a comparative laggard compared to its high-flying Asian and European counterparts in the earlier years.

This was also Prechter's view. In early 1987 he was predicting a final stock market move confined to America and centred on the Dow blue chips as foreign money poured in, sparking a short-lived economic bounce and a temporary rally in the dollar. This would occur in a political climate of impending protectionist legislation which Kondratieff devotees also see as inevitable. The date of 29 October 1929, or 'Black Tuesday', the day that ended the roaring Twenties when shares lost some $10bn. in value or twice the amount of money in circulation in America at the time, was also the day that President Herbert Hoover said he would sign the protectionist Smoot-Hawley Act.

'Black Tuesday' marked the abrupt end of what had been a riotous party. Historians of that crash, Gordon Thomas and Max Morgan-Witts, wrote in *The Day the Bubble Burst*:

> On the day the bubble burst the land was dotted with houses bought on part payments; cars bought on credit; clothes, jewellery, vacations, luxury goods of every kind acquired on the promise to pay in the future – often when stock profits came in.

The inevitable hangover was not shortlived. The Dow did not recover its 1929 high until as late as 1954. However, there are even worse precedents in recent financial history. Prior to the panic of 1837 stock prices reached their highs for the entire nineteenth century. This was a real panic. Mark Faber relates how a financial institution with the impressive name, the United States Bank reached a 1837 high of 122. On 25 November 1841 it was trading at 4. Another financial institution, American Trust, went from 120 to 0 during the same period. These are the ominous precedents facing stock market investors following 'Black Monday' and the crash of 1987.

And what about the comparative debt excesses? Kirkland's book provides some admittedly rough-and-ready numbers. They are not reassuring. The 1920s was also a period of fast money and dubious get-rich-quick schemes. But they pale by today's standards. The trillions in debt created in America during the 1980s, in which Wall Street has been the main beneficiary, has no parallel in magnitude in any previous credit bubble. In America the net issue of debt has been running at ten times the personal savings rate during the 1980s. Americans have been borrowing purchasing power from the future or, in biblical English, putting off the final day of reckoning.

One way of measuring how bad a deflationary financial panic could be in the sense of triggering a sudden scramble for cash is by measuring total dollar debt against hard currency in circulation. Kirkland employs an admittedly crude measure which he calls the debt ratio and which, he argues, has been extremely sensitive in highlighting the ravages of debt deflation during previous cycles. This is the ratio of the total money supply in the banking system in the sense of M1 (currency in circulation and bank current accounts) divided by the amount of gold held by the government. In 1929 at the last peak there was $4.3bn. of gold bullion against a money supply of $58bn., or a ratio of around 15:1. There is now some $138bn. of bullion at the Federal Reserve, valued at $440 per ounce gold, against M1 of $3.55 trillion, consisting of $755m. of domestic M1 (as at 10 March 1988) plus another nearly $3 trillion of Eurodollar deposits offshore in the Euromarkets, a market most Americans do not even know exists. That is a debt ratio of 26:1.

Obviously this particular ratio does not include many other types of debt obligations, be it government debt, mortgage debt, or corporate debt. Defined in a broader way, there is now $338bn. of bullion and greenbacks (adding in the $180bn. of money in circulation – greenbacks – as at May 1988). That can be set against estimated total domestic dollar debt of over $11 trillion to make an even more alarming ratio of 32.5:1. This debt figure includes

America's government and private-sector debt of $8 trillion. It also includes the large amounts of off-balance sheet debt in both the government and private sector. There is, for example, some $2 trillion of such debt issued by federal government agencies. This is not included in federal debt figures though in many cases the bonds are understood by buyers to be guaranteed by the federal government. Examples are federal loans to farmers or Federal National Mortgage Association-backed mortgage securities. It does not include, however, offshore eurodollar debt, nor un-funded government pension plans such as social security, which are promises to pay at some future date.

The worrying Kondratieff point is that the bigger the debt ratio, the more severe the subsequent deflation needed to wipe out the debt. In previous contractions the deflationary process quickly restored the debt to currency ratio to 10:1. At the trough of the Depression, says Kirkland, the debt:currency ratio usually approached 5:1. He writes:

> At this level, the volume of business and consumer lending is at a cyclical low, and the banking system is accumulating monetary gold at a record rate to help forestall massive withdrawals. From this level, robust economic growth is once again able to resume since banking liquidity is high and most of the debt excesses have been removed from the financial system.

Such a deflation would be of a scale that provokes crisis actions like the arbitrary 70 per cent devaluation of the dollar against gold. This is what president Franklin D. Roosevelt resorted to in 1933 when he compulsorily bought gold and gold certificates (but not, to the profit of investors holding them, gold mining shares) from private and foreign holders at $20.67 an ounce and then revalued gold at $32 per ounce. This is why money manager Richard Thornton reckons that ultimately gold will have to be revalued, though this time against the yen in a bid to reliquify the world economy out of deflationary contraction and raise the general price level.

The Investment Conclusions

What are the investment conclusions for those who find this view of the world half credible? The most important is not to live beyond one's means and to avoid debt as much as possible, especially if it is collateralized against overvalued financial securities or inflated asset values such as property located in and around the world's financial centres. For just as property prices crashed in Houston with the fall in the oil price, so they will plunge in London, New York, and Tokyo when paper prosperity evaporates and the money industry withers.

This advice again flies in the face of conventional wisdom. With many governments still encouraging home buyers to go heavily into debt by letting them offset mortgage interest payments against their income taxes, this is a temptation many middle class households still find hard to resist. In America the disease has grown even worse with the arrival of the seductively named 'home equity loans'. These were a product of America's 1986 tax reform which left home equity mortgage financing as the last major tax-deductible item. Home owners who had not already mort-gaged the whole of the current value of their house were able to raise new deductible loans against the remaining equity in their homes to buy cars, boats or, in some cases, just spend since some banks, desperate for loan business, have issued credit cards against home equity loans. If, on a conservative estimate, home values fall only 20–30 per cent in the next downturn (and they have already fallen by some 50 per cent in Houston) then today's home equity fad will prove a disastrous spin-off of tax reform. In reality, however, home values are likely to fall further. In fact so great could be the devastation wrought on middle class wealth that government-enforced mortgage holidays seem a strong prob-ability.

The middle classes and upwardly mobile blue-collar classes tend to have most of their wealth invested in property because a home is the first asset they aspire to own. It is also regarded as a safe investment. Davidson quotes Federal Reserve figures which show that the top 10 per cent of America's income owners owned 85 per cent of outstanding shares but only 30 per cent of outstanding property. The middle classes owned nearly all the remaining property. That means they are over-invested in an investment category which is in a long-term down trend.

For, contrary to another popular conventional wisdom, proper-ty and land do not always increase in value. Farmland has been a disaster in the 1980s, contrary to the perceived wisdom of the inflationary 1970s. Urban property will be the same. In deflation-ary conditions it makes no sense to be over exposed to property, especially on a heavily mortgaged basis. Also because property is such an emotional investment – the 'home' is the last thing most families want to sell – the inevitable liquidation in today's overheated property markets will be excruciatingly slow as home owners hang on desperately in the hope of an upturn. That means recovery will not occur until most of those weak holders are finally shaken out.

So debt, property, and other traditional inflation hedges should be avoided. Conservative investors should stay in cash and safe equivalents. For a depression the best combination is a mixture of holdings in various currencies. Americans, for example, who hold only dollars, risk a massive depreciation in their relative wealth, especially if their government tries to print its way out, perhaps the most likely course of action. Dollar holdings should be in treasury bills bought direct from the Federal Reserve since there is always a risk that banks might go bust.

Gold

What about gold? This is the hardest question. A period of deflation should, at least initially, mean a sharp fall in the gold price. This is what many deflationists expect to happen. They expect gold will fall to as low as $200 an ounce at the depth of the depression. Support for this view was provided by the October 1987 stock market crash. Despite the historic size of the fall and the extent of the global panic the price of gold and gold mining shares actually fell while bonds rose, indicating the financial markets sniffed deflation ahead.

But some long-wave pundits are less sure. They contend that gold is already very cheap, having fallen in terms of hard currencies such as the yen, D-Mark, or Swiss franc. So if it has risen in dollar terms, that may be because the gold market has already begun to discount the long-term depreciation of the dollar. That would suggest that gold should start being accumulated now, while even short-term bears would probably agree that some gold, say 5–10 per cent of total assets, should be held as general insurance against financial or political disasters. Kondratieff followers all expect to buy gold at the depth of the depression since it will then only be a matter of time before it is remonetized, officially or unofficially, as confidence in the dollar and other paper money evaporates.

There is another school of thought, though, which argues that gold should be accumulated now, regardless of whether the nature of the financial collapse is deflationary, inflationary, or an unholy combination of both. These are the 'gold bugs'. As their name implies the only assets they believe in owning are gold bullion and shares in gold mining companies. Otherwise they have a distrust, if not horror, for all forms of paper money. Their case merits discussion not only because they predict that the world is on the verge of one of the biggest transfers of wealth ever seen between those who hold gold and those who do not, but because gold bugs have grown rich in the past thirty years by practising what they preach.

George Soros describes gold, somewhat sarcastically, as 'useful for people who do not believe in the system'. The problem with this view is that the world's central banks own about 35 per cent of the world's gold supplies and have done so for years. If gold is so antedeluvian, why do central banks still own so much of it? The reason is that history shows that gold never defaults. Robert Holzach, who retired as chairman of U.B.S., Switzerland's biggest bank, in April 1987, said to me in an interview in September 1987: 'I believe in gold.' He explained: 'There is a strong belief in many countries in gold. Declarations can be made by central banks that gold is demonetarized but people pay no attention.' So human beings view gold, not paper money, as the ultimate store of value. Gold is not just another commodity. As Richard Thornton says, you cannot have a glut of gold.

A doyen or 'granddaddy' of the gold bugs, as he has been called, is John Exter. A long-term resident of New Jersey, now in his seventies, Exter is a lively, if crustly individual who has adhered stubbornly to his views on sound money. Unlike many gold bugs he is also not an outsider, addicted to conspiracy theories. Rather he spent six years as a vice-president of the Federal Reserve of New York, including spells advising the central banks of Ceylon and the Philippines, and another six years at National City Bank (now Citibank).

Exter is, therefore, acquainted with both the central banking and commercial banking mentality. He has become a wealthy man putting his money where his mouth is by investing in gold. He bought his first gold coins and gold shares in the spring of 1962 as the Kennedy administration embarked on the policy of massive dollar debt financing which has grown, seemingly inexorably, ever since. Since 1965 he has bought nothing but gold-related investments. With gold then fixed at $35 Exter told his wife she could buy all the gold jewellery she wanted as he simply could not conceive of the price of gold not going up. As gold has subsequently climbed in value she has had to remove the jewellery to the safety deposit box.

Exter piled into gold in the 1960s because he was convinced that the Americans would have to close what was known then as the 'gold window' and let the price of gold float. This duly happened on 15 August 1971. Until that date holders of dollars could exchange their dollar bills for gold at the fixed price of £35 an ounce – a great deal. With too many dollars in the system thanks to the burgeoning Eurodollar market and the Vietnam debt-financed war, this is precisely what an increasing number of dollar holders were doing. The result was a sharp drop in America's official gold supplies. These had fallen from $25bn. to $9bn. by the time Richard Nixon made his historic announcement that August day. This was the first official action on gold since Roosevelt had effectively nationalized it when, at the depth of the recession, he raised its price from $20.67 to $35 in 1933 in a bid to reliquify the economy. He also ordered that all gold coins be turned in to the Treasury under the threat of criminal sanctions. The Federal Reserve and banks dutifully handed over their gold bullion though, according to Exter, many private people did not obey what amounted to outright confiscation.

The Nixon move effectively ended the dollar's position as a reserve currency backed by hard money. Despite this the dollar has ever since retained the perception and status of a reserve currency. This has allowed America to enjoy the considerable luxury of borrowing its own money from the rest of the world. The consequence has been a reckless piling up of dollar debt. To Exter, that long-tolerated self-indulgence will be regretted since it has simply postponed and so made worse the day when the bill falls due. For the bigger the dollar debt grows, the worse will be the deflationary implosion when confidence in the currency disintegrates and the system contracts. This is why Exter expects gold to go through $1,000 'almost certainly in 1988'. It is also why he has never sold any of his gold investments; not even in 1980 when gold touched $850 (he admits to thinking about selling then), even though it subsequently fell back to under $300. Exter is then no trader. A true believer, he is in for the long haul though, as he admits, it can sometimes seem more like a roller-coaster ride. For in a world of floating exchange rates the gold price has been extremely volatile.

Why is Exter so convinced? His investment policy rests on his conviction that America's central bank in the form of the Federal Reserve has shamelessly abused the dollar's privileged status as the world's reserve currency, a position which, despite some talk of a move to a yen world, is still taken for granted. Exter argues that when foreigners lose faith in the dollar the consequences will be both devastating and deflationary since it will precipitate a scramble for liquidity. He comments: 'The worldwide confidence in the dollar as a reserve currency is a time bomb that could explode in our faces at any moment.'

Exter is, therefore, an arch deflationist, which makes him an unusual type of gold bug. Most believers in gold fret about the return of double-figure inflation. His belief that gold will benefit from deflation needs some explaining. He argues that gold will rise because it is the only true money left since cash, in contrast to the position in the 1930s, is no longer backed by gold. Instead, to borrow Exter's graphic phrase, paper money has been reduced to an 'I.O.U. nothing'. In his view the next deflation will be much worse than the Great Depression precisely because the dollar is the biggest reserve currency ever seen and because other countries have foolishly continued to believe in it for so long, despite the escalation of dollar debt. In early 1987, in a paper entitled 'The end of the Dollar as the world's reserve currency', Exter wrote:

> For the rest of the world living with the dollar is like being in a rowboat with an elephant . . . A run on the dollar will bring the great contraction, and one far greater than the Great Depression, simply because there is no lender of last resort to the Fed. That is where the buck stops. A paper money system works as long as it explodes, but collapses when the explosion becomes implosion.

One of the seminal experiences for Exter in arriving at this conclusion occurred at the Fed. Already a believer in the gold standard, despite having Keynsianism 'pumped' into him at Harvard, Exter was shocked when in 1958 he was instructed to pay out $2.25bn. of gold – 2,250 tons of at it at $35 an ounce – because the authorities wanted to use the money raised to buy government securities and so boost the money supply to help combat a mini-recession. All Exter could see was the net result; that the Fed had substituted $2.25bn. of paper for its equivalent in gold. This confirmed him in his view that central banks should only hold gold and that, if they insisted on holding paper money, it should at least be in foreign currencies not their own currency which they could simply print. Exter cites Taiwan's central bank, where he has for years played an advisory role, as a virtuous example. The Central Bank of China, as it is known, has no domestic currency assets whatsoever. The government and the commercial banks lend to the central bank not, as in most countries, the other way round. By mid-1987 Taiwan, a country of only 19 million people, had foreign exchange reserves of around $70bn. and only $3bn. of foreign currency debt. Naturally Exter would prefer these foreign-exchange reserves to be held in gold rather than in depreciating dollars, as they mostly are, though as a man of the world he appreciates the political realities that make this necessary. The Taiwanese central bank has run such a conservative policy for the same reason as West Germany's Bundesbank still does. Like Germany in the 1920s under the Weimer Republic, China suffered terrible hyper-inflation in the 1940s prior to the Communist revolution in 1949.

Despite his 1958 experience at the Fed, Exter recalls that the escalation of dollar debt did not really get under way until the arrival in power of the Kennedy administration, which is also when he started buying gold himself. Since then the Fed has been printing money and creating dollar credit exponentially. It has got away with this because the dollar has been treated by foreigners as a reserve currency. Exter likens the process to a number of reservoirs connected to each other by channels. If water is poured into one reservoir it will then flow into the others until a new equilibrium is reached. The same holds true with foreign currencies. Money, like water, runs between all currencies. If one country creates more of its money than the others, as the Fed has consistently done, then dollars will flow out of that country into the others. Hence the Eurodollar market.

If, as Exter defines it, the acid test of a true reserve currency is that the rest of the world is willing to buy and hold it in the face of the growing profligacy of its own central bank and government, then the dollar has continued to pass that test, making sure the final resolution of the imbalance will be even worse. Contrast that with France after François Mitterand came to power in 1981. Socialist policies led to a sharp fall in the franc and double-figure interest rates as the foreign-exchange market voted with its feet. The French government was soon forced to return to more orthodox policies. Another example is Britain in the 1960s and 1970s, a country which was continuously punished by the financial markets with intermittent sterling crises and currency devaluations.

The dollar situation reached its logical absurdity between 1981 and 1985, despite America's soaring balance of payments' deficit, as Exter describes in his paper:

From 1981 to February 1985, for example, foreign central banks and private people bought even more dollars than we lost through growing payments' deficits, so the dollar actually appreciated against foreign currencies by as much as 70–80 per cent. That could never have happened to any other currency. And we shall never see it happen again in the dollar.

To Exter, a sign of just how sick the system had become occurred in 1984 with the bail-out and effective nationalization of Continental Illinois. The run on the Chicago bank, during which some \$20bn. worth of deposits was withdrawn, was the biggest in commercial banking history. The Federal Deposit Insurance Corporation stopped the run only by going far beyond its statutory duty and guaranteeing all depositors and creditors of the bank, not just individuals with deposits of up to \$100,000. That meant the American tax payer bailing out offshore Eurodollar deposits held in Swiss and other bank accounts, as well as all certificates of deposit issued by the Chicago bank. Even then the authorities were lucky because the run did not extend to other banks. So though the Continental episode might show good crisis management by former Fed chairman Volker (Exter's former colleague at the New York Fed) in that the run did not extend to other institutions, no one can pretend that the resolution of the crisis was exactly satisfactory. It does not take great guts to agree to print billions of dollars which is what the Fed effectively did to save Continental. The tough decision, politically and financially, is to say no.

To the financial markets, Continental Illinois was both precedent and signal that American banks would always be bailed out, whatever the final cost to the taxpayer and the budget deficit. To Exter, this episode underlined the lengths to which the authorities will go to avoid a financial crisis, even if putting off pain today only means more pain tomorrow. This led him to change his opinion on what would precipitate the scramble for liquidity he is forecasting. It would no longer, as he once thought, be caused by a particular bank or country defaulting because the Fed will always bail out the defaulter, printing more paper dollars, however many billions are required. That means the collapse will be triggered by a loss of confidence in the dollar and so a run on the Fed itself. And it has no lender of last resort.

This process of collapsing confidence in the dollar is already under way. In his February 1987 paper Exter said:

Over the last twenty-five years the United States has become by far
the world's largest debtor, most importantly to central banks that,
instead of gold, have bought dollars and put them mostly into
treasury bills as reserve currency backing for their own currencies.
But private foreigners have bought even more dollars than central
banks and have invested them differently, mostly in bonds, stocks,
real estate, plant, and equipment. The grand total runs into
hundreds of billions.

We can now see private foreigners beginning to get out which is
weakening the dollar itself and also all markets in which they have
invested. The bigger and stronger foreign central banks in the
Group of Five, or Seven, will try to support the dollar by buying
more, (in 1987 they bought more than $100bn. worth of dollars) but
they dare not buy enough to stem the private tide, so will at some
point give up and let the marketplace take over. The dollar will
weaken more than ever.

When that crisis of confidence finally sets in, marking the end of
the post-1945 economic order based on a dollar world and with it
the end of Pax Americana, the Federal Reserve will be powerless
to thwart the deflationary contraction. The mass scramble for true
liquidity, in Exter's view, will at some point turn into a demand
for gold as people gradually comprehend that paper money is not
backed by anything and, therefore, has no intrinsic value. As that
rush for liquidity gathers pace, the banking system will contract.
Banks will stop lending. Borrowers will stop borrowing. In these
circumstances the Federal Reserve can print all the dollars it
wants but it will increasingly be pushing on a string. Nor is it
even that long a piece of string. Contrary to the status it was
accorded at the height of Paul Volker's tenure when the Federal
Reserve was perceived as all powerful if not the saviour of America
and world capitalism, the twelve Federal Reserve banks form
only a minuscule part of the international monetary system,
partly as a result of the mushrooming of the offshore financial
markets.

This was shown by James Grant in his newsletter in May 1987
when he compared the size of the Federal Reserve's assets to that
of certain private financial institutions. He wrote:

At year-end 1986, Citicorp reported almost $200 billion in assets, no
less than 74% of the Fed's total. To put the matter in another light,
the Fed at year-end was not quite as big as Salomon Brothers,
Shearson Lehman Brothers, Merrill Lynch, First Boston and
Goldman Sachs combined.

Or put another way, Grant noted that the Fed's $252.7bn. of assets at the end of 1986 was less than the $252.7bn. reported by Dai-Ichi Kangyo Bank, Japan's largest bank, on 30 September 1986.

Once set in, depressions have a habit of hanging around. It is hard to persuade banks to start lending again and companies to resume borrowing. Referring back to the 1930s Exter writes:

> The economy was so liquid that the treasury bill rate fell to one eighth of a percentage point. As late as 1940 we still had falling prices, deflation. Only the enormous government borrowing and spending of World War II made them rise at last.

So in such parlous circumstances war can appear one obvious way out.

In fact Exter reckons the dollar system have already begun contracting despite (until early 1987) a loose money policy in America and the largest government deficits ever. The growth of the big American banks' reserves at the Fed has slowed sharply during the past year. If banks are lending less they will not need to tap all their reserves which means the Fed could at some stage find itself pushing on that proverbial string.

If we are already in underlying deflation readers of the financial press in 1987 would have been forgiven for thinking that gold rose that year because of renewed inflation fears. North American (mostly Canadian) gold shares soared in an atmosphere which to many deflationists looked like a classic speculative top. The mining shares were helped on their way by American investors' reluctance to hold South African gold shares, less because of moral concerns than so far exaggerated worries about political risk. The gold euphoria was also reflected in a huge increase in gold production worldwide. In Australia, for example, gold production in 1987 was up fourfold since 1981. World production is now running at a record 1,375 tons a year compared to just 700 tons after the Second World War. Rising prices and rising production in the gold industry have triggered, as always, a flurry of unsavoury 'promoters' on to the scene pushing dubious mining ventures, another normal sign of a cyclical top. A *Barrons* article in June 1987 titled 'Glut In Gold' remarked:

> It is difficult these days to find a spot on the globe – from South Korea to South Carolina, from Ireland to Saudi Arabia, from Zimbabwe to Brazil – where someone is not looking for gold . . .

While it may have taken $850-an-ounce gold to get this exploration juggernaut rolling in 1980, stopping it may take prices far lower than any gold bug can envision.

This is why other long-term deflationists with similar views of the world to Exter are predicting a much lower gold price short-term as a recession sets in. And, sure enough, when share-prices crashed last October the price of gold mining shares collapsed too, and have continued to be weak since. Indeed, they fell more than many other shares indicating that the market sensed lower gold prices ahead. Kirkland estimates that the historical value of gold *vis-à-vis* other commodities is about $200 an ounce which means it was trading for most of 1987 at more than a 100 per cent premium. No wonder gold mining is hot. Producers of other metals have been switching to gold production because it is so much more profitable.

The key question then is, if the deflationist view is right and the credit system contracts and there is a rush for cash, how long will it take people to realize in an 'I.O.U.-nothing' world the best refuge is gold. Exter writes: '*Gradually* they [Americans] and foreigners, too, will realize they are caught in the collapse of the whole paper I.O.U.-nothing money system.' How long is gradually?

To died-in-the-wool gold bugs like Exter, already well up on their money (if well down from the 1980 high), timing is not the issue. For that reason he is unlikely to panic if gold prices fall sharply when investors suddenly realize, as they did after October's stock market crash, that they should be worrying more about encroaching deflation than raging inflation. Indeed that to Exter would be merely a sign to load up on more gold as he confidently awaits 'the greatest run on gold ever seen'. It will be the greatest, he argues, because this will be the first depression to occur where no major currency is gold-backed. In the 1930s most countries remained on gold.

If Exter's views seem extreme it should be stressed that, as an American, he does not revel at the prospect of the looming destruction of the dollar. He is simply pointing out the consequences of the actions he has been warning against for the past twenty-five years. Whatever one may think of the analysis, one stark fact seems unassailable. If the world does suffer another severe economic contraction, and inflation breeds deflation as the long wave suggests, then it is mere common sense that the flight to quality will include a flight to gold if cash (unlike in the 1930s) is no longer back by gold. That means that anyone who worries about such an outcome should start buying gold now, unless they think that human beings have, for some mysterious reason, abandoned their centuries-long love affair with the yellow metal, or some new technology will be discovered to manufacture gold. Central banks will, sure enough, soon start adding to their gold supplies for the first time since the gold window was closed.

As for those worried about short-term price movements, a substantial decline from recent euphoria at the $500 level seems probable but a break to under $200 less so. To see why look at a chart of the gold price in yen or the Swiss franc. It has barely risen against either currency. The reason is that the dollar is not what it was and the gold market, as one of the financial world's most sensitive indicators, is already reflecting that fact. But perhaps the last grim word on what could be coming should be left with Exter. 'If that Depression [the 1930's] lasted for more than a decade, you can see that this one will be worse. I remember that one well, but shall not live to see the end of this one.'

LENDING

*'Nobody can be indebted for ever. No person,
no country, no government. No one.'*
Dr Robert Holzach, chairman U.B.S.
(Union Bank of Switzerland), 1987

Third World Debt

The occasion was an annual meeting of one of those supra-national do-gooding organizations, the likes of the International Monetary Fund (I.M.F.) and the World Bank set up after the Second World War to police the international financial order. Sitting in a hotel lobby in early 1987, the banker leaned over in a conspiracy of frankness and whispered: 'Listen the only game in town is who can get to zero first.' His subject was what has become known as *the* debt crisis, though there is more than one such crisis. He was referring to his fellow commercial bankers' continuing efforts to put their Third World debt exposure behind them in as painless a manner as possible without having to lend the debtor countries any more money.

The remark may have been cynical but it had the merit of being honest. For the banker had put his finger on the basic flaw of the American-sponsored Baker Plan (named after the then Treasury Secretary James Baker) which was still the subject of much rhetoric at this same meeting. This sought, as a quid pro quo, that in return for debtor countries' good behaviour in terms of practising 'orthodox' economic management, the banks would go on lending them more money to finance long-term growth.

The plan failed first because the banks did not want to lend new money after bad unless they knew it was coming straight back to them in the form of interest payments and second, because the most heavily indebted countries were near reaching the end of their tether. They have suffered a net outflow of capital of $140bn. between 1983 and 1987 through paying interest to foreign bankers to service their debt and yet they find their countries more in debt than ever as the principal they owe the banks continues to grow. Their predicament is not a short-term cash flow problem but a structural one. Without any improvement in their fundamental position and with their populations increasingly restless, having lived through a depression worse in terms of a decline in living standards than they endured during the 1930s, it is hardly surprising that politicians in power in these countries have increasingly realized that the best way of dealing with the banks, Washington, the World Bank and the I.M.F. is by applying leverage. That usually means threatening to default.

By September 1987 and the annual I.M.F. meeting in Washington the Baker Plan and the make-believe game of Third World debt rescheduling was, at least tacitly, laid to rest. This amounted to a change in the ground rules. The show had run five years. The problem is that, with the Baker Plan fundamentally flawed because the banks will not lend the necessary new money, there is nothing to replace it. Ever since 1982 and the onset of the Third World debt crisis when Mexico came to the brink of default and Paul Volker arranged his first rescheduling bail-out, these I.M.F. meetings have become more than ever media events, the money world's equivalent of the 'Group of Five' talking shops, and a surreal symbol of the rescheduling fantasy where both creditors and debtors argue over basis-point spreads while back home the debtor countries slide inexorably towards default.

Brazil brought the game temporarily to a halt in February 1987 by unilaterally freezing interest payments on the $68bn. of debt it then owed foreign banks. Three months later Citicorp, the biggest creditor bank, responded. Because it was no longer receiving interest income from its biggest creditor and so one of its major source of profits – Brazilians in recent years have grown used to joking that Citicorp is the country's biggest shareholder – chairman John Reed announced the bank was making a special loan-loss reserve of $3bn. in the second quarter against its Third World debt exposure of $14.8bn. This forced all of America's other major banks, including the weakest financially such as Bank of America and Manufacturers Hanover, to follow suit. The result was that in the second quarter of 1987 American banks reported their worst results since the 1930s, their combined losses totalling $10.3bn. Although few noticed, this amounted to classic deflation.

Misappropriated capital in the form of money badly lent, led to the destruction of wealth. The bankers would dispute this. Technically reserves against Third World debt form part of a bank's 'primary capital' though regulators will soon amend this make-believe definition of capital. That will bring practice in line with common sense. As the bank credit ratings' agency, International Bank Credit Analysis, commented in a report: 'No mildly intelligent individual would dream of agreeing that reserves for L.D.C.s (less-developed countries) debt should be part of a bank's capital.' Indeed stock market investors have long taken the view that the only capital that counts, in the sense of representing real value, is shareholders' equity and retained profits. The rest is just funny money. That is why when Citicorp announced its $3bn. provision, its share price rose. Investors welcomed the long-overdue recognition of reality.

America's big banks are still not yet out of the woods. In the case of the money centre New York banks their reserves still only cover about 25–30 per cent of their Third World debt exposure, whereas most of America's regional banks raised their loan-loss reserves to 50 per cent of Third World debt exposure at the beginning of 1988. They did so because they could afford to. To reserve is a sign of strength in banking because it is clear to everyone involved that the final losses will be greater than 25 per cent. This is also understood by the small, secondary market in Third World debt. Prices fell throughout 1987. By the end of the year the paper of all three big debtor countries – Brazil, Mexico, and Argentina – was trading at a more than a 50 per cent discount to face value.

It does not take a financial genius to appreciate that in such circumstances it could one day be in the interests of the debtor countries to make militant noises (i.e. declaring they will not pay interest and threatening default) in order to drive down the value of their debt. When the situation becomes sufficiently dire, as with Peru whose debt in September 1987 was valued at 6 or a 94 per cent discount to face value, the country then has the option of buying all its debt in (i.e. retiring it) at the market price. This is just what tiny Bolivia proposed, a neat free-market solution to solving the debt problem if not a palatable one to the bankers. (In March 1988 Bolivia brought back $308m. of its foreign debt of $620m. for $34m, or a price of 11 cents for every dollar of back debt.) It makes sense because there are no other buyers for the debt, save for the already exposed banks which might want to swap, say, their Brazilian debt for Mexican debt or vice versa.

Another option is that the big debtor countries will look increasingly to securitize their debt, converting it into bonds at a discount according to the prevailing market rate. Banks may not want to swap their loans for such discounted debt securities but in a deadlock anything is better than outright default, which would mean they get nothing back. And outright default is the established historical precedent of sovereign lending.

In hindsight, the sudden headline-news discovery of the Third World debt problem in August 1982 becomes a tale of extraordinary naivety. It also displays a shocking ignorance of history. The story invites ominous parallels with those financiers in the 1980s who seemed to believe in the limitless potential of the global capital markets to work good, just as in the 1970s it was once fashionable to believe in the infinite possibilities of sovereign lending as a cure-all for the Third World's ills.

In the 1970s the fashionable job in the money business was to be a lending officer travelling the globe recycling OPEC's petro dollars to naturally welcoming Third World regimes, corrupt or otherwise. The more loans the lending officer made, the more successful he was. Few worried if the same loans would go sour five years later, least of all the loan officer who was not a shareholder in the bank.

By contrast, the hot area in the money business in the 1980s has been investment banking, which often meant peddling, securitizing or swapping some form of debt. The investment banker also won credit for doing deals, not for worrying whether the bond issues he worked on would one day default. There is a practical difference, however. The investment bank sells the bonds; the commercial bank keeps the loans on its balance sheet (though increasingly it now wants to sell them).

Partly because of the embarrassment of Third World debt hangovers the label 'commercial banker' had by the mid-1980s become a term of almost snobbish disdain among investment bankers. As for the specialist practice of sovereign lending, it existed only in diminished form. There is a legitimate reason for investment bankers' scorn for the hole the commercial banks dug for themselves in Latin America. It had all happened before. Back in 1936 Freeman Tilden remarked on the risks of lending to foreign countries, especially to Latin America where, as he put it, the money often ends up 'for the pocket benefit of the borrowing country's leading men'. Tilden, neither an economist nor a banker, analysed the dangers and consequences of sovereign lending with admirable clarity, employing an argument few would now dispute.

> When a nation borrows from the individuals of another nation, it is usually in the form either of a bank loan or the flotation of an issue of bonds. Presumably neither one nor the other can be sold without the tacit concurrence of the lender's government; so such loans . . . are distributed to the capitalist public with the inference that they are sound. This is pure illusion. These loans are probably the least secure, taken as whole, of any in the entire field of debt. If the borrowing state defaults or repudiates, the individual holder of exterior promises is luckless. So, too is even the largest bank, for there are only two ways to get the money back: either to take forcible possession of the defaulting country and operate it for the benefit of the creditors; or to distrain the persons or property of the citizens of the debtor nation when they can be found within the confines of the creditor nation. In theory both of these can be done; in practice neither is often done, for excellent reasons. One means a war, and the modern human baulks at such an extreme measure for debt collection; the other means gross injustice and endless litigation and difficulty.

Tilden was not writing in a vacuum but from recent experience. According to the appropriately titled book, *False Security*, published in 1937 and written by Bernard Reis, of the more than $6bn foreign bonds sold to the public in the years 1923–30 some $2bn-worth were then in default. That lesson was also not lost on contemporary bankers. Former bank chairman, George Moore (who worked through the Depression and retired in 1970) recalls how when he ran America's biggest bank, then called the National City Bank and now Citicorp, the firm policy was that only 10 per cent of the bank's capital could be lent to any single country save for Britain, West Germany, and Japan, where the limit was 20 per cent. The reason was that when banks lend dollars in a foreign country, they are not lending to a particular individual, company, or bureaucratic entity but to that country's central bank.

Continued enforcement of that policy would have reduced Citicorp's exposure to a fraction of what it subsequently grew to. Unfortunately, Walter Wriston, Moore's own chosen and talented successor, was more the technocrat than a student of history. As such he embraced sovereign lending in the now infamous comment: 'Countries do not go bankrupt.' Wriston did many fine things at Citicorp in terms of recognizing what he called the 'information revolution' and masterminding the bank's aggressive expansion into consumer banking, the world of credit cards and automatic teller machines. It is his misfortune that he is likely to be remembered by financial historians more for that one remark and his multi-billion-dollar legacy of bad debt.

Moore, as is to be expected from a Citicorp loyalist, blames the official institutions at least as much as the banks for the debt crisis. He has a point. Bankers may have behaved in their usual sheep-like manner, all rushing into the same area together. About the only major international bank which refrained was the maverick British-run Hong Kong and Shanghai Banking Corporation. But the official organizations, whose employees are the privileged recipients of tax-free salaries, were also guilty of turning a blind eye. Moore writes:

> It is clear that the banking system went too far in performing its duty to 'recycle' the huge funds transferred, on short notice, from oil consumers to oil producers when OPEC suddenly quadrupled the price of oil. This includes the World Bank, the IDB, the regional development banks and the central banks of the world which meet monthly at the Bank for International Settlements . . . Only the IMF and the BIS had the monthly statistics, or should have had them, to know of the extreme heights to which these debts had rapidly risen. Public statistics are available to the banking system at least a year late, after the fact. None of us in the banking business realised that the totals of the LDC debt had reached nearly $1 trillion in 1983.
>
> If the official organisations had acted as they should have, the huge totals we must now deal with would not have been reached. Easy come, easy go – most of the loans processed were wasted, used to permit nationals to export huge amounts of capital (not the Brazilians) or used to finance projects which did not contribute to the growth of export earnings for debt repayment. It was a wonderful party – a trillion-dollar binge; the banks thought they were making a lot of money, the borrowers never had it so good, all ordered more drinks as long as the bar was open. Meanwhile the responsible institutions were looking out of the window when they should have called a halt – stopped the party.

This seems a fair enough summary of the débâcle save for the fact that regulatory oversight does not absolve the banks from blame for their own reckless irresponsibility. At the end of it the biggest American banks had committed 90 per cent of their capital to four countries. But even if the responsibility lies with grasping debtors and over-lax regulators as well as deposit-insurance-cushioned bankers, so far the only ones to suffer the full consequences have been the poor and salaried middle classes in the most indebted countries; the wealthy elite just shifted their dollars offshore. This is why the banks will have to take even bigger losses. For, as deflation strengthens its grip on the world economy, masked until October 1987's crash by a speculative bubble in the financial markets, it becomes ever clearer that the world is not going to grow its way out of the Third World debt problem. Rather, these countries are sinking deeper into the mire. Each rescheduling merely adds on a new layer of debt, making the underlying problem worse, and so compounds the banks' irresponsibility and that of the regulators, be it the central bankers, I.M.F. or World Bank, all of which have collectively collaborated in the absurd fiction that rescheduling alone could solve the problem.

In a 1987 paper published by the Twentieth-Century Fund entitled 'The Mexican Debt Time Bomb', authors Norman Bailey, an economist and former member of Ronald Reagan's National Security Council and Richard Cohen, a Washington consultant, lambasted the wasted five years of rescheduling make-believe:

> Countries structurally unable to handle their debt levels in 1981 and 1982 are that much less able to cope with the substantially higher levels of debt they now have. The situation is very similar to that of the drug addict who requires ever-larger doses of narcotics, until his system breaks down entirely. But there is a difference. In the debt crisis the doctors themselves have been prescribing and administering successively larger doses of fatal drugs.

The parallel with the bail-out of Continental Illinois is clear. Regulators have been patting themselves on the back for 'crisis management' when all they have essentially been doing is throwing money at a problem, not dealing with it. This means that the burning question for the exposed banks is not how long they can keep extracting interest payments out of these faltering countries but rather whether they will eventually have to write off all their exposure, not just 25 per cent of it. That is why the sensible bankers, principally the Germans and Swiss, long ago made substantial provisions whereas the Americans and British only began to reserve in size in 1987. Deutsche Bank, for example, says it has written its Latin American loans down by 70 per cent.

The best form of salvage available is the increasingly faddish debt-equity swap. By swapping their debt at a discount for investment in the private sectors of Mexico, Brazil, Argentina, and other countries the bankers have a best-effort chance of earning their way out, while also investing in these countries as opposed to

158

bleeding them dry through extracting interest payments. Although only of limited application (free market Chile has gone the furthest reducing its foreign debt by some 15 per cent or $3bn. through such schemes) debt-equity swaps offer a preferable approach to hanging on in the fond but forlorn hope that debtor countries will keep up to date with interest payments.

The severity of the debt crisis has not eased despite five years of economic growth and falling interest rates. When America next goes into recession, Congress becomes more protectionist and Latin America is prevented from selling exports to its biggest market, there will be no incentive left for the debtors to keep paying interest. There is little enough already. That will pave the way for outright default. Brazil was in effective default from February 1987 to February 1988 when it agreed to make a goodwill payment of $356m. as a quid pro quo for receiving new money from the banks. It was only the biggest defaulter. Other countries which have not been paying interest include Bolivia, Costa Rica, Ecuador, and Peru.

Sensible bankers long ago accepted reality and looked to salvage as much from a bad situation as possible by investing in debt-equity swaps. They realize there is only a limited supply of attractive deals. With so much debt overhanging the market it made sense to be first in to get the pick of the equity investments available. Longer term the forced promotion of equity investment is likely to be viewed as the one positive outcome of this debt crisis. Still it is no panacea and shifts in political sentiment could at any time sour the climate for these deals in the debtor countries.

Nationalists will oppose them as promoting foreign ownership, as has happened in Brazil. This is important for, as Bailey and Cohen note, both the momentum and the leverage is increasingly shifting in favour of the debtors as it becomes clear that the rescheduling merry-go-round has succeeded only in making the original problem worse. They write:

> The IMF and central banks, which safeguard the integrity of the international financial system, have suffered a serious loss of leverage and moral authority. Today the leverage and momentum lie with the debtors. It is not something that the debtors actively sought, but rather something they were driven to by their inability to stimulate economic growth.

Bailey and Cohen argue that it is inevitable that debt relief will come for Mexico and the other debtors. The only question is whether it will come by desperate and unilateral repudiation – the precedent of history – or through some kind of 'reasoned and multilateral settlement' in which the rich countries such as Japan and West Germany provide billions of dollars in return for liberalization and deregulation of the debtor countries' usually heavily state regulated and protected economies. Writing in January 1987, they concluded: 'We have perhaps another six to 12 months before this question is answered; perhaps less.'

Nine months later in Washington at the I.M.F./World Bank meeting the odds had risen in favour of default. The American banks had increased their loan-loss reserves and Brazil had not paid any interest for six months. Mexico's stock market was booming, fuelled by the last big rescheduling fudge which saw the banks provide over $14bn. of new money in 1986. And in testimony to a maturing crisis, Wall Street investment bankers, including Drexel's junk-bond supremo Michael Milken, were flying around Latin America trying to figure out how to securitize Third World debt in a way that could persuade investors to buy it. If junk bonds or mortgages could turn out to be 1980s securitization bonanzas, they asked, why not Third World debt? These hopes always begged the key question of who was going to buy these securities. Despite steep declines in the prices of debt on the secondary market, investors have yet to be attracted. The reason is that yields are nowhere near high enough to compensate for the all too obvious risk of default. Thus the price of Mexican paper last September implied a yield of only around 15.5 per cent, compared with the 9 per cent which could be earned at that time on American treasury bonds and 13 per cent on Australian government bonds. As an added deterrent, there is also every prospect of further falls in prices rather than spectacular capital gains. Indeed, the only plausible reason to bet on secondary Third World loans is if another country follows Bolivia's example and says it will retire its own debt, creating a natural buyer. When Bolivia made this announcement the price of its paper doubled in a few weeks. That is rank speculation.

Virtually ignored throughout the five-year crisis have been disturbing signs that even the official institutions themselves are becoming part of the debt problem. Take the World Bank. Press reports surfaced in 1987 that the credit agencies were considering downgrading this august institution's bonds. The reason is that the World Bank itself has lent too much money thoughtlessly to the Third World and now risks not being paid back. As at 30 June 1986

$61bn. had been lent by the bank against its theoretically 'callable' (i.e. promised but not paid up) capital of $71bn. Of this total some $31bn. is pledged by the five nations with the largest subscription, America, Britain, Japan, France, and West Germany. Nor at the end of the day are bonds issued by the World Bank formally backed by governments. The bank's charter clearly states: 'Every security . . . issued by the Bank shall bear on its face a conspicuous statement to the effect that it is not an obligation of any government.' This looks suspiciously like another form of funny money, or what gold bugs like John Exter like to call an I.O.U.-nothing. As Franz Oppenheimer, a Washington-based lawyer, observed in the *American Spectator* of October 1987: 'The Bank has become a part of the international debt problem and is poorly positioned to become a part of its solution.'

With America itself heavily in debt, with the official institutions impotent if not also financially embarrassed, and with the creditor nations such as Japan and West Germany unwilling to take up the slack, the prospects for a multilateral solution look slim indeed. Betting men would bet against it and for default. That does not necessarily mean the world will wake up one day and read in the headlines 'Latin America Defaults!' Such an organized debtor's cartel seems unlikely, if only because it is not in the nature of Latin American politicians to be so organized or so united. Rather, the default will be gradual, moving from the implicit to the explicit.

The sequel will be deflationary as the banks will be forced to contract because they will have less money to lend. There will be several consequences, not all of them bad. First, new lenders and investors in these indebted countries may actually start putting money back in. The usually ignored reason is that, with the debt slates wiped clean, these countries will, however gradually, once again become attractive areas for investment because they will be starting from scratch. Most importantly, capital will no longer be sucked out, paying foreign bankers interest. Those who act first taking advantage of bargain-basement prices will profit the most. Bankers will deny this. They claim that if a country defaults no one will invest or lend to them again. The truth is more complicated.

Second, the official, multilateral institutions will be discredited, both for their laxity in ignoring the piling up of Third World debt and, more recently, for their complicity in, if not active encouragement of, the five years of rescheduling make-believe. Third, the commercial banks will be severely weakened. Their vulnerability became only too clear with Citicorp's 1987 $3bn. provision. A year after becoming the first American bank to earn $1bn. in a year, the same bank became the first to lose a billion. However, it is not the most vulnerable. If either San Francisco-based Bank of America or New York-based Manufacturers Hanover raised their loan-loss reserves to 50 per cent of their Third World debt exposure their entire equity would be wiped out.

The banks were even more vulnerable when the debt crisis broke with Mexico's declaration of insolvency in August 1982. Then a full-scale default would have been terminal for many major banks. Now there is a good chance of painful recovery for most providing the other lending areas they have expanded into since, such as credit cards and home mortgages, do not suddenly turn sour at the same time, a development which is not unlikely. This is the only positive outcome of rescheduling. It gave the banks time to put their house in order. That, however, does not compensate for the irresponsibility of letting the debtors sink deeper in hock. It should also be remembered that industrial America has also suffered at the bankers' expense. For the impoverishment of Latin America meant it was no longer a customer for industrial America's goods. This is one, often-ignored reason for the size and duration of America's trade deficit. In the 1970s Latin America was a huge market for American exports. In the 1980s these same countries have been forced to curtail imports at the I.M.F.'s prodding to produce the trade surpluses to pay the interest bills of the foreign bankers. That meant few orders for American industry.

America's 'Money-Centre' Banks

In terms of vulnerability to Third World debt shocks, America's money-centre banks remain by far the most exposed of the world's banks. This is clear from the top American eleven banks' special provisions of $12.7bn. in 1987. These had the effect of virtually wiping out all the equity these same banks had built up since the onset of the debt crisis in 1982. That means the big American banks are not well positioned for further write-offs which look inevitable. After making its $3bn. loan-loss reserve and raising in the nick of time $1bn. of equity on the stock market in September 1987 (a mere month before the crash), Citicorp still only had a hard core (i.e. excluding funny-money accounting items such as goodwill) equity-to-assets ratio of 2.7 per cent. By contrast the strongest New York money-centre bank, J. P. Morgan, had an equity-to-assets ratio of 6 per cent and it did not sell any shares in 1987. Nor is Citicorp the weakest. San Francisco-based Bank of America, Manufacturers Hanover, Chase Manhattan, and Chemical are all more vulnerable than Citicorp to further write-downs. This is why the New York money-centre banks decided not to follow America's biggest regional banks at the start of 1988 and raise their loan-loss reserves to 50 per cent of Third World debt exposure. The system could not have stood the strain, even though both Bankers Trusts and J. P. Morgan could have afforded it. Clearly, any time a bank makes a provision against its reserves, it becomes that much more reluctant to lend any new money to the same countries against which it has already set aside huge reserves on existing loans. If this trend continues the New York money-centre banks will be the only banks left lending new money to Latin America.

It is also instructive to compare the position of the American banks with their Japanese counterparts. A 1987 IBCA study shows how the Japanese banks' assets-to-equity ratios are hugely understated because their large portfolios of Japanese shares are valued at cost rather than market value. Revalued to 70 per cent of their market value (to allow for some of the craziness of the Tokyo stock market) and their equity-to-assets ratios soar close to 10 per cent. Even more striking, the undervaluation of each of the Japanese banks' share portfolios is about as large as the total published equity of the top eleven American banks combined. That may say something about the inflated values of the Japanese stock market. But it also says something about the financial weakness of America's biggest banks.

If the debt crisis has caused a big hole in the major American banks' balance sheets, the demise of sovereign lending has also forced them to find different ways of lending other people's money, as has the loss of traditional corporate lending business to securitization. They have responded by going after the consumer in two main areas: lending on home mortgages and credit cards. Citicorp now makes most of its money in these two businesses. Mortgages are viewed as a safe bet because the home is the last loan most people will default on, while credit cards are much more profitable than any of the banks' other businesses because the interest charged to borrowers is so much higher than the banks' cost of funds. Card holders accept these high interest rates because they are prepared to pay for plastic's sheer convenience. However, the result is that banks have become very exposed to the consumer at a time when consumer debt in America has reached record highs and the savings rate a record low – less than 4 per cent of disposable income in 1987. Tax reform and the 'home equity' mortgage has only compounded the problem. As for plastic, the credit card market is saturated. The more cards the banks push out, the less they go to customers worth having.

By the second half of the 1980s the banks had found another favourite business, namely lending to leveraged buy-outs. This again offers tremendous returns but also large risks since all such deals involve the substitution of debt for equity. In the most aggressive L.B.O.s it can mean the banks and junk-bond investors lending $100 to buyers of a company which ends up with only $10 in equity capital. The exposure of banks to this business is not small. According to a December 1987 report produced by Prudential-Bache, the top twenty-one American banks have a combined exposure to L.B.O.s (and rising) of $17bn. which is about a quarter of these same banks' exposure to Third World debtors. Yet in a slump many of these loans would inevitably go sour.

The banks cannot really be blamed for this deterioration in the quality of their business. Desperate to lend, they are simply reacting to competitive and legal pressures and doing business where they are allowed to. The continued enforcement of Glass-Steagall means that the banks find themselves trying to run a late-twentieth-century business according to early-twentieth-century rules. It has caused them to lose much of their traditional corporate business and their best clients to the investment banks since companies increasingly raise finance by issuing securities rather than borrowing from a bank. Since 1978 the number of corporate bonds has quadrupled. This huge loss of business has forced the big banks banks to push, so far as the law allows them, into the investment banks' business of issuing and dealing in securities. This has naturally been resisted by the Wall Street firms, anxious to preserve their lucrative oligopoly. However, Wall Street is not as united as it once was.

A strange thing happened at the Securities Industry Association's annual meeting in sunny Boca Raton, Florida in November 1986. The investment bankers were holding a debate on their industry when, horror of horrors, James Robinson, chairman and chief executive of American Express (which owns a majority interest in Shearson Lehman as well as a commercial bank) referred to Glass-Steagall as the 'regulatory version of the Maginot

Line'. He continued: 'It offers no real protection against invaders who have the capacity to outflank the defence . . . Banks and bank holding companies have totally outflanked the Glass-Steagall Maginot Line in a true blitzkrieg of diversification, powered by court victories and Fed decisions.'

Two senior representatives from Goldman Sachs and Morgan Stanley were present. They were appalled by the Amex chairman's remarks and immediately called an impromptu press conference to argue the merits of the rusty legal relic. In fact Robinson was only expressing the growing frustration many share with the regulatory anomalies posed by Glass-Steagall. In this respect London's Big Bang served the interest of the commercial banking lobby well. It rammed home two points. First, that Wall Street was losing business to London because it was only a half-free market. Second, it showed that the competitiveness of some of America's key players in the global money business was being undermined because they are not allowed complete freedom to play at home.

If attitudes are changing, they are also hardening. Charles Sanford, the tough chairman of Bankers Trust and formerly in charge of the bank's bond trading, has a neat definition of politics: 'Getting someone to do something for you'. It is, by his own admission, something the big commercial banks have not been good at. After years of being outlobbied by the Wall Street securities firms, which have proved themselves assiduous courters of Congressmen as well as generous contributors to political campaigns, the big money-centre banks are finally marshalling a half-decent lobbying effort. A group called the Financial Services Group represents their interests. Interestingly, firms with retail broking arms such as Shearson Lehman, Merrill Lynch, Pru-Bache, and Dean Witter are all members as well as industrial firms like Ford and General Motors, both of whom have been expanding into financial services through mortgage lending.

This shows that it is Wall Street's wholesale trading firms which are most concerned about preserving the status quo for as long as possible. By contrast, firms like Merrill Lynch and Shearson Lehman are in a more ambivalent position. Because they have a large retail business and take in funds from the general public through their money market accounts and mutual funds, they are more akin to deposit-gathering banks, like a Citibank or Chase Manhattan. Similarly, Bankers Trust, a purely wholesale operation, resembles a Salomon Brothers more than it does a Citicorp. It is all very confusing.

As the lobbying effort intensifies, the real progress to date has been made, as Robinson referred to, either in the courts or through Federal Reserve decisions. Congress has been more obstructionist hanging on to the populist myth that big banks are bad. Still, Glass-Steagall will go, perhaps even in 1988. In March the Senate banking committee overwhelmingly approving a bill which, if enacted, would end the separation of commercial and investment banking. The only issue is how long it will take to fall and whether its demise will be via legislation or, as at present, by gradual erosion in the marketplace.

Too Big To Fail

As the commercial banks are allowed to do more and more in the securities business the impact on the investment banks' profitability promises to be severe. An example is dealing in commercial paper. Dealing spreads have fallen significantly since the banks were allowed into the business, which has been bad news for Goldman Sachs and Merrill Lynch, the leaders in that market. A sign of the times came in September 1987 when Goldman backed down from its former strict policy of not sharing commercial paper deals with other firms. The move compares with Morgan Stanley's rude awakening a few years earlier when it suddenly realized that companies were no longer prepared to tolerate its insistence that it be the sole underwriter of corporate bond issues.

The last untampered bastion of Glass-Steagall is underwriting and trading in corporate bonds and shares. It will be the last to fall but its days are also numbered. If the arguments for dismantling Glass-Steagall are well known (and not even disputed in private save on grounds of self-interest by most investment bankers) the absurdity of present arrangements is best shown by the evolution of one banking institution, Bankers Trust. It has done as much as any lending institution to make the leap from commercial to investment banking to the point that it now likes to call itself a 'global merchant bank'.

This transformation is noteworthy since Bankers Trust did not have the corporate client list of J. P. Morgan, the other large wholesale bank, or the global branch network of a Citicorp to smooth the way. These three banks are the biggest domestic threats – foreigners, especially the Japanese, are another matter – to the Wall Street firms' cosy preeminence in the securities business. Bankers Trust's thrust has been to specialize in sales and trading. In the process it has become selling driven rather than, like most banks, lending driven. The bank uses its balance sheet as a securities and inventory account, just like Salomon does, rather than as an ultimate resting place for 'assets' which in banking means loans. In fact loans are increasingly viewed the same way as securities, as assets to be sold. Bankers Trust and Citicorp are leaders in the fast-growing business of loan selling. They have, for example, both sold billions of dollars-worth of L.B.O. loans to foreign and regional banks. The buyers like these loans because they pay high yields, reflecting the considerable risks. Both banks can be aggressive traders. In 1987 Bankers Trust made nearly $800m. from bond and foreign-exchange trading. Fortunately, Glass-Steagall prevented it from losing money trading shares during the October crash.

The ultimate Bankers Trust goal is to make all its assets as liquid (saleable) as possible. This flogger-of-paper role is only prudent since, as a wholesale bank with no retail deposits, Bankers Trust relies almost completely on the money markets for its funding. By contrast, old-fashioned banks with branch networks and tens of thousands of depositors are in a more comfortable position if only because their deposits cannot disappear as fast.

The speed with which interbank deposits can flee a troubled bank in today's electronic global markets became painfully clear in the Continental Illinois episode. The situation is all the more dangerous since some 50 per cent of the deposits in America's banking system are owned by foreigners, which again reflects banks' dependence on these interbank deposits. Naturally, all the depositors in Continental Illinois were paid off. The consequences of not doing so, in terms of the threat of a mass withdrawal of foreign money out of the American banking system, were simply too ghastly for anyone in Washington to contemplate, as senior officials would freely admit.

This blank-cheque approach may be explicable. But it has its own dangers. First, it confirms yet again how dependent the world's biggest economic power has become on foreign capital. Second, it demonstrates how the original purpose of deposit insurance to protect the needy has been corrupted to an unspoken assumption that the government will always prevent any major bank from going under, regardless of the costs. This 'too big to fail' philosophy has grave implications not only for the future bills facing the American tax payer but also for the integrity of the dollar. For when a central bank rescues a commercial bank on a massive scale, it inevitably means printing lots of dollars.

A conservative traditionalist banker like Hong Kong Bank chairman, Willie Purves, would doubtless view this whole trend with suspicion. The Hong Kong Bank acts as lender of last resort and quasi-central bank in the British colony and as a result has rescued a number of ailing banks. However, it has always opposed deposit insurance, arguing that it would encourage sloppy, risk-averse bank management. Doubtless Purves would find it amusing that Americans still have confidence in a deposit insurance system which holds only about $1 in its insurance fund for every $100 on deposit and which is guaranteed by a government which is itself broke. The financially astute Hong Kong Chinese would long ago have pulled their money out, insurance or no insurance, Hong Kong having a proud history of bank runs.

For the same cautious reasons Purves also views reliance on funding from the interbank market with great suspicion. This is instructive. For, in today's increasingly high-tech money industry it is important to remember that there are some big players who remain more comfortable playing under what others would consider old-fashioned, fuddy-duddy rules. Thus, the Hong Kong Bank's established policy is to be a net lender to the interbank market, not to borrow from it. Purves likes to say: 'We only lend money we have.' By that he means money deposited in the bank's branches, or what some bankers call 'warm-nose' deposits. That policy has stood the Hong Kong Bank in good stead in recent years. With some $92bn in assets, the bank ended 1986 as the world's fourteenth largest bank. Five years ago it ranked seventy-fifth. It is also the largest foreign bank in America with over $24bn. in assets through its wholly owned subsidiary, Buffalo New York State-based Marine Midland. True to Purves' conservative policy, some 25 per cent of the Hong Kong Bank's assets are held in cash or overnight deposits at other banks. That compares with the big American banks which are net borrowers. So when the American banks next run into trouble, be it from more Third World debt write-downs or a recession and an increase in bad loans at home, the Hong Kong Bank should have the financial resources to take advantage of others' weakened positions.

Another banker who believes in keeping his powder dry is Carl Reichardt, chairman of San Francisco-based Wells Fargo. To meet Reichardt, a former property developer, is refreshing because he acts and thinks more like a businessmen who has his own cash on the line than a banker who is playing around with other people's money. He also has lots of common sense, treating banking as just another business, which is, of course, what it is.

In his so far successful tenure at Wells Fargo Reichardt has distinguished himself by riding roughshod over a number of contemporary fads. For example, he substantially reduced Wells Fargo's presence in international and investment banking, two recently fashionable areas, and elected to concentrate on California instead. Reichardt's biggest coup was to buy another Californian bank, Crocker National, from Britain's Midland Bank. At the time the biggest banking merger ever in American history, Reichardt made Midland keep all Crocker's Third World debt. In return he got a clean bank at half the price banks usually sell for in America, almost doubled his market share in California and reduced his percentage of Third World debt from 14 per cent to 5 per cent of total assets. As this deal shows, Reichardt does not have his head buried in the sand on Third World debt. Wells Fargo is among the most reserved of America's major banks. After Citicorp raised its loan-loss reserves to cover 25 per cent of exposure, Reichardt exhibited an almost Swiss-like caution by raising Wells Fargo's to 40 per cent of exposure. Apparently he thought 50 per cent would have been more appropriate but did not want Wells Fargo to appear too much of an odd man out. Reichardt's other claim to fame is that he is one of the few bankers to close down two London offices. He had no sooner closed down Wells Fargo's branch there than he had to shut Crocker's too. Thus at a time when virtually every other financial institution in the world was expanding in London seemingly regardless of cost, Reichardt did the exact opposite. The stock market loved it. Wells' earnings and share price have way outperformed most of America's other big banks. Yet Reichardt is refraining from going on a spending spree, buying other American banks. He believes it is better to bide one's time. Because of the absurd overcapacity in lending which plagues American banking (the result of the long-standing ban on interstate banking as well as deposit insurance which keeps banks which would otherwise fail in business) he sees an inevitable shake-out looming. By way of example, there are 450 banks and 210 savings and loans associations in California alone. Reichardt says: 'My guess is that before this all tends there will be more banks for sale than buyers.' He should again be proved right.

America's Thrifts

The American mix of too many lenders combined with too little risk of failure – the legacy of blanket deposit insurance – is an intoxicating, if dangerous, cocktail. The ultimately disastrous consequences are best seen not in the banks but in the savings and loans associations, more commonly and also comically known as 'thrifts'. These take deposits and lend money for the purpose of house purchase, and so are similar to Britain's building societies. Unlike in Britain, though, the thrifts have become the Achilles' heel of the American financial system. In 1986 the 3,300 federally-insured thrifts made a combined net profit of $894m. Behind that bland figure lay some contrasting performances. Thrifts holding three-quarters of the industry's assets made some $9bn. The other 25 per cent lost $8bn. Estimates of the negative net worth (equity minus debt) of that latter group range up to nearly $70bn., a figure that far exceeds the net worth of the whole industry. The cash needs of these bleeding thrifts had by 1986 caused the thrift industry's insurance fund, the Federal Savings and Loan Insurance Corporation, to go bust too. The result in 1986 was a banking bill which included a $10.8bn. bail out or 'recapitalization' of F.S.L.I.C. This was not new money. Rather it was to be paid for over three years by bonds issued through a shell subsidiary by F.S.L.I.C.'s overseer and the thrift industry's regulator, the Federal Home Loan Banking Board. The interest on these bonds will be financed, in theory at least, by the insurance premiums paid to F.S.L.I.C. by still healthy thrifts.

Wherever the bill ultimately falls that $10.8bn., like a piece of sticking plaster, will barely patch up the thrifts' deficit. By May 1988 the money had been effectively used up.

The thrifts' problems have become so dire partly because of the severe recession suffered in parts of America throughout the 1980s, particularly in the agricultural states of the Midwest, in Texas and other oil states. When these local economies contracted, the thrifts were especially vulnerable, their fortunes rising and falling with the local economy where all their loans were concentrated. But their problems were compounded by their practice of breaking one of the cardinal rules of banking – borrowing short, lending long. The thrifts found themselves funding fixed-rate, thirty-year mortgages with short-term money, the cost of which fluctuated with the market. Thus in 1980, at the height of the Volker monetary squeeze, a thrift may have found itself earning 7 per cent on a thirty-year mortgage when its cost of money was nearer 20 per cent. This was clearly the quick path to insolvency.

This fundamental problem – bankers call it an interest rate 'mismatch' – has since been compounded by regulatory laxity and shady business practices. At the heart of the problem has been blanket deposit insurance in an increasingly deregulated industry which is now allowed to do much more than just provide thirty-year, fixed-rate mortgages. Unlike widget makers who make bad widgets or restaurants which serve poor food, badly run thrifts too often do not go out of business. The reason is not that an insolvent F.S.L.I.C. has gone out of its way to attract private buyers and so avoid the liquidation costs of paying back insured depositors. Sensing an eager seller and a federally insured franchise to exploit, thrifts became a playground for, at best, aggressive entrepreneurs, at worse crooks. Buyers gained control for next to nothing and embarked on reckless expansion, often paying themselves fat dividends and bonuses in the process. It has been a free lunch because deposit insurance removes the natural commercial incentive to control risk. If things go wrong the thrift's owner can keep doubling his bets knowing that the ultimate risks of having to pay back the depositors is not his but F.S.L.I.C.'s or rather the tax payer's.

So too often failed thrifts do not depart the industry. Rather, they go on lending. This has been a recipe for fraud as well as imprudent lending. Take just two examples. Thrift regulators have been trying to recover up to $100m. milked from one failed Texan thrift. The former bosses of another defunct Texan thrift have been accused of inflating its net worth for the purpose of paying themselves more than $20m. in dividends and $15m. in bonuses.

This is a sort of banking system more usually associated with banana republics than the world's premier capitalist power. Given the scale of abuses and the growing publicity devoted to it, it is perhaps astonishing that the depositors in the ailing thrifts have not begun pulling out their deposits *en masse*. The under-secretary of the Treasury, George Gould, and a former Wall Street investment banker, conceded as much in a conversation with me in his Washington office in late 1987. 'I am amazed at the resilience of the depositors' trust in the system,' he said. The reason for that trust is depositors' knowledge that the deposits are backed by F.S.L.I.C. up to $100,000. Few sensible people put more than $100,000 of their savings in an ailing thrift. Still there have been signs of depositor concern. In 1985 there was a run on thrifts in Ohio. The reason was that these thrifts' deposits were insured by the state government, not by the federal government. The problem was solved in the obvious way; by making the thrifts federally insured.

In 1987 deposit withdrawals began in Texas where low oil prices, collapsed home prices (down 50 per cent and more from the top), and sheer mismanagement have caused especially severe problems. To attract depositors some of the state's insolvent thrifts have had to offer six-month certificates of deposit, yielding up to 2.5 percentage points over the going market rate. Indeed, the bust thrifts' need for cash has spawned a new industry. These are the money brokers, who through hard sell, cold-calling tactics work the telephones persuading people to invest in high-yielding deposits. The selling point is always the same – federal deposit insurance. Because they have to try and pay for this more costly money, the bust thrifts have no choice but to embark on even riskier lending which will pay higher interest rates to earn the extra money they require to pay depositors. This breeds a vicious circle where losses cause the making of risky loans which, in turn, cause even bigger losses.

Given the state of affairs in his own state it was perhaps not so surprising when the Republican governor of Texas, William Clements, attacked the $10.8bn. F.S.L.I.C. bail-out in 1987 as 'an absolute fraud'. He went on to forecast that in the end depositors would only get 30 cents in the dollar back of the savings they have invested in these bust thrifts. In sounding a public alarm the governor was doing a service to his constituents, though both the industry and the Treasury resented his comments. The standard response was that Clements' remarks were 'irresponsible' because all thrift deposits up to $100,000 are guaranteed by the good faith of the federal government. The best answer to that is, So what? A prudent man would surely look not at the federal government's protestations of good faith but rather at its actions, and in particular the accumulation of its own debt. The American Treasury is, after all, the world's biggest borrower. He would conclude that it could not be trusted in money matters. To put money in bust thrifts for the sake of a few extra percentage points in interest is sheer folly.

Just how bad is the financial condition of the thrift industry? It is hard to pinpoint because of the funny-money accounting tolerated by the industry's deliberately lax regulators. As good an effort as any was made by McKinsey's Lowell Bryan in a study published in

172

July 1987. McKinsey estimated then that the equity ('tangible net worth' excluding goodwill and other funny-money items) of the entire savings and loan industry equaled only 1.5 per cent of its total end-1986 assets of $1.14 trillion, or a mere $17bn. The report divided the industry into three. About 40 per cent of the industry was flourishing. Another 30 per cent had capital equal to only 3–6 per cent of assets, which is below acceptable commercial banking practice of about 7 per cent of assets. The other 30 per cent or a total of 916 thrifts by McKinsey's calculation, was either bust or on the point of going bust.

Since then the picture has deteriorated. The losses are mounting up daily because the longer sick thrifts are not liquidated, the longer they can go on losing money. And, like compound interest, the losses grow geometrically. In the month of October 1987 alone, for example, Texas thrifts had operating losses of $800m. By the end of the same month the combined net worth of all Texas thrifts had deteriorated from $1.6bn. at the end of 1986 to minus $5.1bn. That was based on the official figures. In February 1988 reports surfaced in the *Dallas Times Herald* that federal regulators have deliberately tolerated laxer auditing standards for the worst thrifts, masking another $6bn. in losses.

Thrifts are not only exposed to the normal credit risk of bad loans. They also face interest-rate risk. The reason is not only that they have lent lots of long-term, fixed-rate money but also because they have speculated in mortgage-backed securities and junk bonds which, like other bonds, rise and fall in value with the fluctuation of interest rates. These securities are valued in thrifts' accounts at their original purchase price, not the market price. In recent years the more aggressively run thrifts have been making lots of money speculating in mortgage-backed securities which amounts to betting on falling rates. But during 1986–7 that game came to a screeching halt. By September 1987 the cost of money in America had been rising for seventeen consecutive months. Thus between mid-March and mid-April 1987, when interest rates rose sharply and unexpectedly, the value of mortgage-backed securities outstanding fell by 7 per cent as treasury bond yields jumped from 8.5 per cent to 9 per cent. That is a bigger move than it sounds. McKinsey reckons that thrifts owned some $135.5bn of these securities at the time. That meant a paper loss of $10bn., or more than 50 per cent of the entire industry's estimated $17bn. of equity. This gives some idea of how exposed the thrifts are to interest-rate moves. Take another statistic. In May 1987 Eric Hemel, an investment banker at First Boston and a former employee of the Home Loan Bank Board, the thrift industry's regulator, told Bank Board hearings in Washington that he estimated the market value of the industry's $633bn. total portfolio of mortgages (including those turned into securities) fell by over $50bn. because of the interest-rate rise. On McKinsey figures that is three times the industry's equity. Then consider that in September and October interest rates once again rose sharply and unexpectedly – treasury bond yields jumped from 9 per cent to 10.5 per cent before falling again. At the time, that can have only made the thrift industry's numbers look even grimmer, though interest rates subsequently fell.

If the red ink is spreading at an alarming rate, the net cost of liquidating the ailing thrifts also keeps on rising. By early 1988 McKinsey's Lowell Bryan reckoned it would cost nearly $70bn. to shut down the worst cases. That covers the net cost of turning assets into cash and paying off all depositors. McKinsey's July 1987 report noted that if there were either a recession or a big rise in interest rates, the bail-out cost could easily jump to $100bn. and over. Remember that the thrifts' problems have accumulated during five years of falling interest rates, economic recovery and, in most areas of the country, rising home values. The question that needs to be asked is what happens when these trends reverse?

Mark Perkins, a Florida-based thrift analyst, wrote in February 1988:

> It seems improbable to us that the financial markets continue to yawn at the crisis in the savings and loan industry. We believe that when history looks at each of these two financial crises, the losses sustained by the system in the savings and loan industry will exceed losses from L.D.C. [Third World] lending.

Perkins added that the crisis was nearer than many thought because deals could no longer be done with F.S.L.I.C. I.O.U.s. 'No one will accept them. As a result, liquidity for the problem thrifts is beginning to dry up.' Thus in December 1987 the Federal Home Loan Bank of San Francisco announced it would no longer automatically accept F.S.L.I.C.'s guarantee for a loan to a problem thrift. While the Federal Home Bank of Dallas demanded $1bn. in cash as collateral for loans to problem thrift.

When such dire warnings are sounded about the financial condition of the thrifts, it is often argued that the banks should take them over, effectively bailing the thrift industry out. That may be perfectly sensible in theory but it begs the question of whether the banks themselves have the money. They have not. After excluding all foreign debt provisions, McKinsey says that bank write-offs of domestic loans grew from $6.6bn. to $17bn. between 1982 and 1986, years when the economy was growing and interest rates falling. The report adds that in a recession these write-offs usually double or triple and are concentrated in the weakest banks. That would be more than sufficient to use up the $18.3bn. in insurance funds held by the banks' own insurance fund, the Federal Deposit Insurance Corporation at the beginning of 1988, leaving nothing left over for the thrifts. Even without a recession there will be more calls on the F.D.I.C. In March 1988 the First Republic Bank of Dallas, Texas's biggest bank, admitted defeat and went cap in hand to the F.D.I.C. This could turn out to be the costliest bank rescue in American history, probably even overtaking the $4.5bn bail-out of Continental Illinois in 1984. If so, that will make a big hole in that $18.3bn. reserve. Yet, amazingly, the news of the failure of Texas's biggest bank was treated by the financial markets as almost routine.

The problem in America's credit system, be it banks' Third World loans, thrifts' home loans or banks' credit card or L.B.O. exposures are, therefore, severe. They are of an altogether more critical nature than those facing lending institutions in other major capitalist countries because America has far too many banks. America's politicians have insisted on preserving a fragmented banking system in opposition to natural market forces and in deference to a strain of folksy populism still evident in the American psyche. Banking in other countries, be it Japan, West Germany, France, or Britain, is far more concentrated and so far safer. You cannot have a safe banking system without adequate capital. And America's is dangerously deficient in capital. To claim that everything is alright because the federal government, the world's biggest borrower, guarantees everything through deposit insurance is simply not good enough. Such a guarantee is only good so long as foreign money is prepared to fund America's debt and buy dollars.

So the problems facing America's credit system show that financial mania and financial excesses are not just confined to stock markets. Indeed, the system which provides the ordinary American with the financing to purchase his home, is probably the weakest point of the lot. The thrift industry, like the sovereign debt issue, is a time bomb as will become clear when home prices fall throughout America and not just, as now, in certain regions. However, nothing fundamental will be done about defusing it because local thrift interests are protected in Congress by their political representatives, while to tamper with deposit insurance in any meaningful manner is beyond the realms of the politically possible. That means the problem will only come to a head and make the front pages when depositors lose confidence in the system and start withdrawing their money. When that will occur is a matter of guesswork since, as gold bug John Exter says: 'Confidence is suspicion asleep.'

When the thrift issue does implode it could make Third World debt seem marginal by comparison, especially to the American home owner and tax payer. Time is running out. When the stock market crashed in October 1987, suddenly poorer investors rushed to move what was left of their money into treasury bills and bonds, money market accounts, or ordinary bank or thrift deposit accounts. In so doing they acted as if they still believed in the system's ability to look after their money. In the next and more serious financial panic people will start questioning the banking system itself. America, overloaded with banks and thrifts and bankrupt deposit insurance, is far more vulnerable than any other major economic power to depositor panic. When currency starts fleeing the banking system, that really is deflationary.

CONCLUSION

*'Go into the street and give one man a lecture on
morality and another a shilling, and see which
will respect you most.'*

Samuel Johnson, 1763

The scene was a Manhattan dinner party in early 1987. Among the
guests was Arthur Burns, distinguished former chairman of the
Federal Reserve and former American ambassador to Bonn.
Burns, who died later that year, was also an academic economist
who had spent a career studying the business cycle. It seemed an
ideal opportunity to ask this highly qualified man what he thought
about the Kondratieff long wave. Burns almost went red in the
face, so distasteful did he find even discussing this preposterous
notion. There was no evidence whatsoever, he asserted, to
substantiate this particular version of voodoo economics. This was
the same man who as Federal Reserve chairman went before
Congress in 1974 to assure America's legislature that the country
was not in a recession. America was by then already in the midst of
its worst, post-1945 economic slowdown.

The discussion was instructive because it demonstrates how
dangerous it is to rely on the analysis of economists, however
technically qualified. They will not help you preserve your wealth,
though they will provide a very eloquent 'on the one hand/on the
other hand' type of analysis. To deny statistical proof for the long
wave may be entirely legitimate since there are only statistics
available historically for the past three such cycles. But to refute it
totally when there is a clear trend of a depression every sixty years
or so smacks of pedantry. And yet most otherwise quite sensible
people continue to do just that. Human beings cannot bear to
admit that economic activity, like all other human activity, is
cyclical and that 'what goes around comes around.'

This is the essence of the long wave. It is not founded on some

177

deterministic superstitious nostrum. Rather, it is based on cause and effect; and in particular on the premise that human beings' collective memory does not extend back further than two generations and that those who cannot remember the mistakes of their grandfathers are condemned to repeat them. As such, belief in the power of the long wave to set the context and illustrate the trend is more likely to be shared by readers of history than students of Keynsian economics which teaches that governments are able to manage destiny.

The chief message of the long wave is that prosperity and easy money gradually lead to higher and higher levels of speculation and indebtedness to the point where the debt burden becomes too great for the economy to bear any longer. The result is depression, by which is meant a fundamental change in the system, as opposed to a recession, which is a mere correction in the business cycle. Only after the previous excesses are corrected through a deflation can the world pick itself up and embark, however gingerly, on a new period of prosperity. It will then take two generations for a similar manic speculative fever to occur because it will take that long to erase the collective folk memories of the previous boom and bust.

To those who were already worrying that the world was slipping towards just such a Kondratieff-style deflationary downturn, the severity of the stock market crash of October 1987 was peculiarly sinister. It only seemed to confirm that grim interpretation. Yet even after this historic event, where the fall in world share prices outside Japan was twice that of 1929, most economists have remained relatively sanguine, while most players in the money business have carried on as if it was business as normal. Hence the extraordinary revival of M.&.A. and 'merchant banking' on Wall Street in early 1988.

This is despite the impressive record of the stock market as a lead indicator of the economy. As the respected Montreal-based Bank Credit Analyst commented in November 1987: 'The economy has never escaped a recession whenever the stock market has fallen as much as it has in 1987.' The contrary, optimistic view was that the crash was a computer-driven aberration, that the stock market finished 1987 at the same level as it began the year, and that America's industrial economy was booming. Exactly the same kind of reassuring sentiments were aired at the beginning of 1930 when the general mood was one of qualified optimism, as is clear from reading the contemporary press. As now, only a small minority thought the crash would lead to a slump. The prevailing view among both industrialists and ordinary investor was that the gamblers in Wall Street or the City had received their come-uppance. The same sentiment is commonplace on Main Street today.

Unfortunately, most investors lost most of their money in the four years which followed October 1929, not during the actual crash. The Dow lost 85 per cent of its value, falling from its post-crash recovery high of 295 in April 1930 (a 50 per cent rally from the October 1929 bottom) to its low of 40 in July 1932. In a post-crash warning to its readers to be wary of the stock market, the Bank Credit Analyst said in November 1987: 'Investors in the 1929 era frequently remarked that it was not the crash in that year that destroyed them but the subsequent action in 1930, 1931, 1932, and 1933.'

It is, therefore, dangerous to indulge in premature bargain hunting. As at December 1988, the Dow Jones Industrial Average had still not recovered to its level prior to the more than 500-point drop on 19 October 1987. Nor had any of the world's other major stock markets, save for Tokyo, which had incredibly made new highs. So it increasingly seemed that, aside from Japan, it had made sense to panic and sell during the October 1987 stock market crash. Investors who were still hanging on, hoping for a recovery in share prices to pre-crash levels, were still hoping. It may prove a long wait. The Dow Jones did not return to its 1929 390 high until 1954.

Ominously, by February 1988, there were already tentative signs that deflation was gathering momentum, though they could not be found by reading the newspaper headlines. The evidence lay partly in America's money supply statistics. These arcane numbers had obsessed both bond and stock investors in the early 1980s, a period during which everyone was a monetarist and when the big question was whether Paul Volker could defeat inflation. The release of the weekly American money supply numbers was then the most widely anticipated event of the financial markets' week. However, by 1987, so dramatically had sentiment changed that the money supply figures were all but ignored save by a few eccentrics. Yet it was the sharp deceleration in the growth of money in America throughout 1987 which was the root cause of the stock market crash, precipitating the rise in interest rates and the fall in the bond market, and so the collapse in share prices.

Remarkably, after temporarily injecting liquidity into the

system in the week of the crash to keep certain Wall Street and Chicago brokers solvent, the Federal Reserve, now under a different chairman, Alan Greenspan, appeared to return to its restrictive monetary policy. The annual growth of real (adjusted for inflation) M2, which consists of current and deposit bank accounts as well as money market funds, collapsed from 8.1 per cent in January 1987 to minus 1 per cent in December 1987. This was the sharpest slowdown in American money growth for nearly twenty years. The slowdown continued throughout 1988.

Tight money is not the usual way for the authorities to respond to a financial panic, especially with a forthcoming presidential election. Yet the Federal Reserve appears to have remained quite tight. This is disturbing. It raises the question of whether the central bank is still in control of monetary policy or whether, far from the Federal Reserve being tight, the system is already contracting regardless of official policy.

Already enough money has been printed during the easy-money 1980s to fuel another dose of inflation if people change their habits and money starts chasing goods again. However, easy money has not led to higher inflation because the velocity of money (the rate at which money passes from person to person) has been falling. This key variable has fallen throughout the 1980s because investors have preferred to hold their money in financial assets where they received a real rate of return, rather than spend it as in the inflationary 1970s. Hence financial asset inflation.

The still mostly anecdotal evidence is that velocity may have begun falling again after October 1987, that banks are lending less, and that consumers are saving more and borrowing and buying less. There were two other indicators in addition to the slowdown in money growth which pointed to the fact that the Federal Reserve may have already begun to push on a string. First, the amount of currency in the system was rising. In the three months up to January 1988 notes and coins in circulation grew 11.4 per cent compared with a rise in M1, which includes bank demand deposits, of only 1.4 per cent. That may indicate that people have begun taking cash out of the banking system and putting it under the mattress or in the safety deposit box, a sign of caution. Second, as at February 1988 total Federal Reserve credit had not increased for ten months. Indeed there have been net-free reserves in the banking system. That means the rate at which the banks have been making new loans has been slowing.

All this may explain, rather than any conscious Federal Reserve policy, why monetary growth continued to decelerate. The Federal Reserve itself may have shown its concern when it announced on 19 February 1988 that it would start reporting weekly, rather than monthly, changes in America's broader money supply aggregates, known as M2 and M3. This was viewed by some as the Fed's way of telling the markets they should be paying more attention to these numbers, which had been coming in below the Fed's targeted growth rate. The implicit message was that monetary growth was less than the Federal Reserve wished and that the central bank would be justified, as a result, in easing policy more aggressively. The Federal Reserve needed to make this gesture because it did not want the markets to react badly to signs of an aggressive easing in monetary policy which, in a presidential election year (Greenspan is a Republican appointee) could only too easily be interpreted as a crude way of pump-priming the economy for a pre-election boom. That sort of bad reaction in the markets would precipitate a sell-off in the dollar and a rise in interest rates, further compounding deflationary pressures. That was why the Federal Reserve found itself in such a precarious position. Because of America's dependence on foreign creditors to fund its trade and budget deficits, Greenspan has had to keep one eye on the dollar and the bond market, and one eye on the economy, an unenviable balancing act.

Whatever its motives, the central bank was right to draw the market's attention to the slowdown in monetary growth since, if everybody rushes for cash at the same time, then the financial system will inevitably contract. The risk is that this will precipitate a debt deflation spiral, as debt created during the speculative years is wrung out of the system. And the more debt there is, the greater the excesses that will need to be purged before recovery is possible.

So even if the Federal Reserve did decide to ease aggressively, the change in policy may not have the required effect. Banks may have more money available to lend but that will not help if they do not want to lend it or consumers and companies want to borrow less. The Federal Reserve would then have lost control of monetary policy. As Mr Charles Eaton, a Kondratieff watcher at Nikko Securities wrote in January, 1988:

> Even if the Federal Reserve does cut the discount rate there is no guarantee that the resulting lower rates of interest will be enough to reverse the decelerating growth trends of money and consumer spending for several more months. The Fed will be pushing on a string.

This is just what happened after 1929. Despite the endurance of myths to the contrary, the Federal Reserve eased aggressively then. The discount rate, which was 5 per cent on 29 October 1929, was cut seven times to 1.5 per cent in early 1931. It did not stop the onset of depression because people were already scared and running for cover. Between October 1929 and March 1933 the level of bank loans in America declined from $24.4bn. to $13.2bn.

The deflationary process was graphically described in layman's language by Philip Manduca, executive director of London-based Daiwa Futures on 1 February 1988 in his weekly doomsday newsletter to clients. He wrote:

> The revenge that money has taken is extraordinary, and turns the whole theory of the need for money in our economic system on its head. Presently anyone with any sense is driving himself to raise cash, with little intention of spending it. This sum of money is for security, not expenditure. So the entire purpose behind the role of money in our environment has changed, and for the recessionary worse. What happens now? Simple but depressing. Investment funds do not come to market but prefer to stay in the bank. Hence, volumes, liquidity and collapse occur in the financial marketplace. In the economy, consumers, fearful of losing their jobs, reduce their spending, raise their savings and hope to survive . . . Down goes money velocity, down goes spending, down go profits, and down goes the economy. It doesn't take an astral projection to draw the obvious conclusion. As profits decline and as turnover collapses, goods begin to be sold at lower and lower prices, just to be shifted. Permanent sales become a common sight on the high streets of urban centres. Unemployment levels soar.

In other words debt deflation will have bred price deflation (i.e. prices will be falling) and we will already be in a depression. The key question for investors will then become how each country's government reacts as the deflation finally becomes apparent to one and all. The lesson of history is that there are two practical ways out of such a predicament. The first is debt default and the second currency depreciation. There is, of course, a third way but as Douglas Kirkland, author of *Power Cycles*, relates, it has never been tried. He writes: 'A third method, actual retirement of debt by repayment, has never been used by any major government to affect large-scale debt reductions.' It is, therefore, imprudent to expect it to happen this time.

Of the two remaining alternatives the most efficient, though also the most immediately painful, is systematic default. Those holding the debt, who can no longer service it, will default. Such a deflationary debt liquidation may be extremely painful but it has the benefit of being relatively short-lived. An example is America in the 1930s. Note, however, two positive aspects of such a slump. First, the currency maintains its value. In a climate of falling prices cash actually appreciates in value. Second, the quicker the liquidation of the previous cycle's bad debt, the quicker the process of recovery can commence.

The other way out, currency depreciation, is superficially more appealing in the short term, though in the longer term it is far more insidious and dangerous. Unfortunately that makes it more appealing to politicians, especially in countries which have lost the political will to make tough decisions. Instead of letting the liquidation occur, the decision is made to print money. The outcome is that the level of debt is reduced in real terms by the decline in the value of the currency. This is the path to hyperinflation and social and political chaos. Any country which embarks down it will eventually lose the faith of foreign creditors and be unable to borrow in the long-term bond market.

Generally, those countries which liquidate the debt load fastest will emerge quickest and strongest from the depression. Those that resort to the soft-option of devaluation will be long-term casualties. The key question in this cycle is what course America will take, as the world's major power and largest debtor nation. The time for decision is nearing. Until early 1988 the country followed the course of competitive dollar devaluation. It can only be hoped that, when the economic contraction does arrive, the Federal Reserve will insist on preserving the integrity of the dollar. The signs under Greenspan in 1988 were that it would, given the relative tightness of monetary policy. However, that resolve has yet to be tested in a severe economic downturn. There must be a serious question as to whether the American political system, based as it is on perennial optimism, will be able to bear the consequences of such a debt liquidation. If America does resort to destroying the value of its debt through extreme dollar depreciation then the consequences extend beyond that country. For it would mean not only destroying the bond market but also the end of the dollar as the world's reserve currency with no obvious candidate to replace it. That could create yet more uncertainty.

How can an individual or family best withstand the coming storm? The conclusions are not complex. Indeed they are plain common sense. At the time of writing (the end of March 1988) the most important point was to build cash and reduce debt in preparation for whatever was coming. The same will be true, only more so, by the time this book is published. Cash or its proxy should make up at least 75 per cent of any investor's portfolio. This is not a time to try and make large capital gains through speculation. That game ended on 19 October 1987. It is a time to try to preserve what one has and, above all, to get out of debt.

Second, shares should be sold. Those who were caught in the crash have been tempted to hang on in the hope of a recovery in prices. Unfortunately that is not likely to happen before the onset of depression though there will inevitably be misleadingly violent bear-market rallies, such as the rally in share prices to April 1930 and again in early 1988. More likely is that the Tokyo stock market will collapse (it could easily happen during this book's gestation period) sending more shock waves throughout the world's financial markets and depressing asset values everywhere.

Mark Faber has a useful if grim analogue for a bear market. He compares it to terminal cancer where a patient is encouraged by intermediate recoveries only, cruelly, to discover his condition deteriorating again. He writes:

> A bear market is a financial cancer that spreads. Intermediate rallies (occasionally very strong ones) keep the hopes of investors alive. Furthermore, by continuously publishing bullish reports, brokers and economists like good nurses keep the flame of hope from burning out. But after 18 to 36 months of continued losses, total capitulation usually sets in and a major low occurs.

Do not buy shares until you see such capitulation. At that point the economy will probably be entering a fully fledged slump. There will then be the buying opportunities of a generation especially if you can pick the companies that will prosper in the next upturn.

Third, property should be sold, especially where the value of the home makes up the major portion of an individual or family's net worth. At the time of writing it is still possible to get good prices for clearly overvalued residential property because there are still so many people around who believe in one of today's favourite maxims, namely that property always goes up in price. Believers in this nonsense, which compares in idiocy with talk in the 1970s of a permanent energy shortage, may be interested to learn that homes took twenty years and more to return to their 1929 levels after the last depression.

184

Especially vulnerable are the financial centres, principally London, New York, and Tokyo and their suburbs. This can be said with confidence because property in such cities has been appreciating by as much as 30 per cent a year during the 1980s, many times faster than the inflation rate, primarily because of the false prosperity enjoyed by those in the money business. So even if there is no depression such property is due for a substantial correction because no kind of asset has ever continuously increased in value faster than inflation. In a depression property in such centres will plummet by at least 70 per cent.

However, unlike the stock market crash, the collapse in property values will be agonisingly slow. The residential market will not bottom out until long after the stock market has reached rock bottom. Those with mortgages they find hard to service will hang on grimly for as long as possible because, understandably, they will not want to lose their home. They will default on every other kind of commitment before they default on their mortgage. Likewise, those who have decided to sell will hang on the hope of getting the price they think their home is worth, as opposed to what someone is prepared to pay for it. Their dilemma will be that the longer they delay, the less they will receive. So sell property as soon as possible while there are still people around willing to buy it, and still banks willing to lend to them against current inflated levels.

Amazingly, some residential property was still being sold in London and New York in early 1988 for the same price the property was valued prior to the stock market crash. This will not last. Already it is clear that it is taking longer to sell a property, a clear sign of weakness not strength.

Fourth, long-term government bonds are the best investment available for those still willing to speculate, since money can be made betting on an economic downturn. Indeed American treasury bonds rallied sharply immediately after the stock market crash as the bond market anticipated a weaker economy and lower interest rates ahead. However, conservative investors in bonds should avoid all corporate and junk bonds, sticking only to government bonds since the government *in extremis* can always print money to pay its creditors back.

But even treasury bonds, or their equivalent in other countries such as long-term gilts in Britain, should be sold once the economy enters a deep recession because at some point there will be a financial panic triggered by the swelling volume of defaults. The

185

demand for cash will be so great, and the mounting fear of default so acute, that it will cause a sharp upward movement or 'spike' in interest rates, as happened between September 1931 and June 1932. Once that has occurred government bonds can be bought again, though only if the investor is confident that the government in question has opted for the default option. Clearly, bonds would be the worst of investments where a currency is being depreciated to reduce the debt load. In those cases bonds should be sold as soon as the economic slump becomes the subject of newspaper headlines, and so becomes obvious to all. By then it will long have been discounted by the bond market.

As for gold, which was discussed in detail earlier, it is clear that it offers a unique hedge against both inflation and deflation. This is because it is both a real asset and also a liquid one, since it can always be sold easily. That said, gold should fall in price in the break into depression as holders of bullion sell to raise much-needed cash. However, the advantage of holding some gold is that, like health insurance, it is the hedge against the unpredictable. The question of whether the way out of the slump will be deflationary (debt default) or inflationary (currency depreciation) will be the most important decision investors will have to make in the next few years. The outcome will vary between country and currency. Gold is a hedge against both.

This last point raises the issue of currency. Here diversification may be the key. Whether a country's currency will be worth holding will depend on which course of action its government and central bank follows. Where currency depreciation is the chosen policy that country's currency is not worth holding. In such cases gold and foreign currencies are essential insurances. Investors should also remember the increased likelihood of exchange controls as governments panic or even, as happened in the 1930s in America, compulsorily purchase gold.

At this point it is impossible to say which governments will behave most responsibly. History suggests that the Swiss franc is as good a survival currency as any since Switzerland has a long tradition of sensible financial management combined with political stability and neutrality. It is also the world's safe which means that many rich and powerful people of all nationalities and all political persuasions keep their money there. For this reason alone Switzerland is likely to remain a relatively safe harbour.

Investors should not be unduly swayed by what interest rate they can obtain from holding a currency. In general the higher the interest rate on offer the weaker the currency since an incentive needs to be offered to persuade someone to buy it. The interest rate paid on Swiss francs, for example, is already nominal. In really dire times it may even turn negative which means you would have to pay the Swiss for the privilege of owning it. There is a reason for the low interest rate. Switzerland has low inflation and the Swiss franc a long history of appreciation. A depression is not a time to chase yield.

This raises an obvious problem for anyone who lives off investment income. Obviously dividend income from shares cannot be counted upon in the next few years. Therefore, the best option for those who need income is to lock in the high real interest rates still on offer by buying government bonds. When the depression begins they can then decide whether to sell or hold depending on whether they see resort to the printing press. The point is that just as no one should count on remaining employed during a slump, so no one should count on investment income.

Clearly, there are numerous other points which could be discussed, for example, the relative safety of different countries' banking systems. Here again there are no guarantees or panaceas in an uncertain world. Thus, it could transpire that offshore banking centres may not prove quite the ideal places to hoard money as many now believe. Consider these two points. First, no government is going to bail out an offshore bank, since offshore depositors have no natural political constituency. Second, many of the Swiss private banks and similar offshore banks which cater to rich individuals lend out their deposits by investing in Euromarket instruments such as certificates of deposit and bonds. In a really bad situation many of these could default. It might, therefore, be concluded that the safest banks are each country's biggest national banks, be they Swiss, West German, British, American, or Japanese, simply because political reality would demand the government nationalizes the bank rather than let it go under, as happened with Continental Illinois, whatever the cost.

This may all sound apocalyptic stuff. It is not the purpose of this book, however, to fuel paranoia or to write survivalist charters. It is merely to point out what may be the consequences of the 1980s speculative fever, a fever which is best comprehended by understanding what was going on in the money business.

There will be those who ask if a depression is coming and why this view is not shared more widely by the professional experts of the investment world and the financial markets. One answer is that it is not in their commercial interest to play the role of public Cassandras. The few who do are often regarded as irresponsible mavericks. The second point is that in my experience bankers, brokers, money managers, and the rest tend to be a lot more cautious with their own money than they do with their clients'. Ultimately there is no shirking each individual's responsibility for his financial affairs. *Caveat emptor* is the only investment law or regulation that counts.

There will also be those who find talk of another depression simply unbelievable. This reflects a fundamental difference in outlook. Human beings tend to divide into two cultures; those who believe in the efficacy of governments and their ability to solve problems, and those who are suspicious of official assurances. The former group have grown with the influence of Keynsian economies and the practice of Big Government, though Keynes himself was one of the twentieth century's great sceptics. These scoffers should consider this. If the deflationary view is wrong and they follow the above advice, the worst that will happen to them is that they will have rearranged their affairs in an admirably conservative and prudent fashion and, in a way, their Victorian forbears would have approved of.

The other good news is that a depression creates fantastic opportunities as surely as it creates devastating losses. Moreover, the sooner the debt liquidation begins, the sooner the world can embark on a new period of prosperity. It is during the early stages of such a recovery that technological innovation is usually at its most rapid. But first we have to destroy the bad debt created so eagerly by the pushers and pedlars of the money business. The yuppies will disappear and the baby boomers will grow up.

SUGGESTED READING

Auletta, K., *Greed and Glory on Wall Street*, Random House, New York, 1988.

Bailey, N., and Cohen, R., *The Debt Time Bomb*, Twentieth Century Fund, New York, 1987.

Batra, R., *The Great Depression of 1990*, Simon & Schuster, New York, 1987.

Brooks, J., *The Takeover Game*, Truman Talley Books, New York, 1987.

Bryan, L., *Breaking Up the Bank*, Dow Jones Irvine, New York, 1988.

Davidson, J. D., & Rees-Mogg, W., *Blood in the Streets*, Sidgwick and Jackson, London, 1987.

De Voe, Talley M., *The Passionate Investors*, Crown, New York, 1987.

Exter, J., 'The End of the Dollar as the World's Reserve Currency', a presentation at the Fifteenth Annual Conference for Monetary Research and Education, New York, 27 February 1987.

Faber, M., 'Business Cycles and the Future', a presentation at the Securities Institute of Australia, 11–12 December 1986.

Ferris, P., *Gentlemen of Fortune: World's Merchant and Investment Bankers*, Weidenfeld and Nicolson, London 1984.

Frieden, J., *Banking On The World*, Harper & Row, New York, 1987.

Grant, J., *Bernard Baruch: The Adventures of a Wall Street Legend*, Simon & Schuster, New York, 1983.

Goldenberg, S., *Trading: Inside the World's Leading Stock Exchanges*, Sidgwick and Jackson, London, 1986.

Hamilton, A., *The Financial Revolution*, Viking, London, 1986.

Hayes, S., *Wall Street and Regulation*, Harvard Business School Press, 1987.

Kaufman, H., *Interest Rates, the Markets and the New Financial World*, Times Books, New York, 1986.

Kirkland, D., & Kirkland, W., *Power Cycles*, Professional Communications, Phoenix, Arizona, 1985.

Mackay, C., *Extraordinary Popular Delusions and the Madness of Crowds*, Farrar, Straus and Giroux, New York, (Original Edition 1841).

Moore, G., *The Banker's Life*, W. W. Norton, New York, 1987.

Prechter, R., *The Major Works of R. N. Elliot*, New Classics Library, Gainesville, Georgia, 1980.

Reich, C., *Financier: The Biography of Andre Meyer*, William & Morrow, New York, 1983.

Reis, B., *False Security*, Equinox Cooperation Press, New York, 1937.

Rothchild, J., *A Fool and His Money: the Odyssey of an Average Investor*, Viking, 1987.

Rowley, A., *Asian Stockmarkets: The Inside Story*, Dow Jones Irvin, 1987.

Sarnoff, P., *Jesse Livermore, Speculator-King*, Traders Press Inc, 1985.

Smith, A., *The Money Game*, Michael Joseph, London, 1968.

Soros, G., *The Alchemy of Finance*, Simon & Schuster, New York, 1987.

Tilden, F., *A World in Debt*, Funk & Wagnalls, New York, 1937, (reprinted by Freidberg Commodity Management Inc, Toronto).

Thomas, G., & Morgan-Witts, M., *The Day the Bubble Burst*, Arrow Books, London, 1980.

INDEX

191